BOLLYPOLITICS

WORLD CINEMA SERIES

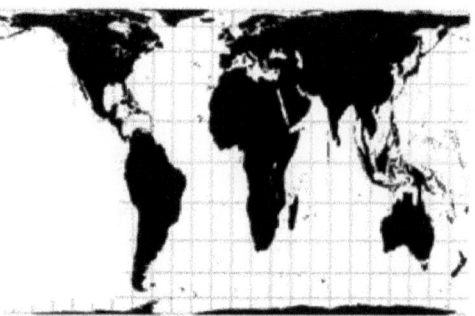

Series Editors:

Lúcia Nagib, Professor of Film at the University of Reading
Julian Ross, Research Fellow at the Leiden University

Advisory Board: Laura Mulvey (UK), Robert Stam (USA), Ismail Xavier (Brazil), Dudley Andrew (USA)

The *World Cinema series* aims to reveal and celebrate the richness and complexity of film art across the globe, exploring a wide variety of cinemas set within their own cultures and as they interconnect in a global context. The books in the series will represent innovative scholarship, in tune with the multicultural character of contemporary audiences. Drawing upon an international authorship, they will challenge outdated conceptions of world cinema and provide new ways of understanding a field at the centre of film studies in an era of transnational networks.

Published and forthcoming in the World Cinema series:

Allegory in Iranian Cinema: The Aesthetics of Poetry and Resistance,
Michelle Langford

Animation in the Middle East: Practice and Aesthetics from Baghdad to Casablanca,
Stefanie Van de Peer

Basque Cinema: A Cultural and Political History,
Rob Stone and Maria Pilar Rodriguez

Brazil on Screen: Cinema Novo, New Cinema, Utopia,
Lúcia Nagib

Brazilian Cinema and the Aesthetic of Ruins,
Guilherme Carréra

Cinema in the Arab World: New Histories, New Approaches,
Edited By Philippe Meers, Daniel Biltereyst and Ifdal Elsaket

Contemporary New Zealand Cinema,
Edited by Ian Conrich and Stuart Murray

Cosmopolitan Cinema: Cross-cultural Encounters in East Asian Film,
Felicia Chan

Documentary Cinema of Chile: Confronting History, Memory, Trauma,
Antonio Traverso

East Asian Cinemas: Exploring Transnational Connections on Film,
Edited by Leon Hunt and Leung Wing-Fai

East Asian Film Noir: Transnational Encounters and Intercultural Dialogue,
Edited by Chi-Yun Shin and Mark Gallagher

Eastern Approaches to Western Film: Asian Reception and Aesthetics in Cinema,
Stephen Teo

Impure Cinema: Intermedial and Intercultural Approaches to Film,
Edited by Lúcia Nagib and Anne Jerslev

Latin American Women Filmmakers: Production, Politics, Poetics,
Edited by Deborah Martin and Deborah Shaw

Lebanese Cinema: Imagining the Civil War and Beyond,
Lina Khatib

New Argentine Cinema,
Jens Andermann

New Directions in German Cinema,
Edited by Paul Cooke and Chris Homewood

New Turkish Cinema: Belonging, Identity and Memory,
Asuman Sune

On Cinema,
Glauber Rocha, edited by Ismail Xavier

Pablo Trapero and the Politics of Violence,
Douglas Mulliken

Palestinian Filmmaking in Israel: Narratives of Place and Identity,
Yael Friedman

Performing Authorship: Self-inscription and Corporeality in the Cinema,
Cecilia Sayad

Popular Ethiopian Cinema: Love and Other Genre,
Michael W. Thomas

Portugal's Global Cinema: Industry, History and Culture,
Edited by Mariana Liz

Queer Masculinities in Latin American Cinema: Male Bodies and Narrative Representations,
Gustavo Subero

Realism in Greek Cinema: From the Post-War Period to the Present,
Vrasidas Karalis

Realism of the Senses in World Cinema: Th e Experience of Physical Reality,
Tiago de Luca

Stars in World Cinema: Screen Icons and Star Systems Across Cultures,
Edited by Andrea Bandhauer and Michelle Royer

The Cinema of Jia Zhangke: Realism and Memory in Chinese Film,
Cecília Mello

The Cinema of Sri Lanka: South Asian Film in Texts and Contexts,
Ian Conrich

The New Generation in Chinese Animation,
Shaopeng Chen

The Spanish Fantastic: Contemporary Filmmaking in Horror, Fantasy and Sci-fi,
Shelagh-Rowan Legg

Theorizing World Cinema,
Edited by Lúcia Nagib, Chris Perriam and Rajinder Dudrah

Queries, ideas and submissions to
Series Editor: Professor Lúcia Nagib—
l.nagib@reading.ac.uk

Series Editor: Dr. Julian Ross—
j.a.ross@hum.leidenuniv.nl

Publisher at Bloomsbury: Rebecca Barden—
Rebecca.Barden@bloomsbury.com

BOLLYPOLITICS

Popular Hindi Cinema and Hindutva

AJAY GEHLAWAT

BLOOMSBURY ACADEMIC
LONDON • NEW YORK • OXFORD • NEW DELHI • SYDNEY

BLOOMSBURY ACADEMIC
Bloomsbury Publishing Plc
50 Bedford Square, London, WC1B 3DP, UK
1385 Broadway, New York, NY 10018, USA
29 Earlsfort Terrace, Dublin 2, Ireland

BLOOMSBURY, BLOOMSBURY ACADEMIC and the Diana logo are trademarks of
Bloomsbury Publishing Plc

First published in Great Britain 2024

Copyright © Ajay Gehlawat, 2024

Ajay Gehlawat has asserted his right under the Copyright, Designs and Patents Act, 1988,
to be identified as Author of this work.

For legal purposes the Acknowledgements on p. x constitute an
extension of this copyright page.

Cover design: Ben Anslow
Cover image: Top © Shilpa Thaku / Pacific Press / Alamy Live News; Middle /
Bottom © Arpan Basu Chowdhury / Pacific Press / Alamy Live News

All rights reserved. No part of this publication may be reproduced or transmitted
in any form or by any means, electronic or mechanical, including photocopying,
recording, or any information storage or retrieval system, without prior
permission in writing from the publishers.

Bloomsbury Publishing Plc does not have any control over, or responsibility for, any
third-party websites referred to or in this book. All internet addresses given in this
book were correct at the time of going to press. The author and publisher regret
any inconvenience caused if addresses have changed or sites have ceased to
exist, but can accept no responsibility for any such changes.

A catalogue record for this book is available from the British Library.

Library of Congress Cataloging-in-Publication Data

Names: Gehlawat, Ajay, author.
Title: Bollypolitics : popular Hindi cinema and Hindutva / Ajay Gehlawat.
Description: London ; New York : Bloomsbury Academic, 2024. |
Series: World cinema ; vol 35 | Includes bibliographical references and index.
Identifiers: LCCN 2023051465 (print) | LCCN 2023051466 (ebook) |
ISBN 9781350401884 (hardback) | ISBN 9781350401921 (paperback) |
ISBN 9781350401891 (ebook) | ISBN 9781350401907 (pdf)
Subjects: LCSH: Motion pictures–India. | Nationalism in motion pictures. |
Motion pictures–Political aspects–India.
Classification: LCC PN1993.5.I8 G43 2024 (print) | LCC PN1993.5.I8 (ebook) |
DDC 791.430954—dc23/eng/20240108
LC record available at https://lccn.loc.gov/2023051465
LC ebook record available at https://lccn.loc.gov/2023051466

ISBN: HB: 978-1-3504-0188-4
PB: 978-1-3504-0192-1
ePDF: 978-1-3504-0190-7
eBook: 978-1-3504-0189-1

Series: World Cinema

Typeset by RefineCatch Limited, Bungay, Suffolk
Printed and bound in Great Britain

To find out more about our authors and books visit www.bloomsbury.com
and sign up for our newsletters.

CONTENTS

List of Figures viii

Acknowledgements x

    Introduction: The Modi-fication of Bollywood 1

1 From Metatext to Fascist Aesthetics: The Case of Sanjay Leela Bhansali 45

2 Modi's Ad Man: Akshay Kumar 79

3 Modi's *Bhakt*: Kangana Ranaut 113

4 The Kashmiri Pandit: Anupam Kher 141

5 Hope from the Hinterlands? Ayushmann Khurrana 167

    Conclusion: The Modi Question 209

Notes 217

Filmography 237

Bibliography 241

Index 255

FIGURES

I.1	Bollywood group selfie with PM Modi	38
1.1	Hindutva groups burn effigy of Sanjay Leela Bhansali in 2017	63
1.2	The ritualized uniformity of the "Ghoomar" sequence in *Padmaavat* (2018)	67
1.3	Moving in perfect synchronicity towards *jauhar* in *Padmaavat* (2018)	69
1.4	Shahid Kapoor showing off his dancing skills in *Haider* (2014)	72
1.5	Deepika Padukone displaying her midriff in *Happy New Year* (2014)	73
2.1	Akshay explains the value of shit in Swachh Bharat PSA, 2018	85
2.2	Akshay joyfully flings fertilizer in Swachh Bharat PSA, 2018	86
2.3	Modi hails (cheap) success of Mars mission in *Mission Mangal* (2019)	90
2.4	Fawning Kumar asks Modi about his fashion style in BJP video (YouTube, 2019)	91
2.5	Fully saffronized Kumar in *Kesari* (2019)	96
2.6	Encroaching saffronization of Kumar's *soch* in *Mission Mangal* (2019)	99
2.7	Muslims safely placing Ganesha statue before their mosque in *Sooryavanshi* (2021)	104
2.8	Aryan appearing to walk on water in *Ram Setu* (2022)	109
3.1	Child bride Manu with much older Gangadhar Rao in *Jhansi Ki Rani* (1953)	120
3.2	Shankar prepares Rani's corpse for cremation in *Jhansi Ki Rani* (1953)	121

3.3 Beatific Rani engaging in *jauhar* in *Manikarnika* (2019)   128
3.4 Becoming one with the Absolute in *Manikarnika* (2019)   128
3.5 Art Karat's "Padmavati" jewelry collection (2018)   132
3.6 The heroine's blissful leap into the *jauhar* pit in *Samrat Prithviraj* (2022)   133
4.1 Gandhis scowl as Singh speaks in *The Accidental Prime Minister* (2019)   146
4.2 Party members in the Family's hand in *The Accidental Prime Minister* (2019)   147
4.3 Spectral presence of Indira Gandhi in *The Accidental Prime Minister* (2019)   149
5.1 Kartik gives a lesson about homophobia in *Shubh Mangal Zyada Saavdhan* (2020)   185
5.2 Joshua walks through rows of imprisoned boys with bound hands in *Anek* (2022)   197
C.1 Excised shot from "Besharam Rang" song, 2022   213

ACKNOWLEDGEMENTS

I would like to thank a number of individuals for their ongoing support throughout the completion of this book, including my parents and brother for *Anek*; Asha and Jaya for numerous small favors and reminders; and Sylvie for her good suggestion regarding the order of the chapters. At Bloomsbury, I would like to thank my editor, Veidehi Hans, for her useful advice and assistance throughout the process of completing the book, and the peer reviewers for their collective input. I am grateful to Philip Lutgendorf for a useful discussion about Sanjay Leela Bhansali during a car trip in 2017. At my university, I am thankful to Dawnelle Ricciardi for all her assistance with the many interlibrary loans needed in the course of this study. Portions of the Introduction and Chapter 1 previously appeared in *Studies in South Asian Film & Media* 9:2 (2019) and *South Asian History and Culture* 8:3 (2017)—my thanks to the editors for their kind permission to include the material here.

Introduction: The Modification of Bollywood

As the air in India's capital grows increasingly unbreathable, another toxic specter haunts the nation today, the growing specter of Hindutva, or Hindu nationalism, which has overwhelmed India since the election of Narendra Modi as prime minister in 2014. India is not alone in this chauvinistic rightward turn—witness the rise of nationalist strongmen around the world, including in the United States, Europe, Brazil, Turkey, Russia, and the Philippines—yet, the situation in India has grown particularly dire since Modi's election, and reelection in 2019. In the ensuing period, one witnesses a dramatic rise of intolerance in the subcontinent, embodied by a growing number of hate crimes perpetrated by extremist Hindu groups against Muslims and other minorities. Since Modi assumed office, literally hundreds of cases of such vigilante violence have occurred (Baksi and Nagarajan 2017), the overwhelming majority of which have been directed against Muslims (Mohan 2018: 35). Compounding this spate of violence has been the resounding silence that more often than not accompanies it, particularly from Modi, who is an otherwise avid Tweeter. As media scholar Shakuntala Banaji has observed:

> Kidnapping, rape, gang-rape, molestation, lynching, extra-judicial killings of and pogroms against Muslims, Dalits, Adivasis, Buddhists, Christians,

Sikhs, Kashmiris and populations of contested regions of the North East occur regularly (Taltumbde 2010; Mander 2015; Puniyani 2017). State and central governments often collude. So, why is it that, even when reported extensively, these crimes have drawn little opprobrium from the vast majority of India's literate population?

2018: 334

This is a key question and one that largely informs this study. The dramatic rise in recent years of sectarian violence and intolerance in India is matched, or compounded, by the lack of condemnation frequently greeting it, particularly from those in power, and neither shows any sign of abating. Indeed, it could be argued that one (form of violence) directly feeds into, or stems from, the other. Simultaneously, collaborations between Bollywood, the colloquial term for the popular Hindi cinema industry, and Modi's Hindu nationalist Bharatiya Janata Party (Indian People's Party, hereafter BJP), have substantially increased in the past several years, with numerous Bollywood stars frequently utilizing their celebrity status to endorse Modi's agenda. Alternatively, those who have been identified as critics of the ruling party within Bollywood, including two of the three Khans who have dominated the industry for several decades, have faced repeated attacks on social media (for being anti-national) as well as calls to boycott their films. As Arkotong Longkumer notes, "The rise of Hindu nationalism and the studies that have accompanied it have grown exponentially in the last few decades (Basu et al. 1993; Benei 2008; Doniger and Nussbaum 2015; Froerer 2007; Ghassem-Fachandi 2012; Gopal 1991; Hansen 1999; Hasan 1994; Jaffrelot 1998; Ludden 1996; McKean 1996b; Rajagopal 2001; Sarkar and Butalia 1995; van der Veer 1994)" (2021: 6). Yet, only one of the fourteen studies he cites—Rajagopal's—discusses Hindu nationalism in relation to media and that, too, is primarily focused on television and now over twenty years old. What arguably remains missing is a sustained examination of the effect of the rise of Hindu nationalism, or Hindutva, on Bollywood, and of Bollywood's negotiations of such an ideology. While recent studies by social scientists and journalists, including those of Jaffrelot (2021), Chowdhury and Keane (2021), and Komireddi (2019), make passing references to Bollywood, none include any sustained discussion of the film industry and its involvement with Hindutva.[1] In a country in which this film industry plays an outsized role, this is a particularly glaring omission and one which the current study seeks to address.

The outsized role that Bollywood plays in India is a crucial point here. As film historian Vijay Mishra observes, "The massive size of Indian cinema is obvious from the statistics: eight hundred films a year shown in more than thirteen thousand predominantly urban cinemas, viewed by an average of 11 million people each day" (2002: 1). "Cinema," as fellow film scholar Asha Kasbekar notes, "is the most important form of popular entertainment in India. With an annual production of 800–1,000 films, India is the world's largest producer of films, and this wealth of production informs all aspects of Indian cultural life" (2006: 179). This all-pervasive influence of the popular Hindi film form is important to bear in mind when considering the recent rise of Hindutva and its related impacts on the industry and the film form itself. Until only very recently, the *masala* format of the Bollywood film—an indigenous culinary term used to refer to the spicy blend of generic elements frequently included in the popular film—was frequently derided by critics and the films more often than not dismissed as escapist fare. Yet, the recent rise of fervently nationalist and/or Islamophobic fare from the industry—films like *Padmaavat* (2018), *Panipat* (2019), *Kesari* (2019), *Manikarnika* (2019), *Uri* (2019), and *The Kashmir Files* (2022)—reflects a shift away from the earlier Bollywood model. This shift in the form and content of Bollywood in the past nine years has been accompanied by increasing crackdowns on viewpoints deemed anti-nationalist or anti-Hindu (terms which themselves have become increasingly conflated by Hindutva forces) and a related expansion of what may constitute such an offense. This increased sensitization, particularly among the majority Hindu population, towards what may cause or give offense (in films) is directly correlated to the government's censor board and its expansive criteria. As author Karan Mahajan (2021) notes:

> Unlike in the US, writers and directors in India must contend with a finicky and paternalistic government-appointed national censor board, which arbitrarily forces directors to snip content that might be against 'the interests of the security of the State, friendly relations with foreign States, public order, decency or morality, or involves defamation or contempt of court or is likely to incite the commission of any offense'. Basically, *anything* that offends *anyone*. Individuals and groups that sniff offense are ready to cry foul, sue filmmakers, and go on a rampage against productions and cinemas (emphasis in original).

Furthermore, as Mahajan (2021) goes on to note, the censor board has a long history in India, dating back to the 1952 Cinematograph Act, itself a "holdover from British public morality laws," which consolidated "a single, government-appointed censor board tasked with protecting cinema-going Indians from salacious or inflammatory content."

The increasing crackdowns by the censor board, and the increased sensitization towards content considered offensive, has been accompanied by a spate of attacks on Bollywood actors, directors, producers, and films in the past nine years. To provide just a brief overview, these include massive backlash in 2015 against the so-called "King of Bollywood," Shah Rukh Khan, for allegedly claiming there was "growing intolerance" in India. BJP leaders attacked the Muslim actor, calling him a "Pakistani agent" and urging boycotts of his subsequent film, *Dilwale* (2015) (Sahadevan 2015). Khan, colloquially known as "SRK," was forced to retract his statement, claiming that he had never called India intolerant (*Hindustan Times* 2015). The same year, fellow superstar (and Muslim) Aamir Khan was attacked for publicly expressing his own concerns about growing intolerance in India. This resulted in a "social media backlash" against Snapdeal, an e-commerce platform Khan had endorsed and, within months, Snapdeal decided not to renew Khan's contract (Subramanian 2022). In the fall of 2022, Khan's comments were again brought up to fuel another boycott of his most recent film, *Laal Singh Chaddha* (2022) which, in turn, fared poorly at the box office.

In 2016, Bollywood producer Karan Johar was forced to make a substantial donation to an Indian army fund and issue an "abject apology" after casting a Pakistani actor, Fawad Khan, in a film he produced, *Kapoor & Sons* (2016) (Komireddi 2019: 149). Johar was additionally forced to pledge that he would never again "engage with talent" from Pakistan and the principal Indian film producers association subsequently placed a blanket ban on any Pakistani actors or technicians working in India (ibid., 150). Later that same year and again in the following year, director Sanjay Leela Bhansali was physically attacked by right-wing Hindu groups on the set of his film, *Padmaavat*. In the first instance, Bhansali was slapped by these protestors and, in the second incident, in March of 2017, protestors burned down his set (Hebbar 2017). Even after the film's production was completed, its release was repeatedly held up due to claims of historical inaccuracy (this in a film based in part on a myth). Simultaneously, right-wing Hindu groups and BJP politicians issued death threats against both Bhansali and the film's lead actress, Deepika Padukone, whose effigies were burned at several protests. Such groups also threatened to burn down any theatres which screened the film (*Hindustan Times* 2017). The reason for these protests? A rumor that the film included a dream sequence featuring the Muslim villain, Alauddin Khilji, and Padukone's character, a mythic Hindu queen. The Central Board of Film Certification, or CBFC, required Bhansali to make several alterations to the film, including to its title, and to include additional disclaimers at the outset. Nevertheless, the film was initially banned in several BJP-controlled states, including Rajasthan, Gujarat, Madhya Pradesh, and Haryana.

In 2020, following the suicide of a young Bollywood actor, Sushant Singh Rajput, the BJP attempted to weaponize rumors about foul play and drug use involved in Rajput's death to "strengthen its grip on power in Bihar," where Rajput was from and where the BJP was contesting state elections that fall (Nandy 2020). After old WhatsApp messages between Rajput's girlfriend and fellow Bollywood actor, Rhea Chakraborty, and Rajput's staff were produced, which seemed to suggest that she procured marijuana for him, the Narcotics Control Bureau (NCB) opened an investigation and arrested Chakraborty, who was denied bail and spent one month in jail (Nandy 2020). Later that year, in September, WhatsApp messages were again mysteriously leaked, this time apparently suggesting that Deepika Padukone had asked her manager to buy drugs for her. Padukone, who, in January 2020, took part in a student protest at Jawaharlal Nehru University (JNU) against the BJP-sponsored Citizen Amendment Act (CAA), which threatened to strip Muslims of their citizenship, was summoned by the NCB for questioning, with some speculating that this was an act of retaliation by the government for her involvement in the JNU protest (Nandy 2020). The following year, 2021, SRK's son, Aryan Khan, was arrested by the NCB for purportedly possessing drugs and, even though no drugs were found on him, he was denied bail and kept in jail for nearly a month (Subramanian 2022). As Samanth Subramanian (ibid.) recently observed in *The New Yorker*, "Shah Rukh Khan said little during those weeks," even as "the rest of Bollywood ... absorbed the news as the most cautionary tale of all: if they could do this to the king, imagine what they could do to us."

The acceleration of such attacks on Bollywood actors, producers and directors (and their loved ones) has resulted in a split in the film industry, with some who "swear by the Modi government" and others who "fear the space for them to be true artists and challenge rising majoritarianism in the country is shrinking" (Subramanian 2022). This is precisely what *Bollypolitics* intends to explore—the particular negotiations of such recent "Modi-fication" as embodied by the work of multiple leading artists in the industry —but, in order to do so effectively, I will first provide a series of interrelated overviews of relevant developments and their related histories, including of Hindutva, of

Bollywood, their interrelationships and related theories of (Hindu) viewership, in order to come to a better understanding of how precisely we have arrived at the present moment, which did not materialize out of thin air.

Hindutva

"Hindutva," as historian Sumit Sarkar notes, "has had a long gestation period" (1993: 164). The Hindu nationalist movement began with the formation of the Rashtriya Swayamsevak Sangh (RSS), or National Volunteer Organization, by Keshav Baliram Hedgewar in 1925. The concept of Hindutva was developed by V. D. Savarkar in his 1923 work, *Hindutva: Who is a Hindu?* As South Asian religions scholar Ellen Goldberg notes, for Savarkar, Hindutva was "an emphatically geographical, political, ethnic, and cultural designation defined much more broadly than simply religion" (2020: 116). India, in Savarkar's view, was the "Hindu Homeland," thus Muslims, or any group perceived to be of "foreign religious or cultural affiliation," could never be considered truly Indian (Goldberg 2020: 116). The political model for the second leader of the RSS, M. S. Golwalkar, was "Germany and its 'political writers' who concocted an ethnic definition of nationhood" (Jaffrelot 2021: 14). Golwalkar was "strongly opposed to the idea of a secular state" which "would not discriminate on the basis of religion" (Guha 2007: 35) and in his book, *We, or Our Nation Defined*, first published in 1938, he stated:

> The non-Hindu people of Hindustan must either adopt Hindu culture and language, must learn and respect and hold in reverence the Hindu religion, must entertain no idea but of those of glorification of the Hindu race and culture ... in a word they must cease to be foreigners, or may stay in the country, wholly subordinated to the Hindu nation, claiming nothing, deserving no privileges, far less any preferential treatment—not even citizens' rights.
>
> Qtd in GUHA 2007: 35

Golwalkar, in an eerily prescient decision, had settled upon the cow as the key mobilizing agent for the realization of a Hindu *rashtra*, or Hindu nation. In his view, the "mother cow" deserved to be "the sole object of devotion and worship" which, in turn, would inspire "devotion to the motherland" (qtd in Guha 2007: 624).[2] After Mahatma Gandhi was killed by a former RSS member in 1948, the group was banned by the new Indian government (ibid., 110). As historian Ramachandra Guha notes, though the group was not directly involved in the assassination, it had been "active in the violence in the Punjab," and its world view was similar to that of Nathuram Godse, Gandhi's assassin (ibid.).[3] However, one year later, the ban on the RSS was lifted and Gowalkar agreed to ask its members "to profess loyalty to the [secular] constitution of India," and to "abjur[e] violence" (ibid., 111).

In the 1950s the RSS, which Modi himself joined as a young man, spawned "a whole series of affiliates," including the forerunner of the BJP, the Jana Sangh, and the Vishwa Hindu Parishad (VHP), or Hindu World Council (Sarkar 1993: 164). These groups combined physical training of young men with indoctrination, with numerous schools built up over the years—what Sarkar calls a process of "building up hegemony through molecular permeation" (ibid.). All of these developments culminated in many ways with the so-called Ram Janmabhoomi (Ram's birthplace) movement and the ensuing destruction of the Babri Masjid, or mosque, in Ayodhya by members and affiliates of these Hindutva groups in December 1992. According to Hindu myth, Ayodhya was the birthplace of the Hindu deity Ram, hero of the Hindu epic, the *Ramayan*.[4] Guha notes how, two years after India achieved its independence in 1947, "an official sympathetic to Hindu interests allowed an idol of the child Ram to be placed inside the mosque" (ibid., 576). This was done "under cover of darkness," and devotees were, in turn, "persuaded that it had appeared miraculously," and that its sudden presence in the mosque amounted to "a sign that the displaced deity wanted to reclaim his birthplace" (ibid.). In the early 1980s, the VHP began a campaign for the "liberation of the spot where Ram was born" (ibid.,

577). Working closely with the RSS, the VHP embarked upon a movement to reclaim this sight, a movement which would simultaneously unite the various Hindu factions.

Ayodhya

The destruction of the Babri Masjid in Ayodhya in December 1992 is arguably the key flashpoint in the subsequent rise of Hindutva forces in India today. Mishra has also noted the significance of this event, claiming that "Ayodhya" can be read "both as a temporal marker (i.e., December 1992) and as a process that has been part of the Indian unconscious for more than two millennia" (2002: 214). As Guha notes, there were two "contingent events" that "immeasurably helped" the Ayodhya movement: the first of these was the ritual suicide by immolation, known as *sati*, of a young woman from Rajasthan, Roop Kanwar, in 1987, following the death of her husband (2007: 579). Though the practice of *sati* had been outlawed for some time, Kanwar's performance of this ritual suicide "inspired a groundswell of devotion" by Hindu groups in Rajasthan and beyond, for whom Kanwar became "an exemplar of Hindu womanhood" (ibid.).[5] The second and "more significant event" that aided the Ayodhya movement was the telecast on the Indian state television station of a new series based on the Hindu epic, the *Ramayan* (Ram's journey), beginning in 1987 and ending in mid-1988 (ibid.). This televisual *Ramayan* was enormously popular—its success "exceeded all expectations," and its "appeal and influence contributed enormously to the VHP's movement to 'liberate' the birthplace of Ram" (ibid., 579, 560).[6]

This period also saw the rise of the BJP which was formed from the older Jana Sangh, a party first established in 1951 whose aim was "to consolidate India's largest religious group, the Hindus, into one solid voting bloc" (ibid., 145). The Jana Sangh stood for the "reunification of the motherland through the absorption (or perhaps conquest) of Pakistan" and accused the ruling Congress Party of "appeasing" Muslims (ibid., 145–6). After being routed in elections in 1980, members of the Jana Sangh broke away and formed a new party, the BJP, yet, as Guha observes, "the new name could not really disguise a very old aim," namely, to advance Hindu interests (ibid., 558). The formation of the BJP resulted in "a wave of religious violence in northern and western India," including Hindu–Muslim riots in Uttar Pradesh (1980, 1982), Bihar (1981), Gujarat (1981–2), Andhra Pradesh (1983), and Maharashtra (1984) (ibid.). As Guha notes, these riots tended to adhere to a familiar pattern, "set off by a quarrel that was in itself trifling" but that quickly metastasized through rumor (ibid., 558–9). One sees how rumor, further propelled and accelerated by the advent of social media, has continued to play a key role in the spread of communal violence in India (and elsewhere) in the twenty-first century. Regardless of who may have started any particular quarrel, Guha notes that "it was always the Muslims and the poor who were the main victims" (ibid., 558).

The BJP, which had only won two seats in the 1984 elections, decided to "hitch its wagon" to the campaign to build a Ram temple at the site of the Babri Masjid in Ayodhya and, as this movement's popularity grew, so, too, did the political fortunes of the BJP (ibid., 588–9). By the time of the next general elections, in 1989, the BJP's popularity had grown substantially and it won eighty-six seats. Thus, as Guha notes, in the 1980s, "a single holy place in a single small town was able to accomplish what a ubiquitous holy animal could not," with the Ayodhya movement gaining "widespread appeal" during this decade (ibid., 625). Such widespread appeal was furthered by a series of actions taken in 1990, beginning with the BJP's decision to launch a *rath yatra*, or chariot procession, led by party boss L. K. Advani, from Gujarat to Ayodhya.[7] A week before it reached its destination, however, the BJP procession was stopped by the authorities and Advani placed in preventive detention. Nevertheless, his followers made their way to Ayodhya and, even though as many as 150,000 were detained, nearly 75,000 still managed to arrive in Ayodhya, where they battled with the police and members of the paramilitary Border Security Force, or BSF (ibid., 626–7). The battle lasted for three days and at least twenty supporters of the Ram Janmabhoomi movement were killed (ibid., 627). These deaths, in turn, led to calls for revenge and resulted in "Hindu mobs attack[ing] Muslim localities" as well as stopping trains to remove and kill anyone who appeared to be Muslim (ibid.). The BJP went on to win even more seats in the 1991 parliamentary elections and now held power in four northern Indian states (ibid., 628). Later that year, the VHP and RSS began acquiring and leveling the land around the Babri Masjid, in anticipation of building a temple at the site.[8]

The VHP announced December 6, 1992, as the date that had been chosen as the "auspicious" day on which the building of the Ram temple would begin (ibid., 629). By this time, over 100,000 supporters of the Hindu temple movement had assembled in Ayodhya, carrying *trishuls* (tridents), bows and arrows, iron rods, and axes (ibid., 629–30). By midday on December 6, these Hindu supporters had invaded the mosque and, over a period of five hours, proceeded to demolish it. As Guha observes, "A building that had seen many rulers and dynasties come and go, that had withstood the furies of 400 or more monsoons, had in a single afternoon been reduced to rubble" (ibid., 630). Though approximately 20,000 Indian paramilitary troops had been assembled on the outskirts of the town, they were not sent in to stop the attack on the mosque, due to the government's fear of being labeled "anti-Hindu" (ibid., 631). Yet, the aftermath of the demolition of the Babri Masjid proved to be even more deadly, with riots breaking out "in town after town," in an "orgy of violence" that lasted two months and led to more than 2,000 deaths (ibid., 632). Hindu mobs celebrated the destruction of the mosque by burning Muslim homes and neighborhoods, with riots spreading throughout northern and western India. One of the worst-hit cities was Bombay, India's commercial center and home to the Hindi film industry, which until then had enjoyed a cosmopolitan reputation. Throughout December of 1992, BJP-led "victory rallies" descended upon Muslim homes, mosques and businesses, which were attacked and burned (ibid., 632). Though a curfew was imposed and the army brought in, it took ten days to quell the violence in Bombay. Peace held for only three weeks, however, with a new spate of attacks breaking out in January 1993, with Muslims bearing the brunt of violence; of the nearly 800 people who died in these riots, at least two-thirds were Muslim, even though they only constituted fifteen percent of the city's population (ibid., 633). While a shaky peace was again established and managed to hold for two months, a sequence of bombs subsequently rocked the city in March of 1993, with over 300 people killed in the blasts (ibid.).

The demolition of the Babri Masjid and its violent aftermath raised questions about the state of Indian democracy and secularism. Writing in the *Economic and Political Weekly* in January of 1993, Sumit Sarkar speculated that these events were "frighteningly evocative" of the horror of fascism, characterizing these incidents as "the most widespread round of communal violence since the Partition years" (163). In Sarkar's view, "the drive for Hindu Rashtra has put in jeopardy the entire secular and democratic foundations" of the Indian republic (ibid.). Along with the broader contours of violence, he noted particular incidents, including "the beating up of journalists on December 6"; members of another Hindutva group, the Bajrang Dal, frequently and "openly declar[ing] that anyone who criticizes the destruction of the Babri Masjid will have to go to Pakistan"; and police officers who had "rounded up all Muslim men in some areas" and "beaten them up unless they agreed to say Jai Shri Ram [Hail Ram]," as further instances of impending fascism in India (ibid.). "What is making all this possible," Sarkar felt, "is evidently a wide, though very far from universal, degree of consent" (ibid., 164). The central element, in his view, of "Hindutva as a mass phenomenon (or for that matter to Fascism) is the development of a powerful and extendable enemy image [...]; the Muslim here becomes the near-exact equivalent of the Jew—or the Black ... in contemporary White racism," reduced to "second-class citizenship at best" through "constant fear of riots amounting to genocide" (ibid., 165–6).

Writing in the immediate aftermath of Ayodhya, Sarkar did however note "one major distinction between the Hindutva of today and European Fascism, particularly of the Nazi variety," namely, "a very different relationship with established religious traditions" (ibid., 166). While Nazis "sought to ground identity on race, not religion … the Sangh Parivar [the broader family of Hindutva groups], by very definition, has to preach total adherence and deference towards Hindu traditions even while fundamentally transforming them" (ibid.). Indeed, returning to his earlier point concerning the consent which made such events possible, Sarkar writes of such groups' "effort to transform what millions of Hindus sincerely believe … to be a supremely tolerant and Catholic religion into a terrifying instrument of vandalism, murder, and usurpation of political power" (ibid.). How did this become possible? To some extent such confusion may very well stem from a misunderstanding of Hindutva. Writing recently about Hindu nationalism, the scholar of far right extremism Eviane Leidig notes that, "when it comes to India, scholars of right-wing extremism in the West have misrepresented Hindutva as a type of nationalism that is primarily religious rather than ethnonationalist" (2020: 218). Though Hinduism does play a "significant role," Hindutva, in Leidig's view, "is not centered on religion … but rather on how religion is politicized in such a way that being a Hindu generates belonging as an ethnonationalist identity" (ibid., 220). Hindutva, in other words, is "misunderstood as a religious phenomenon rather than as the politicization of religion" (ibid., 235). Thus, while Hindutva may have a "very different relationship with established religious traditions" than Nazism did (Sarkar 1993: 166), it is nevertheless at heart a political movement that "parallels right-wing extremism in the West," particularly in its demonization of Muslims (Leidig 2020: 221) who, to return to Sarkar, have become "the near equivalent" of Jews (1993: 165).[9]

One is reminded of Aime Cesaire's *Discourse on Colonialism* (2000 [1955]) when reading Sarkar's descriptions of "what millions of Hindus sincerely believe[d]" to be the "supremely tolerant" nature of their religion, and their ensuing perplexity in light of the events of Ayodhya and its aftermath. Describing the rise of Nazism in Europe, Cesaire wrote:

> People are surprised, they become indignant. They say, 'How strange! But never mind—it's Nazism, it will pass!' And they wait, and they hope, and they hide the truth from themselves, that it is barbarism, the supreme barbarism, the crowning barbarism that sums up all the daily barbarisms; that it is Nazism, yes, but that before they were its victims, they were its accomplices.
>
> Ibid., 36

Relatedly, Cesaire wrote that:

> it would be worthwhile to study clinically, in detail, the steps taken by Hitler and Hitlerism and to reveal to the very distinguished, very humanistic, very Christian bourgeois of the twentieth century that without his being aware of it, he has a Hitler inside him, that Hitler inhabits him, that Hitler is his demon, that if he rails against him, he is being inconsistent.
>
> Ibid.

These two elements—surprise and complicity—in many ways resurface in the aftermath of Ayodhya; as Sarkar has noted, what made all of this possible is "a wide, though very far from universal, degree of consent" (1993: 164). As Banaji observes, the events of 1992–3, which were examined at length in the Sri Krishna Commission Report, constituted "an orchestrated pogrom by Hindu chauvinist cadres with the support of those in power" (2018: 340). Yet, it is arguably not just "those in power" who become implicated in such attacks—as scholar and critic Rustom Bharucha, also writing about the carnage of Ayodhya and its aftermath has noted, "Somewhere within and outside ourselves, we need to confront that dangerous border where nationalism becomes fascism, not by denouncing the other and subjecting ourselves to further aggression, but rather by questioning our own complicities in the legitimization of violence around us" (1994: 1389).

Bharucha, like Sarkar, notes the "difficulties involved in naming fascism in the Indian context," as well as how attempts to distinguish the Indian context from those of Germany and Italy in the 1930s "could very well be a wish-fulfilment on our part, an evasion of responsibility in confronting symptoms of fascism in India today" (1994: 1389). While acknowledging the "boldness" of Sarkar's intervention, Bharucha nonetheless argues that, "one would have to acknowledge that it is, perhaps, easier to name the fascism of the Sangh Parivar than its allies, whose 'connivance and implicit sustenance from within the highest corridors of power' have almost legitimized fascism within the framework of democracy" (1994: 1389). Beyond the complicities of those in power, as both Banaji (2018) and Bharucha (1994) have noted, I am concerned here with the broader complicity of the mass public, and how such complicity can be given and traced. This is precisely where the outsized role of popular Hindi cinema, and the large numbers of Indians who regularly patronize it, become relevant. As Kasbekar has observed, "The centrality of Indian cinema to Indian lives cannot be overemphasized" (2006: 179). How, then, did popular Hindi cinema respond to the events of Ayodhya and its aftermath? If these events were indeed the key flashpoints in the subsequent rise of Hindutva forces in India today, can we trace a similar transformation of the Bollywood film during this period?

Bollywood, 1990s–2000s

Bharucha, writing in the early 1990s, argues that "it is only in recent years, with the communalization of popular culture in India, that 'enemy images' in cinema have been marked with specific political signs in the Indian context" (1994: 1391). He points to Mani Ratnam's film, *Roja* (1992), as an instance of such a shift, arguing that in this film—"the first dubbed film to achieve widespread national success" (Ganti 2013: 209)[10]—one witnesses a deviation from "villains in the earlier sense," who are replaced by "enemy figures who are specifically marked as 'Kashmiri' and 'Muslim'" (Bharucha 1994: 1391). Ratnam, in Bharucha's view, was "selling the hottest brand of nationalism," not only making it "palatable but desirable" (1994: 1392). This was due in part to "the film's cinematography, lighting design, and song visualizations," as well as the innovative soundtrack by newcomer A. R. Rahman, all of which "ushered in a new aesthetic regime in Hindi cinema" (Ganti 2013: 209–10). Yet, it is precisely these elements that Bharucha finds problematic, particularly as they are utilized to buttress nationalism in ways that, at times, "borders . . . on fascism" (1994: 1392).[11] Ratnam's follow-up to *Roja*, the second installment in his so-called "terrorist trilogy," was *Bombay* (1995), a film that deviates from the standard Hindi cinema template in featuring an interfaith couple (Hindu man and Muslim woman) and in positioning their story not within some older timeframe but very clearly within the context of the destruction of the Babri Masjid and its immediate aftermath.[12] For both of these reasons, the film generated a degree of controversy, with Bal Thackeray, founder and head of the Shiv Sena, another Hindutva party based in Maharashtra, demanding a number of changes to the film before it could be released (Vasudevan 2001). With *Bombay*, one also witnesses an instance of the strategies the Hindu Right adopted in the aftermath of Ayodhya, which included "negative pressures, primarily from the Shiv Sena leader Bal Thackeray and his cohorts," as well as "establishing dialogues with important [film] industry members" (Bose 2009: 28). In a particularly compelling instance of the latter, it was Bollywood superstar Amitabh Bachchan who "organized a meeting between Mani Ratnam and Bal Thackeray," which, in turn, attached a "slanted sense of political negotiation" to *Bombay* (Vasudevan 2001: 198).[13]

Such negotiation accords with film scholar Nandana Bose's broader point regarding "the BJP/ Shiv Sena's decade-long intervention to promote a Hindu nationalist ideology in the Bombay film industry" (2009: 28), as well as Guha's claim that, in the 1990s, "the BJP came to define the political agenda in a way the Congress once did in the 1950s and 1960s" (2007: 639). The popular Hindi cinema played a particularly outsized role in defining such an agenda. "No political party," Bose notes, "had spent as much time and effort establishing dialogue with the cine-world as the BJP-Shiv Sena Combine did in the 1990s" (2009: 31). Beyond blacklisting "'anti-national' stars, such as the popular action-hero Sanjay Dutt," and "boycotting and even bann[ing]" the films of "Pakistani and Indian artistes collaborating with such artistes" (Bose 2009: 29), one also sees how the events of Ayodhya were themselves weaponized by these Hindutva groups at this time. As Bose notes: "In May 1993 the *Trade Guide* reported a joint meeting between the BJP and members of the Film Makers Combine (FMC) supposedly leading to a secret deal [...] Among the conditions accepted were: 'No ridiculing of Hindu sentiments in any film' and that 'Members of the industry should not criticize or condemn Hindus involved in the Ayodhya movement'" (2009: 33). In a subsequent press release sent to the *Trade Guide*, the BJP "Film Cell" noted that "we warn such producers that even if they manage to get a censor certificate, our *janandolan* [mass agitation] would not let them show these films in theatres" (qtd in Bose 2009: 33). Thus, one can see how the threat of violence stemming from Hindutva groups became increasingly palpable in the years immediately following the destruction of the Babri Masjid, as well as how groups like the BJP and Shiv Sena increasingly leveraged such threats of violence to control, or dictate, the content of films. As Bose notes, of the deputy chief minister's claim at an inaugural BJP Film and Television Forum in 1996, that such gatherings would "'play a constructive role in bridging the gap between the government and the film industry,'" such phrases—"bridging the gap"—were "euphemism[s] for overt interference by the right-wing in the industry" (ibid.).

At the same time, as Indian film historian Sumita Chakravarty has observed, "Ratnam's terrorism trilogy" [*Roja*, *Bombay*, *Dil Se* (1998)] is "mediated and filtered through the exigencies of internal and external censorings and the conventions of entertainment cinema with its emphasis on music, spectacle, and romance" (2000: 218). This is a key point and I would extrapolate from it to argue that the same is true to varying degrees of all Bollywood films. One sees such mediation in the subsequent "spate of films—*Border* (1997), *Fiza* (2000), *16 December—All Forces Alert* (2002), *LOC—Kargil* (2003), *Ab Tumhare Hawale Watan Sathiya* (2004), *Fanaa* (2006), among others" that were released in the ensuing years and featured "characters and events caught up in terrorism and warfare" (Kaul 2009: 193). Even as one could frame such mediation as aiding the proto-Hindutva film in maintaining some semblance of banal ideological cover, one could also point to such mediation as an instance of the Bollywood form attenuating or, indeed, reconfiguring, such Hindutva ideology. In numerous films dealing with such themes that were released during this period (1990s–2000s), one can consistently trace such a "mediating and filtering" within the films via the conventions of the Bollywood form that Chakravarty mentions. Thus, even as the RSS urged Indians at the turn of the century to watch the films of the "up-and-coming" Hindu actor Hrithik Roshan rather than those of the three leading Muslim actors (Shah Rukh Khan, Aamir Khan, Salman Khan) (Guha 2007: 640–1), and while Roshan starred in a number of films featuring terrorism and warfare, he at times played a sympathetic Muslim character, as in *Mission Kashmir* (2000), or a man whose decision to join the Indian army is motivated more by a desire to impress his girlfriend, as in *Lakshya* (2004). Relatedly, whether the protagonist in such films is played by Roshan or one of the Khans, he frequently engages in song and dance, with the films more generally hewing to the Bollywood conventions Chakravarty (2000) has described. Additionally, as Hindi film music theorist Alison Arnold has observed, music directors frequently employ "both 'overt' and 'covert' means of musical fusion" in film songs, including: "(1)

the mixture of a recognizable Hindu or Muslim musical form with contrasting, that is, Muslim or Hindu, lyrics and/or screen characters; (2) the combination of recognizable Hindu and Islamic musical features within one song; (3) lyrics that openly express Hindu–Muslim brotherhood and unity" (qtd in Chakravarty 1993: 167). In other words, Bollywood's syncretism and hybrid approach arguably undermine any ostensible Manichean framing, particularly one pitting Hindu against Muslim. Such facile framing is belied by the Bollywood form itself which, as Chakravarty notes, is informed by "the dialectics of juxtaposition and contamination" (ibid., 5).

Thus, even as one detects a shift in the 1990s—a period during which the BJP and Shiv Sena applied growing pressure on the film industry to conform to its Hindutva template—from the villain being the West to being Pakistan,[14] the response of the industry to "the nativist definitions of 'Indian' culture offered by proponents of Hindutva" was not entirely "wholehearted" but more or less regularly 'mediated and filtered' by the exigences of the Bollywood film form (Viswanath 2002: 41; Chakravarty 2000: 218). Similarly, while it was "under the aegis of the Bharatiya Janata Party (BJP)-led government" that Bollywood was granted industry status in 1998," and while critics have argued that this was granted as a way for the BJP-led state to control Hindi film production (Bose 2009: 23, 28), the films produced during these years did not uniformly adhere to the BJP template, whether with regard to choices in casting or storyline. The period during which the BJP first led the Indian government (1998–2004) was paradoxically marked by the enormous popular success of the Muslim triumvirate so despised by the RSS, with one or more of the Khans starring in the biggest blockbusters of each of these (BJP-led) years. This was also the period that witnessed the acceleration of liberalization, begun in 1991, and readily on display in the increasingly diasporic- and consumer-oriented themes of Bollywood films. While one could point to films such as *Aa Ab Laut Chalen* (1999) or *Kabhi Khushi Kabhie Gham* (2001, hereafter *K3G*) with their non-resident Indian (NRI) protagonists as "supportive of the

Hindutva ideology" (Viswanath 2002: 47), one could also argue, to return to and invoke one of Chakravarty's (1993) defining metaphors for popular Hindi cinema, that such films' ostensible nods to what could be considered "jingoistic nationalism" (Bose 2009: 36) could also be seen as "imperso-nations" of such ideologies, delivered in a tongue-in-cheek manner and not meant to be taken at face value (4).[15] A case in point could be the scenes from *K3G* which some critics point to as "exemplif[ying] how a Hindi film could be exploited to serve jingoistic nationalism" (ibid.)—in one, the film soundtrack plays "Vande Mataram" (Hail Mother India), a nationalist song, as one of the film's (Hindu) protagonists (Hrithik Roshan) arrives in London; in another, a rendition of the Indian national anthem is performed by the young child of NRI parents and his English classmates at a school function. Both scenes, while ostensibly including nationalist songs, do not invite uniform readings; indeed, one Indian film theorist claimed that "the nationalist refrain of the sound track seems rather ridiculous" (Mazumdar 2007: 140), while another described the sequence as "highly suggestive and highly ironic," going on to argue that "hearing this nationalist mantra sung over a montage of the main sights of London is, for me, laugh-out-loud funny" and, furthermore, "suggests a radical criticism of categorical identity" (Hogan 2008: 179).

In this way, one can see how Bollywood's "imperso-nating" style, even during this period of BJP-led governance, can reformulate (and critique) what might be considered an homage to the Hindutva playbook, or to rearticulate Bose's (2009) sentiment, how a Hindi film could appear to serve such interests even as it (implicitly or explicitly) undermines them. Writing about such films, film scholar Gauri Viswanath argues that, while "political compulsions" may have forced the BJP to "put its hard-core issues on the backburner," its "hidden agenda has been cleverly hijacked by Bollywood filmmakers of the 90s" (2002: 50). For this reason, she goes on to conclude, "the 90s films can at best be read as cinematic translations of the rhetoric of the Hindu Right" (ibid.). Yet, per the above readings of the ostensibly "nationalist" scenes in *K3G*, one could alternatively describe this phenomenon, with Bollywood's "clever hijacking" functioning as a form of "cinematic translation" of the BJP agenda that results in a "mediation" of this agenda via Bollywood conventions, that is to say, its Bollywoodization. Such translation could indeed be considered "clever," as it requires close attention to, and familiarity with, Bollywood's cinematic conventions and, more broadly, its impersonating ethos, in order to be appreciated. Yet, such a (counter)reading of such cinematic moments provides a counternarrative to the overhasty conclusion that films from this period (1998–2004) including such moments, that went on to become box office successes, must be read as vindications of a Hindutva ideology. If anything, per Chakravarty's metaphor of imperso-nation, which arguably informs the majority of these films, the success of such films, including those "caught up in terrorism and warfare" (Kaul 2009: 193), was due, at least to some extent, to their playful engagement with such themes, in which characters frequently step "out of character" to, for example, perform a song and dance, or otherwise deviate from (and thus destabilize) a straightforward, nationalist narrative.[16]

Disclaimers

Nevertheless, a key shift occurred during this broader period and one that was utilized by the BJP and the Sangh Parivar to mobilize their supporters around the Ayodhya movement, what film scholar Raita Merivirta describes as "a change in public historical consciousness in India," through which "history became central to religious national identity in the late 1980s" (2016: 457). While "Bollywood has traditionally not insisted on historical accuracy," the rise and consolidation of Hindutva forces in the 1980s and 1990s, with a concomitant deployment of Hindutva-ized history, for example, regarding the birthplace of Ram, has led to "'History' as a way of knowing the past gain[ing] increasing currency," particularly with regard to contemporary Hindu–Muslim relations (ibid., 457–8). This resulted in a resurgence of what has arguably become one of the key conduits of Hindutva ideology in Indian cinema in the twenty-first century, namely, the historical film. While "Historicals of the Nehru period (1947–64) 'drew on the Congress Party's idea of history' and ... emphasized the Nehruvian 'unity in diversity,'" the genre "dwindled with the end of the Nehru era" (ibid., 459). It is in the twenty-first century that one witnesses the resurgence of this genre, which has arguably become one of the more popular, and Hindutva-ized, in Indian cinema today. The re-introduction of this refurbished and Hindutva-ized genre in the twenty-first century also brought with it the advent of another key element directly related to the shift in (Hindu) viewers' newly "historicized" sensibilities and their corresponding engagement with cinema, namely, the cinematic disclaimer. Beginning in 2001, with the film *Asoka*, one can trace not only an increase of Bollywood historicals but, in turn, increasingly lengthy disclaimers accompanying such films. These disclaimers, more than the films themselves, highlight in many ways the shift in consciousness that Merivirta (2016) describes as well as how such a shift has, in turn, led to what has arguably become a key feature of the contemporary cinematic landscape in India: the highly, one might even say overly, sensitized (Hindu) viewer.

Starring SRK and directed by Santosh Sivan, *Asoka* is an epic historical drama about the early life of the eponymous emperor who ruled much of India in the third century BCE. It is also decidedly a Bollywood production, co-starring Kareena Kapoor and featuring a number of catchy songs and highly choreographed dance routines, some of which have little to do with the storyline. Preceding the film is a disclaimer which reads: "This is a story based on legends. Some characters, events and places have been fictionalized for greater dramatic appeal. This film does not claim to be a complete historical account of Asoka's life. It is an attempt to follow his journey." The film fared well, both critically and commercially, and generated no controversies. Four years later, the film *Mangal Pandey: The Rising* (2005), was released. This film is a historical biographical drama about the eponymous figure, an Indian soldier known to have helped spark the 1857 Indian rebellion against the British, starring Aamir Khan as Pandey. Like *Asoka*, the film begins with a disclaimer, this time slightly longer, which reads:

> This story is based on actual events. In certain cases, incidents, characters and timelines have been changed or fictionalized for dramatic purposes. Certain characters may be composites or entirely fictitious. Some names and locations have been changed. The scenes depicted may be a hybrid of fact and fiction which fairly represent the source materials for the film, believed to be true by the filmmakers.

Despite this rather detailed disclaimer, distinguishing between fact and fiction and openly acknowledging the film has altered certain elements for dramatic purposes, the BJP demanded the film be banned, claiming that it depicted falsehoods and tarnished the image of Pandey (Rediff News 2005). Following demands for the film to be banned, there were protests staged in the district where Pandey had been a native, where a shop selling CDs of songs from the film was attacked (ibid.). Though the government of the state of Uttar Pradesh considered banning the film, ultimately it was not.

Three years later, director Ashutosh Gowariker released *Jodhaa Akbar* (2008), a lavish historical drama about the purported marriage between the titular characters, a (Hindu) Rajput princess and the Muslim emperor Akbar, played by Bollywood superstars Aishwarya Rai and Hrithik Roshan, respectively. As with *Asoka* and *Mangal Pandey*, *Jodhaa Akbar* also begins with a disclaimer which states:

> Historians agree that the 16th century marriage of alliance between the Mughal emperor Akbar and the daughter of King Bharmal of Amer (Jaipur) was a recorded chapter in history ... But there is speculation till today that her name was not Jodhaa ... Some historians say her name was Harkha Bai,

others call her Hira Kunwar, and yet others say Jiya Rani, Maanmati & Shaahi Bai … But over centuries her name reached the common man as Jodhaa Bai. This is just one version of the historical events. There could be other versions and viewpoints to it.

The film was a critical and commercial success, featuring a number of songs scored by A. R. Rahman, however, despite its success and lengthy opening disclaimer, the film was greeted by protests from members of the (Hindu) Rajput community, who claimed the film contained numerous historical inaccuracies, including that Jodhaa was Akbar's wife rather than his son Salim's (Bollywood Hungama 2008). These Rajput groups subsequently claimed they would cease their protest "only if a selected group of historians give clean chit to the film" (Bollywood Hungama 2008). In the meantime, protests by Rajput groups in numerous states, including Madhya Pradesh, Rajasthan, Gujarat, and Punjab, took place, with protestors threatening to burn down cinemas screening the film (Gupta 2008). The film was subsequently banned in several states and, while these bans were ultimately lifted by the Indian Supreme Court, what is noteworthy here, beyond the protests and violence that accompanied the film's release, is the protestors' recourse to history. Here one witnesses a compelling instance of the shift Merivirta describes taking place following the events of Ayodhya—an appeal for a "clean chit" from historians—something she labels a "novelty" in the Indian context (2016: 457).

As critics were quick to note, *Jodhaa Akbar* was not the first filmic adaptation featuring these historical figures. Writing in the Indian newspaper *The Hindu*, Rishi Vohra (2008) noted that "there was no uproar when K. Asif's 1960 classic, *Mughal-e-Azam* featured 'Jodha Bai' (Durga Kote) as the Rajput wife of Akbar (Prithviraj Kapoor)," further observing that Indian audiences continue to watch this earlier film up to the present day "without raising a question about the historical facts."[17] Vohra is right to conclude that such "public intolerance is a new trend" (ibid.) and, furthermore, one that illuminates Merivirta's thesis concerning the newfound appeal to history by, in this case, Hindu Rajput groups, as a criterion for assessing a film's legitimacy. One can begin to trace the growing importance that "History" is accorded by Hindu chauvinist groups stemming back not only to the attacks on the Babri Masjid but, indeed, preceding and in many ways fueling those attacks. One simultaneously witnesses how such a newfound role of "History" becomes increasingly utilized by Hindutva groups as a way of reframing "debates about contemporary Hindu–Muslim relations" and "influenc[ing] Bollywood film-making" (Merivirta 2016: 458). One can see how the disclaimer preceding the film reflects an awareness of this increasing fixation with "History," itself acknowledging the multiple names by which Jodhaa was known and, more relevantly, by including explicit reference to "historians." Compared to the earlier (and shorter) disclaimers accompanying *Asoka* and *Mangal Pandey*, one can see how the makers of *Jodhaa Akbar* may have felt increasingly compelled to include such minute details and acknowledge "there could be other versions and viewpoints to it." Such efforts, both in creating such a disclaimer and in responding to Rajput groups' protests against the film, reveal a growing awareness on the part of Bollywood not only of the necessity of such disclaimers but, via their direct appeals to "history" and "historians," of the need to hew to this newfound criterion of authenticity (in a work of fiction).

In the ensuing years, one sees a major expansion of such disclaimers, as in the case of the one preceding Sanjay Leela Bhansali's *Bajirao Mastani* (2015):

This Film is based on the Marathi Novel titled 'Rau' (written by N.S. Inamdar) based on the life of the legendary warrior 'Peshwe Bajirao' and his second wife 'Mastani'. Some of the incidents, characters, events etc. contained in the Film have been changed and altered for the dramatic/cinematic appeal and effect.

This Film, though made in consultation with eminent historians, does not warrant, represent or claim to be historically accurate. The Filmmaker fully acknowledges and respects other perspectives and viewpoints with regard to the subject of the film. The Filmmaker does not intend in any manner to belittle, disrespect, impair or disparage the beliefs, feelings, sentiments and susceptibilities of any person(s), community(ies), society(ies) and their culture(s), custom(s), practice(s) and tradition(s).

What one sees here is both an increasing usage of legal jargon ("does not warrant, represent or claim to be") and an explicit notice that, despite being made "in consultation with eminent historians," the film makes no claim to historical accuracy. Also worth noting here is the additional language, absent from previous disclaimers, disavowing any bad intentions on the filmmakers' behalf. Why did Bhansali feel compelled to include such details? Again, it is important to bear in mind, as noted at the outset, just how widespread film viewing is, and has been for many decades, in India. As Kasbekar has observed, "India is the worldwide leader, by far, in the quantity of movies produced, *and watched*, each year" (2006: 180, emphasis added).[18] Why is it that filmmakers in a country with the highest number of films produced and viewed by its citizens, feel compelled to note what one could assume would be obvious to anyone who has even seen just one film, namely, that it is a work of fiction, featuring actors and sets?[19] Why have numerous Hindu groups become increasingly sensitized to filmic portrayals of purported historical events? As Vohra (2008) aptly observed, no such sensitivity seemed to manifest itself in 1960, when *Mughal-e-Azam* played in Indian theatres. No theatres were threatened with arson because *Mughal-e-Azam* represented Jodha Bai as being the (Hindu) wife of the (Muslim) Emperor Akbar, nor did the film itself begin with any disclaimer, save that the film was, essentially, a work of art. Is Merivirta's thesis, concerning the growing weight that "History" has taken on, particularly for Hindu groups since the agitation around the Babri Masjid, the only plausible explanation for such heightened sensitivity? How did such an impulse—to take offense—override an earlier impulse to be entertained by a work of art?

These questions become all the more complicated given that Bollywood films in the twenty-first century, unlike most of their twentieth century predecessors, include such increasingly detailed disclaimers. How, in other words, could a viewer claim to be offended by a work of art (for being a work of art) when it explicitly purports to be nothing but a work of art?[20]

Darsan

Related to these questions is whether, and how, a film could be considered a Hindutva film and whether or not such a film form has manifested itself in India today. In the process of addressing this issue, we must turn to the field of Bollywood studies, which also saw its consolidation during this period (1990s–2000s). Underlying my foray into this field is an indigenous theory of spectatorship that has been promulgated by numerous academics, including art historians, film theorists, visual anthropologists, sociologists and religious scholars, as being key to understanding the dynamics of visual interaction in an Indian context. This is the theory of *darsan*, or devotional viewing. We shall see how this religiously inflected paradigm frequently informs many of the ensuing speculations about the implied Indian viewer, particularly regarding works of art that could be considered to connote or otherwise manifest, explicitly or latently, some "Hindu" content. In one of the first book-length studies of Bollywood, Vijay Mishra claims that "the Bombay film can endorse the dharmic order even as it accommodates the modern and transgresses that order" (2002: 33). Alternatively, another leading Bollywood film scholar, Rachel Dwyer, begins her book-length study of Indian cinema, *Filming the Gods*, by arguing that "the decline of religion as a feature of modernity may well be true only of western modernity" (2006a: 4). "Hindu iconography and its relationship of the image and the viewer," Dwyer claims, "have, perhaps, an ever greater affinity with cinema and the conventions of Indian cinema, whether or not the operation of a melodramatic mode or its sequence of 'attractions'... subordinate the spectacular to the other requirements of cinema" (ibid.).

Meanwhile Mishra, in an echo of Chakravarty's earlier point about Bollywood "mediating and filtering" content through its own conventions (2000: 218), finds that "there is some evidence that the cinema is being deconstructed... to question those essentialisms in the Hindu world view that lend themselves to a fascist politics of idealized projection," which is why he finds "no direct, unmediated connection between the popular and Hindutva politics" (2002: 233). Rather than suggesting that Bollywood has been "complicit" in "espousing fundamentalist practices," he argues that this cinema has "confirmed" certain forms of "spectatorial identifications" which may correspond to a Hindu world view (233). "The danger this poses," Mishra goes on to note, is "one of the greatest threats to precisely the nationalist secular ideal that Indian cinema has fostered" (233). This point is also echoed in a way by Dwyer when she notes that "it would be surprising if the Hindi films from the 1990s on ... did not manifest Hindutva ideology, just as nationalist and Nehruvian ideologies dominated earlier films" (2006b: 274). At the same time, Dwyer claims that "it is not clear what a Hindutva film would be" and that "the Hindi cinema has yet to produce a truly Hindutva film" (ibid., 276, 282). Setting aside for the moment the question of what constitutes, or how one could define, such a film form, it is worth noting that Viswanath locates the emergence of what she calls the "right-winged," or "saffronized," Bollywood film in the 1990s (2002: 41). She posits such films as *Hum Dil De Chuke Sanam* (1999), *Aa Ab Laut Chalen* (1999), and *Pardes* (1997), all of which feature NRI figures, as "wholeheartedly" responding to "nativist definitions of 'Indian' culture offered by proponents of Hindutva" (2002: 41). Even as the precise definition of a Hindutva film remains in question then, one already sees a divergence among Hindi film scholars regarding not only whether such a film form has indeed manifested itself by this time but, even more interestingly, whether such films "mediated" or "wholeheartedly" embraced such content.

Dwyer prefaces her inquiry into this subject by noting her reluctance in examining the role of religion in Indian cinema "due to wanting to avoid seeing religion as the essence of India" (2006a: 5). Nevertheless, she finds that "Hindi cinema's very disavowal of certain forms of realism and its unique modification of the melodrama allow the eruption of the religious" (ibid.). At the same time as she claims that Indian cinema may have "specific traits that incline it more towards the religious than other cinemas," Dwyer also notes that "of course it is not just the text itself, but the way the audience perceives it," that does or does not make it so religiously inflected (ibid., 163–4). Nevertheless, she concludes, "these films, however cynical critics may be, do create religious sentiment in viewers and audiences," which, in turn, "raises the question of a Hindu imagination" (ibid., 164). It is worth noting Dwyer's terminology here: she does not claim that such films *may* create religious sentiment in *Hindu* viewers but that they *do* create religious sentiment in (all) viewers. Dwyer also claims that "scopophilia, the pleasure of looking," is "associated with the practice of darshan in much of Indian experience" (ibid., 149). Nevertheless, she argues that making such claims "does not imply any necessary associations with Hindutva or Hindu nationalism" (ibid., 165).

The issue of darsanic viewing is further developed by art historian Preminda Jacob, who notes that "this is, by no means, a trivial topic," given its bearing on "the social evolution of societies and the political evolution of the state" (2009: 227). She claims that "anecdotal evidence" suggests that, "in the viewing of Indian cinema the communal, participatory dimension may supersede the individualized, private experience of viewers of Western cinema" (ibid.). In such a darsanic engagement, Jacob further argues, the "exchange of gazes between the star and the fan disrupts the scopophilia (both voyeurism and fetishism) that is normally associated with cinematic spectatorship" (ibid., 231–2). Here we begin to see fissures between these respective theorists (and theories) of *darsan*. While Dwyer claims that scopophilia is "associated with" *darsan* (2006a: 149), Jacob believes the latter "disrupts" scopophilia and that the "technology of cinema is put in the service of a *darshanic* gaze" (2009: 231–2). Indeed, as she goes on to note, "rather than dissipate the power of *darshan*, cinema's introduction into India ... added yet another context in which the faithful could experience the divine" (ibid., 250). While Jacob, unlike Dwyer, distinguishes between "the faithful" and general "viewers and audiences" in theorizing such cinematic effects, she also believes a distinct viewing paradigm is appropriate for theorizing the implied (Hindu) viewer of Hindi cinema, whether or not such a paradigm is "associated with" or "disrupts" cinematic scopophilia.

Jacob's conclusion is, in turn, supported and furthered by contemporary visual anthropologists and sociologists. Christiane Brosius, for instance, in an essay on "Hindu intervisuality," argues that "rather than de-sacralizing an object, as is often assumed in the context of mass reproduction, new audiovisual technologies [in India] may well affirm, and even increase, the gazing subject's perception of an invisible, overwhelming and intimate presence in the images and their display" (2002: 292). Sociologist Lakshmi Srinivas, in turn, proposes what Dwyer argued no one had yet defined, in her discussion of what she labels a "devotional aesthetic" (2016: 218). Such an aesthetic, she claims, "may be described as 'pentecostal' (viewing or) engagement with the film, a crossing over from social respect (of the star) to worship" (ibid.).[21] The cinema viewing experience in India, Srinivas claims, is shaped by "an aesthetic of watching live entertainment" (ibid., 168). Echoing Jacob's point about "the communal" possibly "superseding" the "individualized private experience" (2009: 230), Srinivas argues that film in the Indian cultural context "is not viewed by atomized individuals" but instead is framed by what she calls a "social aesthetic" (2013: 381).[22]

It is in the subsequent work of art historian Kajri Jain (2021) that one sees a direct engagement with what is arguably implicit in the work of Brosius (2002), Dwyer (2006a, 2006b), Jacob (2009), and Srinivas (2013, 2016), namely, the arguments made by German philosopher and cultural critic Walter Benjamin

(2019 [1936]) regarding the mechanically reproduced work of art. Jain begins her study of monumental statue-building in India by noting both that "it is not enough to simply ascribe this phenomenon to Hindu nationalism, or Hindutva,"[23] and Benjamin's "legendary artwork essay, which … is centrally concerned with the politics of new image technologies at a moment of increasingly authoritarian right-wing populism" (2021: 4–5). While acknowledging the rise of such right-wing Hindu forces in India today, Jain also feels that subsequent theories that try to make sense of cultural artefacts such as Hindutva films or statues employ "the familiar trope of cultural dupes" (ibid., 83). Rather than relying upon "cynical intent, bad faith, faulty reason, dysfunctional psyches, moral evil, and regressive ideology," and projecting these upon human actors (politicians, the public), Jain alternatively argues for a methodological approach that "attend[s] to the material registers (technological, formal, generic)" of such forms in understanding both the interactions and subsequent theorizations of such mechanically reproduced works of art and their implied publics (ibid.). To do so, and particularly "given that Benjamin's ideas are focused on the fate of the bourgeois artwork and geared to the political situation in early twentieth-century Western Europe," Jain feels the German philosopher's theories "require some revision" (ibid., 174). Jain suggests "a modification" to Benjamin's ideas, particularly to his concept of "aura," in the Indian context (ibid., 174–5). Previously, according to Benjamin, the work of art found expression in the cult and "in the service of a ritual"; mechanical reproduction, in turn, "emancipates the work of art from its parasitical dependence on ritual" (2019: 174). While Benjamin defines aura as "the unique phenomenon of a distance, however close it may be" and argues that it is this aura which withers in the process of mechanical reproduction (ibid., 173, 171), for Jain, "aura is a product of the very mass reproduction that was supposed to do away with cult" (2021: 178). Such a paradigm shift would reinscribe aura within the cinematic, which, in turn, would reposition the film viewer within the realm of ritual and the cult or, in this case, the darsanic.

Yet, as Benjamin pointed out over eighty years ago, "aura is tied to [the actor's] presence; there can be no replica of it" (2019: 180). Consequently, in the mechanically reproduced film, "the aura that envelops the actor vanishes, and with it the aura of the figure he portrays" (ibid.). However, Benjamin notes, "cult value does not give way without resistance" and, as he observed of the period in which he was writing, a period in which the forces of fascism were already mobilizing across Europe, "ultrareactionary authors give the film a similar contextual significance—if not an outright sacred one, then at least a supernatural one" (ibid., 178). A particularly compelling instance of this in Benjamin's era is Leni Riefenstahl's film, *Triumph of the Will* (1935, hereafter *Triumph*), her so-called "documentary" about the Nazis which the director herself infamously claimed was not propaganda but "history—*pure history*" (qtd in Bharucha 1994: 1391, emphasis in original). As film theorist Daniel Mourenza has noted, "Riefenstahl thus created a mythical image of National Socialism," in which the images of her film "reinforce the cultic" (2020: 140). This, as Mourenza notes, results in *Triumph* being "a corrupted representation" (ibid.), precisely because, as Benjamin noted, the cinematic "apparatus is pressed into the production of ritual values," a "violation" of the apparatus which finds its counterpart in "the violation of the masses" (2019: 194).

I do not mean to imply that contemporary authors espousing theories of darsan are necessarily "ultrareactionary" but rather that such theorizations may unwittingly perform the work of the right in an era in which, as in Benjamin's time, such ideologies are gaining traction. Given the increasing consolidation of Hindutva both on- and off-screen in India, and particularly since the time of Dwyer's earlier ruminations on such (im)possibilities, such speculations are no longer hypothetical but have become all too real which, in turn, makes a careful (re)consideration of the ramifications of darsanic models and the use of such models to re-ritualize the filmic experience all the more necessary. The theorization of the implied Indian viewer via the darsanic paradigm, that is, of the former as a "devotional viewer," calls to mind Sarkar's observation that "an uncritical cult of the 'popular' or 'subaltern' [...] can lead even radical historians down strange paths" (1993: 165). The darsanic viewing model becomes an instance of what theorists have labeled 'common sense', or what film theorist M. S. S. Pandian described as the "pre-existing cultural practices of the subaltern classes" (1992: 139).[24] What we have here, then, is an instance of what Banaji (2018) characterizes as Hinduvta "cannibalis[ing] and harness[ing] the tactics and vocabularies of ... older Hindu scopic regimes" (6). That academics have given their imprimatur to such "common sense" only provides an additional form of ideological cover for what is essentially a "hijacking" of Hindu concepts by forces of the Hindu right, aided and abetted (unwittingly or otherwise) by the intellectual elite. Such appropriation can and should be read in tandem with other contemporary tactics, including "the persistent effort by Hindu nationalists to present their mythology as history" (Jaffrelot 2021: 171). Such efforts, and related theorizations of viewers, as well as the implicit collapsing—very much in keeping with the Hindutva agenda— of Hindus (and a Hindu religious mentality) with all Indians, are what have led to the increasing Hindutva-ization of Bollywood, something that has only intensified since Modi's rise to power.

Intensification of Pathologies

Modi's use of holograms becomes another way these tendencies have manifested themselves in India today. Apparently the first Indian prime minister to employ 3D holograms, Modi's use of such a technological device is described as "mesmerizing the illiterate masses with technological-driven affect" (Rai 2019: 324). Film and media scholar Swapnil Rai describes how the projection of Modi's 3D hologram at various venues creates, for these "mesmerized" masses, the sense of "a leader who is seemingly directly accessible" (ibid., 336). Film theorist Ravi Vasudevan has also described how

Modi's hologram has been used "to relay the leader's aura" (2022: 360). Technically, however, as Vasudevan goes on to note, "Modi's performance of liveness [via such holograms] is a fiction" (ibid., 380).[25] Yet, such a "fictionalization of address and reception" is part of what Vasudevan labels "the Modi effect," one which "claims a complete lack of human mediation" (ibid., 380, 382). Here we see what Benjamin described as "the phony spell of a commodity" (2019: 182), or what Mourenza (2020), in turn, labels "simulated aura" (127), being employed to create a "fantastical reciprocity," converting "a mediated experience into one of liveness and co-presence" (Majumdar 2022: 509). Such obfuscation of detail accords with the fascist impulse to conceal technological mediation (Mourenza 2020: 142), even as Modi's ensuing "fauxra" helps buttress his cult of personality, particularly amongst the allegedly "mesmerized" masses.[26] Here, again, we see how "the violation of the masses ... has its counterpart in the violation of an apparatus which is pressed into the production of ritual values" (Benjamin 2019: 194).

In a recent piece entitled "The Cult of Modi," Guha notes that several authoritarian leaders today, including Putin, Erdogan, Orban, Bolsonaro, Modi, and Trump, have "constructed, and been allowed to construct, personality cults around themselves" (2022). "One would not expect the population of a free country to be so cravenly worshipful of a living individual," Guha writes, "but, tragically, they are" (ibid.). Guha's words, in turn, reference those of Aldous Huxley who, discussing Hitler in 1958, describes the latter's authoritarian order as being imposed upon the masses "with the hypnotized consent of the majority" (2000 [1958]: 271). Describing Hitler's presumption of the masses as easily manipulable, Huxley writes, "To those of us who look at men and women as individuals rather than as members of crowds ... he seems hideously wrong. In an age of accelerating over-population, of accelerating over-organization and ever more efficient means of mass communication, how can we preserve the integrity and reassert the value of the human individual?" (2000: 276). To paraphrase Huxley over half a century later, how can we explain the current phenomenon of Hindutva and Hindutva-ized films (and their ensuing successes) while preserving the integrity of the implied subject, that is, not reducing him or her to a "hypnotized" fool? This becomes particularly salient in light of contemporary theorizations of Indian film viewers which seem to echo earlier cynical assessments of humans' capacity for reason. Writing in an established, peer-reviewed film journal, two academics of Indian origin recently claimed:

> Advocates of art would call for as much possible freedom to media and films on religious transgressions and wish for an emancipated, tolerant society that sits back and enjoy [sic] films without letting their sentiments hurt [sic], come what may. A review of controversial cinema and subsequent protests suggests that such notions are far-fetched in the context of India.
> BARTHWAL and SHARMA 2023: 706–7[27]

One hears a disturbing echo of the sentiments Huxley previously described in such an assessment, which relatedly finds that filmic representations "may be taken as reality by the larger [Indian] population," as "most people do not have the expertise, will, or time to enquire and validate such representations and assume them to be true" (ibid., 706). Nevertheless, an answer to my earlier question regarding the heightened sensitivities of (Hindu) viewers in India today is provided, namely, that "the present society is even more sensitive to films' depictions" due to "the right-wing Hindu nationalists bringing history to the forefront and building a political narrative in the context of contemporary Hindu–Muslim relations" (ibid., 710–11). We have now come full circle—or to a self-fulfilling prophecy—as, for these authors, it is the propagation of history by the BJP that has caused the shift in audiences' reactions to "historical films," and to their increased sensitization to such material. Such a conclusion becomes rather ironic given how arguably desensitized these same audiences have apparently become over the same time to images of sectarian violence in real life. In other words, such (implied, Hindu) viewers are (now) more outraged by fictitious representations than by actual representations. Such a form of transference, or sublimation, may be seen as providing a response of sorts to the question posed by Banaji (2018) at the outset but also reveals the ensuing justification for the variety of phenomena increasingly on display in the Bollywood ecumene, from increasingly lengthy disclaimers to increasingly virulent protests accompanying the release of one or the other film. If "the masses" are essentially framed as blind victims, then the conclusion that logically follows is that "censorship of films is … needed" (Barthwal and Sharma 2023: 719). This, in many ways, is where India finds itself today, yet this is not the only possibility. Near the end of his study of South Indian film star and politician MGR, Pandian describes MGR's "success story" as simultaneously "the failure of a people" (1992: 144). Nevertheless, Pandian concludes, "politics is always a contested terrain and that even among the devoted followers of MGR there exist indelible marks of dissent … are [sic] quite important," as "therein lies the possibilities of constituting […] a new progressive common sense" (1992: 145).

At the same time, if "the [Gujarat] pogrom of 2002[28] … offers a template for the consolidation of a vigilante public" and the Hindutva narrative has "achieved hegemonic status" in India today, then the development of a fascist consciousness which accepts such a narrative becomes inevitable, to a certain extent (Banaji 2018: 342). This study intends to examine the particular roles Bollywood, and the viewing of Bollywood films, play in such a process. If Modi "represents the open vocalization of certain desires that lay immanent before 2014" (Baishya 2021) and his arrival in Delhi has "only intensified the media pathologies that have long been on display" (Chowdhury and Keane 2021: 251), how has Bollywood intensified such pathologies and what role do viewers play in this process? This is precisely where facile models of the "hypnotized masses" become insufficient in providing a full account for the interactive nature of such processes. I would like to reframe Banaji's (2018) notion of a vigilante public as a viewing public. Such a public cannot merely be reduced to certain audiences' tendencies to become vocal spectators; as with Modi, it is the silence of the film audience in the wake of overt propaganda and related violence that implicates them in such a process. One could describe this as a suturing process, in which one becomes imbricated within the psychodynamics of a fascist consciousness which can manifest itself in varying iterations and with regard to multiple narratives and discourses, whether they be Hindu–Muslim conflict, Hindu myth and/or history, Hindu ideologies including caste and gender roles (encompassing practices of *sati* and *jauhar*), or, more broadly, a growing insistence, reflected through increasingly lengthy disclaimers, on "authenticity." Simultaneously, a diminution of quintessential Bollywood elements—those "mediating and filtering" content (Chakravarty 2000)—arguably results in an attendant diminution of *viewers* engaging in such "mediating and filtering." A fascist, or Hindutva-ized, consciousness alternatively overrides the basic cinematic premise (in bad faith) and insists that Hindutva must trump *masala*. Hence no dream sequence can be permitted between Padmavati and Alauddin Khilji; hence Padukone's midriff must be digitally covered because Padmavati would not show skin; and hence, even more recently, Padukone cannot wear an orange dress while dancing with SRK.[29]

Such an altered ecumene creates a scenario where Bollywood may plausibly believe "the average member of their audience now truly likes everything the BJP likes, and abhors everything it abhors" (Subramanian 2022). If a fascist consciousness is gleaned from, or surmised to inform, such sentiments, then the (erstwhile) Bollywood film, too, undergoes related transformations—witness the increase in the Modi era of Hindutva-ized historical epics, of jingoistic war films, and of collaborative enterprises that are mutually enforcing, with Bollywood endorsing a BJP project or platform and the BJP, in turn, endorsing the Bollywood film, whether via tax breaks, official endorsements or combinations thereof. Such collaborations occur at both the individual level, on- and offscreen and at an industrial level, as in the recent group selfie taken

FIGURE I.1 *Bollywood group selfie with PM Modi (2019). Source: Public domain, 2019. Photo by Karan Johar / Twitter.*

with Modi featuring multiple Bollywood stars which, in turn, is posted and shared (and "liked") on social media platforms (Figure I.1).

Such collaborations also extend to the financiers of films who "are often politicians themselves or have ties to them" (Sharma 2019). Thus, in an ecumene in which, to remain viable Bollywood must remain marketable, such "Modi-fications" become forms of coercion, fed by capital, chauvinism and myth that, in turn, increasingly inform "common sense." Yet, such "Modifications" remain uneven—as Basu (2020) notes, identifying Hindutva as a, or perhaps, the, key ideology informing (and reshaping) Bollywood today does not mean that every film released adheres to such an ideology in equal measure. Rather, Hindutva now functions "as a normative information ecology," in which "the range of possibilities pertaining to narration, aesthetics, or ideology" is already narrowed (Basu 2020: 201–2). This newly shaped cinematic world, with its uneven, unsure and frequently contested trajectories, is what *Bollypolitics* traces. Through a series of case studies, this book examines how contemporary Bollywood films at times obliquely critique, at times blatantly endorse, Hindutva ideology—or, to paraphrase Arnold, how Bollywood oscillates between "overt" and "covert" strategies with regard to such "Modi-fications" (qtd in Chakravarty 1993: 167). The ensuing case studies, detailed below, examine not only how particular films and filmic representations conform to or violate such a "normative information ecology" but also how actors' offscreen personae, informed by social media engagements, collaborations with Modi and the BJP or, alternatively, by threats of boycotts and physical harm, inflect readings of their films. In other words, *Bollypolitics* is concerned with how Bollywood is changing as India grows increasingly Hindutva-ized, that is, how Bollywood is and has been responding to such shifts. Simultaneously, this study explores how audiences and theorists from a range of disciplinary backgrounds have helped inform, digest or at times repudiate, such "Modi-fications." The primary objective of this book is the textual analysis of contemporary films, and how these films embody recent shifts in Indian politics, supplemented, when relevant, with discussion of related social media discourses. The case studies, in turn, are a structuring device employed to consolidate and analyze a certain body of films. Thus, while it may not yet be entirely clear what a "Hindutva" film may be, it is my hope that its constitutive elements, in all their multifariousness, including how they are shaped and deployed by the cinematic, are made clearer through this study.

Chapter Overview

Chapter 1, "From Metatext to Fascist Aesthetics," examines two of Sanjay Leela Bhansali's recent films, *Bajirao Mastani* (2015) and *Padmaavat* (2018). I begin by considering how Bhansali paradoxically employs the historical genre to provide a critique of contemporary Hindutva which, I argue, can be read as *Bajirao Mastani*'s metatext. Following an overview of this concept, based on film theorist Robert Stam's (1992) broader discussion of intertextuality, the chapter engages in a reading of the film in light of contemporary events, including the rise of sectarian violence in India. This is accompanied by a close reading of one of the film's crucial song sequences, "Gajanana," which I analyze both in relation to the filmic plot and the broader social context of the film's release. The chapter then proceeds to a discussion of Bhansali's subsequent film, *Padmaavat*, with particular attention devoted to what I characterize as the film's fascist aesthetics. Beginning with an overview of the multiple challenges Bhansali faced while making this film, including physical attacks on production sets as well as death threats issued by various Hindutva groups, my discussion then moves to an overview of fascist aesthetics, based on the analysis of Susan Sontag (1980) and Frank Tomasulo (2014) regarding Riefenstahl's *Triumph* (1935). The chapter then engages in a close reading of key sequences from *Padmaavat* that deploy such an aesthetic, including the culminating *jauhar* sequence, which features the mass immolation of the titular heroine and her female followers. The chapter concludes with a discussion of how *Padmaavat* deviates from a Bollywood aesthetic as well as what the broader ramifications of such a shift are, both for the Bollywood film form and for its reception by contemporary Indian audiences.

Chapter 2, "Modi's Ad Man," turns the focus to Bollywood star Akshay Kumar and his on- and offscreen relationships with Modi and the BJP, including two films made in collaboration with Modi's government, *Toilet: Ek Prem Katha* (2017, hereafter *Toilet*) and *Mission Mangal* (2019). Drawing upon Pallavi Rao's (2019) analysis of the film, my discussion of *Toilet* revolves around how it employs caste-based logic to frame the issue of sanitation as well as provide its Brahmin protagonist, played by Kumar, with a way to resolve this issue. The chapter also explores how *Toilet* benefitted from its partnership with the BJP's Clean India campaign as well as how the filmmakers and the Modi government collaborated in a mutually beneficial media campaign. The chapter then examines Kumar's subsequent film, *Mission Mangal*, which dramatizes the development of India's Mars orbiter mission and similarly engages in a pro-government portrayal. Relatedly I consider Modi's brief cameo near the end of the film as well as Kumar's filmed interview with Modi during the latter's re-election campaign the same year. Building on Sreya Mitra's (2021) analysis of star power and "Brand Modi," I analyze how such filmic and extrafilmic collaborations function as public relations exercises for the Modi regime, in which Kumar, in turn, operates as Modi's ad man. My discussion then moves to another recent Kumar film, *Kesari* (2019), in which the actor plays a Sikh warrior in a dramatic reenactment of the 1897 Battle of Saragarhi, in which twenty-one members of the 36th Sikh regiment held off thousands of Pashtuns attacking the fort before their ultimate demise. Like *Padmaavat*, this film can be seen as part of the broader "saffronization" of Indian history. My discussion then turns to another recent Kumar blockbuster, *Sooryavanshi* (2021), which rearticulates the more recent history of violence following the attack on the Babri Masjid in December 1992. Even as the ensuing violence in Bombay serves as backstory and motivating force for Kumar's character, the eponymous super (Hindu) cop, in his pursuit of modern day (Islamic) terrorists, the film alternately elides and celebrates the underpinning violence perpetrated against Muslims. I conclude by looking at one final film, *Ram Setu* (2022), in which Kumar plays an atheist archaeologist tasked with determining whether the so-called Ram Setu, a chain of natural limestone shoals between India and Sri Lanka, is a manmade formation. Drawing on IMAX aesthetics, the film engages in what I describe as immersive Hindutva as a way of reimagining a mythical Hindu past, in this case, relating to the *Ramayan*.

Chapter 3, "Modi's *Bhakt*," explores the case of Kangana Ranaut, a younger actress turned director who has quickly become one of Prime Minister Modi's most strident supporters, particularly via social media, where she has a large following. Following an overview of Ranaut's career and social media controversies, this chapter engages in a detailed study of her 2019 historical epic *Manikarnika: The Queen of Jhansi* (hereafter *Manikarnika*), which she co-directed and in which she also plays the titular role. I begin by examining earlier cinematic depictions of this historical figure, including Sohrab Modi's *Jhansi Ki Rani* (1953). Building on Harleen Singh's (2014) analysis of the Rani of Jhansi, the chapter engages in close readings of key sequences from these earlier adaptations, before moving to a detailed analysis of Ranaut's *Manikarnika*, exploring how this most recent iteration reimagines key events and, in the process, how Ranaut, as both director and star, frames her character as a martyr for a Hindutva-ized nation. I conclude my discussion by briefly looking at Ranaut's forthcoming film, *Emergency* (2024), a biopic about former Prime Minister Indira Gandhi, in which Ranaut again plays the lead character and directs. Due to be released just ahead of the 2024 general election, I consider how Ranaut's film, in reimagining the earlier era of the Congress matriarch and her notorious period of Emergency (1975–7), paradoxically helps buttress the Modi regime in the contemporary moment.

Chapter 4, "The Kashmiri Pandit," examines recent films of renowned Bollywood actor Anupam Kher, as well as how he has become a key ally of Modi and the BJP. My discussion begins with a brief overview of Kher's film career, which includes appearances in a number of international, English-language films including *Bend It Like Beckham* (2002). I then explore the subsequent evolution of Kher's career following Modi's ascendancy to the post of prime minister, including Kher's performance as former Prime Minister Manmohan Singh in *The Accidental Prime Minister* (2019), based on the book by Sanjaya Baru. Kher's portrayal of the former Congress prime minister, following Baru's depiction, is that of a weak man manipulated, in turn, by the party president, Sonia Gandhi, and her son and heir apparent, Rahul Gandhi. This is followed by a discussion of the recent Hindutva blockbuster *The Kashmir Files* (2022), which features Kher in his newly Hindutva-ized avatar and depicts the tragedy of the Kashmiri Pandits, who were forced from their homeland in the early 1990s. Heavily promoted by the Modi government and also issued tax breaks, the film has become a box office success, with Modi himself exhorting Indians to watch it, even as he rescinded Article 370, abrogating Kashmir's status of semi-autonomy. I examine how the film, in an uncanny reinvocation of D. W. Griffith's *The Birth of a Nation* (1915), demonizes Muslims as savages and, in the process, recreates this historical period as a hyperbolic horror show, deploying incendiary visual tactics that simultaneously brutalize and work to inflame (Hindu) viewers. My discussion of the film is supplemented by an exploration of Kher's invocation of his own Kashmiri Pandit identity as well as how such an invocation coheres with the film's underlying rhetoric and revisionist history.

In the final chapter, "Hope from the Hinterlands?," I consider three recent films starring newcomer Ayushmann Khurrana, all of which deviate from Bollywood's typical formula, shifting the focus to contemporary issues including caste-based violence, homophobia, and the Northeast region of India. Significantly, all of these films take place outside the cosmopolitan centers of India, focusing instead on denizens of smaller towns and utilizing such contexts to expose and confront provincial mindsets regarding such issues. Through close readings of each film, this chapter explores how these films present, to varying degrees, viable alternatives to the contemporary Hindutva-inflected big-budget Bollywood film. Like Akshay Kumar, Khurrana has also paid obeisance to Modi via social media, yet his filmic endeavors reveal a cannier approach to mediating Modi's politics. The chapter begins with an analysis of Anubhav Sinha's *Article 15* (2019), whose title invokes the provision of the Indian Constitution banning caste-based discrimination. Building on Anwer and Arora's (2022) study of caste and couple formation in New Bollywood, my discussion of Khurrana, as an upper caste police officer who travels to the state of Uttar Pradesh to investigate the rape and lynching of two Dalit girls, focuses on how the film and its resolution become contingent upon a Brahminical savior complex in which Khurrana functions as the key agent enabling justice. Khurrana takes a different turn in the following film I examine in this chapter, *Shubh Mangal Zyada Saavdhan* (2020), in which he plays a middle-class gay man who accompanies his boyfriend on a trip from

Delhi to Allahabad, to attend a wedding. While there, Khurrana and his boyfriend are outed which, in turn, exposes provincial prejudices and allows Khurrana to enlighten his boyfriend's conservative Hindu family about homosexuality and gay rights. The film also directly references the Indian Supreme Court's landmark decision, in 2018, decriminalizing homosexuality which, in turn, becomes a key element of the story. I conclude this chapter with a discussion of *Anek* (2022), Khurrana's second collaboration with Anubhav Sinha, which explores the nebulous political and cultural issues of the Northeast region as well as its complex relationship with, and continued estrangement from, India. All three of Khurrana's films discussed here engage with salient political issues that generally remain unaddressed by mainstream Bollywood, making these films, in turn, even more significant.

I conclude by briefly considering the recently released BBC documentary, *India: The Modi Question* (2023), which was subsequently banned in India, as well as Bollywood superstar SRK's recent comeback film, *Pathaan* (2023), which has gone on to become an enormous blockbuster. Considering these films in tandem, I examine *Pathaan*'s release, preceded by Hindutva-generated controversy, as a microcosm of the contemporary situation Bollywood finds itself in, as well as how this industry and its so-called "King" have responded to the questions Modi has posed. Concluding his magisterial tome on the history of modern India, Ramachandra Guha writes, "So long as Hindi films are watched and their songs sung, India will survive" (2007: 759). The question this study seeks to address, even as Guha has subsequently changed his tune,[30] is whether a Hindutva-ized Bollywood would still ensure such an outcome—and, if so, what kinds of sounds and visions of contemporary India its "Modi-fied" content provides.

1

From Metatext to Fascist Aesthetics: The Case of Sanjay Leela Bhansali

Director Sanjay Leela Bhansali provides one of the most compelling instances of what I call the "Modi-fication" of Bollywood. In this first chapter, I set out to analyze two of his most recent films, *Bajirao Mastani* (2015) and *Padmaavat* (2018), both blockbusters and both indicative, in multiple ways, of the fraught negotiations filmmakers tackling issues relating to Hindu–Muslim conflicts, whether real or mythical, have faced within the contemporary political context. *Bajirao Mastani* (hereafter *BM*) follows Bhansali's previous film *Goliyon Ki Rasleela Ram-Leela* (2013, hereafter *RL*) in utilizing an earlier narrative to (re)tell a contemporary story. However, while the ur-text of *RL* was *Romeo and Juliet*, transplanted, in turn, to a contemporary Gujarati setting, *BM* invokes a more religiously inflected storyline—that of Brahmin and Peshwa warrior Bajirao and his love for Mastani, the fiery daughter of a Rajput king and Muslim *tawaif* (courtesan), herself trained as a warrior and marked as Muslim in the film. While Bhansali takes great pains at the outset to disavow any intention of religious critique, I argue that such a critique—of fundamentalist Hindu forces—indeed, forms, and can be read as, the metatext of *BM*. Such a metatext becomes particularly apparent in the contemporary Indian context, in which the always fraught relations between Hindus and Muslims have been further exacerbated since the election in 2014 of the Hindu nationalist Bharatiya Janata Party (BJP) leader Narendra Modi to the post of prime minister. Modi has been a divisive figure in India since becoming chief minister of the state of Gujarat in 2002, when fierce clashes between Hindus and Muslims broke out, leading to the deaths of approximately 2,000 people, the overwhelming majority of whom were Muslims (Marino 2014: 117). The ruling BJP Party and Modi in particular were widely accused of "tacitly, and sometimes actively, supporting some of the worst attacks on Muslim neighborhoods for political gain" (Singh 2013: 687). Though Modi has thus far remained clear of all charges, he has also widely been held responsible for the violence, in particular due to his failure to speak out forcefully against it. Since Modi became prime minister, and particularly in the past years, there has been an increase in activism from right-wing Hindu nationalist groups in India, including not only Modi's own BJP Party but also aligned organizations such as Shiv Sena. In this chapter, I intend to read *BM* in light of these current events, excavating in the process the film's metatextual critique of such activism and intolerance and arguing that, in an interesting corollary to Modi's purported silence, it is Bhansali's strategy of indirection—addressing contemporary events via an historical tale—that has paradoxically resulted in the film's overwhelming success. If the tale of the doomed lovers Bajirao and Mastani provides insights into "the socio-cultural processes, moral values and even political events" of the eighteenth century (Vanina 1999: 101), then a metatextual reading of *BM* can similarly provide illuminating insights into the political events and underlying values of the contemporary era, in which the film has been realized and received.

Disclaimers

Before proceeding with a discussion of *BM* and its metatext, however, I would first like to make a disclaimer, itself stemming from Bhansali's disclaimer. *BM* begins with a lengthy statement, appearing onscreen in both English and Hindi and read in voiceover in Hindi, proclaiming that, while the film is based on the book *Rau* by Marathi novelist N. S. Inamdar, it does not profess to be historically accurate and, furthermore, that no slight is intended in any way towards any "group(s), community(ies)," and so on. Such a statement might be understood as coming in response to India's rather restrictive laws governing artistic expression, which forbid any work from causing or giving offense to the religious sensibilities, in particular, of any group. The particular groups this disclaimer may have been geared towards may very well have been those who did, in turn, protest the film's screening, namely, Hindu-right organizations such as the BJP, who burnt an effigy of Bhansali and shouted slogans against the film in Pune, leading to the local theatre canceling some of the film's initial screenings (*Times of India* 2015). Such backlashes have become increasingly common in recent years, and have frequently targeted both Bollywood personnel and their films. To cite just one of several such instances, when Bollywood superstar Shah Rukh Khan (SRK) asserted in 2015 that there was "growing intolerance" in India, BJP leaders attacked him, calling the Muslim actor a "Pakistani agent" (*Hindustan Times* 2015). SRK's subsequent film, *Dilwale* (2015), was, in turn, also boycotted by various groups in response to his comments (Sahadevan 2015). Thus, to reiterate and build upon Bhansali's claim, I am not claiming that such a metatextual reading—of *BM* as critiquing contemporary fundamentalist Hindu forces—is either Bhansali's intention or that it is the only possible way of interpreting the film (Indeed, given the alacrity shown by the Hindu right in effecting punitive measures against its perceived critics, one could see why openly declaring such an intent, particularly in light of India's draconian laws governing speech, would be avoided by the film's director). If anything, such a metatextual reading is catachrestic, given that it deliberately "mis-reads" its auteur's professed intentions. Yet, it is paradoxically the very vehemence of such a disavowal on Bhansali's part that gives rise to the catachrestic reading I am suggesting. It is precisely in order to excavate what has otherwise gone unremarked upon—the film's bearing on the contemporary situation regarding Hindus and Muslims, a topic that, in many ways, cannot be directly addressed by mainstream Hindi cinema[1]—that I employ such a critical framework here.

Such a deliberate misreading can further be articulated in two ways. First, Bhansali himself, in a manner akin to Milos Forman in *Goya's Ghosts* (2006), can be seen as making an intervention into a contemporary issue (the rise of Hindu fundamentalism since the election of Modi) by reverting to a previous historical period—the eighteenth century background against which *BM* unfolds—and using this earlier historical epic to say something about the current political situation.[2] Furthermore, as he did in both *Devdas* (2002) and *RL*, Bhansali imbues this earlier historical narrative with contemporary discourses, for instance, injecting a degree of feminist critique into *Devdas* and its depiction of the courtesan figure Chandramukhi. In the process, one could describe Bhansali's cinematic treatments more as updates or reconfigurations of the earlier tales (and the discourses informing them). Second, such a (mis) reading of *BM*—as transhistorically critiquing Hindu intolerance in India—in turn, problematizes the boundaries governing/ constituting the nation as well as the ensuing discourses surrounding/ informing such allegorical readings as, for instance, those suggested by Frederic Jameson (1986) regarding "Third World texts." To engage in such a metatextual reading does not necessarily entail remaining within Jameson's paradigm of (reading) Third World texts as (national) allegory. It is entirely possible to read *BM* as "just" a story, that is to say, non-allegorically, and precisely for this reason that such a metatextual reading of the film can be seen as catachrestic: blatantly contradicting its author's professed claims, synchronically critiquing the present and, in the process, problematizing contemporary discourses shaping the reading of a "Third World text." It is by "misreading" the film in precisely this manner that such an approach can paradoxically constitute a productive intervention into the contemporary socio-political context. To invoke another Jamesonian concept, one could say that the (meta)text of *BM* lends itself to a process of *transcoding*, in which the same film can be seen as articulating two moments—the (past) time in which the film takes place and the (present) time in which the film is released—which are collapsed even as they remain distinct.[3] Before commencing with such a reading, I would also briefly like to address the concept of the metatext that I will be employing here.

Metatext(s)

My discussion of the metatextual stems from the broader discourse concerning intertextuality. As Robert Stam has noted, the concept of intertextuality suggests that "every text forms an intersection of textual surfaces where other texts may be read" (1992: 20). Key to such a concept is the ensuing notion of the implied audience which, in turn, can be said to possess a degree of spectatorial competence premised upon "all the semiotic systems with which the reader or spectator is familiar" (Stam 1992: 21). Thus, in the context of my discussion of *BM*, one could assume that the contemporary Indian viewer of the film would have, at the very least, a familiarity with the conventions of Bollywood cinema, itself quite intertextual. The particular notion of the metatextual stems from the further nuanced notion of transtextuality, defined by Gerard Genette as "all that puts one text in relation, whether manifest or secret, with other texts" (qtd in Stam 1992: 22–3). Genette subdivides transtextuality into five particular forms, the third of which he calls "metatextuality" and defines as "the *critical* relation between one text and another, whether the commented text is explicitly cited or silently evoked" (Stam 1992: 24, emphasis in original). This latter notion—of silent evocation—is particularly relevant to my discussion of *BM* which, I argue, engages with contemporary socio-political events in precisely such a manner. Again, the notion of silence becomes crucial here as it signifies in multiple ways. On the one hand, it is Modi who, as critics frequently note, has remained silent in the face of ongoing and increasing acts of intolerance instigated, in many cases, by members of his own political party. On the other hand, it is *BM* which silently evokes, via its metatext, a critique of such acts and, in turn, of such silence. Related to the concept of the metatextual and relevant to my discussion here is also Genette's fifth form of transtextuality, which he calls "hypertextuality" (Stam 1992: 25). This term refers to the relation between one text—the hypertext—and an anterior text, or "hypotext," which the former "transforms, modifies, elaborates, or extends" (ibid.). As Stam notes, the two concepts—metatextuality and hypertextuality—have much in common and, for the purposes of this discussion, both concepts will be utilized. *BM* may be said to have two metatexts, one explicit (the history of Bajirao and Mastani), aka the hypotext, and one implicit (the rise of contemporary Hindu fundamentalism) whose readability, in turn, is contingent upon the audience's intertextual competence, that is, its ability to read the semiotic system Bhansali employs in *BM* in light of contemporary events.[4] It is precisely in this way that *BM* can be said to signify its (metatextual) meaning to its (implied, Indian) audience which can be said to engage in a form of mediation that "presupposes [one's] sense of the relative autonomy of each of the sectors or regions in question" (Jameson 1981: 43).[5] Even as this metatext relies upon such spectatorial competence, however, it is also precisely what Bhansali must disavow, as noted in the earlier section, in order to have his film screened without creating the attendant controversy that such an overt metatext might bring about, particularly in the charged sociopolitical atmosphere of India today.[6]

Bajirao Mastani

While the historical tale of Bajirao and Mastani is familiar to students of Indian history, most scholars, as Eugenia Vanina notes, "would, at best, treat it as a minor episode more suitable for a ballad" (1999: 101). At the same time, as Vanina observes, "a different approach is possible" (ibid.) and, indeed, Bhansali does much more than merely provide a ballad. His adaptation, again, based on Inamdar's *Rau*, is a larger-than-life spectacle, incorporating cutting edge video effects (VFX), stunning scenery and costume design and a number of impressively choreographed song and dance sequences, one of which in particular will be discussed below. The film begins with the ascent of Bajirao (Ranveer Singh) to the position of Peshwa (prime minister) in the empire of Chhatrapati Shivaji, founder of the Maratha state, followed by a montage sequence which establishes his prowess on the battlefield and consolidation of power over the ensuing decade. As K. M. Panikkar notes, Bajirao utilized two "powerful instruments" in his quest to build a Maratha empire in Hindustan: the Maratha cavalry and the conception of a *Hindu Pad Padshahi*, or Hindu empire (1961: x). At this point in Indian history, the power of the Mughals was declining and it was precisely in such a context that Bajirao consolidated Maratha power and, by extension, the Hindu empire, in central India. The excavation of the metatext I have in mind begins with this commitment to make India a Hindu state, or "Hindu swaraj." Like Bajirao, Modi, with his "long-standing record as an assertive Hindu nationalist," has also made no secret of his aspiration to create such a state in contemporary India and, in the process, "to polarise society along religious lines" (Manor 2015: 748).

It is shortly after the opening credits montage, visualizing Bajirao's prowess and exploits over a period of roughly ten years, that we are first introduced to Mastani (Deepika Padukone). As scholars have noted, Mastani's origins are not clear (Srinivasan 1961: 79). The daughter of a Rajput emperor, Chatrasal Bundela, and one of his Muslim consorts, Mastani was "endowed with beauty and various talents" and was "equally skilful in arts and in arms" (Vanina 1999: 103). Along with her singing and dancing skills, Mastani "knew how to ride a horse and could handle sword and spear" (ibid.). In historical accounts, Mastani accompanied Bajirao back to Pune after the latter assisted her father in defeating the army of Muhammad Khan Bangash. However, here, too, accounts vary; as Vanina notes, "We do not know whether Mastani was presented by Chatrasal to the Peshwa as a slave, or whether some marriage ceremony was performed" (ibid.). In *BM*, meanwhile, Mastani dramatically makes her entrance as the very messenger sent by her father to summon Bajirao. The Peshwa, upon hearing that a messenger has arrived outside his battleground tent seeking succor, tells his aid to rebuff the messenger. Suddenly, however, the messenger enters Bajirao's tent and, in the process of fighting off the latter's men, her (female) identity is revealed when her mask and helmet fly off, revealing her long hair and face. Though Bajirao seems intrigued by this woman warrior, he still refuses her request for military aid, at which point Mastani places her sword at his neck, insisting that she vowed to return with assistance or not return at all. Impressed by her nerve, the Peshwa relents and returns with Mastani to help defeat Bangash's armies. During the battle, Mastani saves Bajirao's life and Bajirao, in turn, carries Mastani off the battlefield after she suffers a minor wound and collapses.

Upon visiting her quarters at her father's palace, Bajirao asks to see Mastani's wound and, upon doing so, presses his dagger, made hot by a nearby flame, to her wound so that Mastani cries out and clutches Bajirao tightly. In subsequently being given his dagger Mastani, following Rajput tradition, assumes that she and Bajirao have entered into a (marital) union. Shortly thereafter, Bajirao returns, alone, to his kingdom in Pune, where he is greeted by his (Hindu) wife Kashibai (Priyanka Chopra). We are then shown Mastani informing her parents of her decision to go to Bajirao (armed with his dagger), even though her mother cautions against it, pointing out that she is a Muslim and thus would not be welcomed by the Brahmin Marathas. Nevertheless, Mastani sets off for Pune, where she is first met by Bajirao's mother Radhabai (Tanvi Azmi), who inquires about Mastani's background, noting that she is Muslim when the latter tells her who her mother is, and also about the purpose of Mastani's visit. When Mastani shows Radhabai Bajirao's dagger, explaining the implication of her being in possession of it, Bajirao's mother dismisses the claim, stating that such a gesture is not recognized by the Brahmin Marathas. Yet, Mastani remains as a guest at the Peshwa's residence, even though she is relegated to the court dancers' chambers, and even performs a song and dance one evening before Bajirao and his assembled guests.

However, Radhabai, as well as Bajirao's brother, Chimnaji Appa, "aware of the delicate situation created by the presence of Mastani," first attempt to relegate the latter to the position of dancer and, when this fails, to "impress upon the Peshwa ... the need to abandon Mastani" (Srinivasan 1961: 80). Rather than doing so, Bajirao decides to make Mastani his wife and, after she gives birth to his son, to move them both into his house, a decision that creates enormous ripples throughout the orthodox Brahmin community, despite the fact that Mastani conducts herself as "a *pativrata* Hindu wife" and not as a concubine (Vanina 1999: 103). Both she and Bajirao want their son, originally named Krishna, to be brought up as a Hindu, however the Brahmin priest refuses to perform the sacred thread ceremony and so Bajirao changes the child's name to Shamsher Bahadur and decides to raise him as a Muslim. Nevertheless, in marrying a non-Hindu woman—the Muslim Mastani—Bajirao commits a "double sin" in the eyes of his fellow Brahmins and other orthodox Hindus: first, as Vanina notes, by "polluting" himself by the union with an impure (non-Hindu) woman and, second, by "stoop[ing]" to marry a courtesan's daughter (ibid., 105). While relations with such women were typical amongst the nobility, to legitimize such a relationship was tantamount to scandal. Here, again, one can trace a parallel to Modi, during whose tenure divisions between Hindus and Muslims have been exacerbated, including, paradoxically, when attempts are made to overcome such divisions. One particularly relevant instance of such exacerbation can be seen in the "widespread campaign" increasingly waged since Modi has come to power against so-called "love jihad," that is to say, perceived attempts by Muslim men to dupe Hindu women into marrying them (Manor 2015: 750). It is important to note that, in the case of *BM*, we are conversely presented with an instance of a woman who herself engages in syncretic religious practices being defined (solely) as Muslim and engaging in an amorous union with a Hindu man.[7] Yet, despite this distinction the parallel between these moments rests upon the similar intolerance displayed towards interreligious unions by Hindu chauvinists.

Crucial to such a view was the Brahmin notion of the house, or *ghar*, that Bajirao, as Peshwa, should occupy (Vanina 1999: 105). In accordance with his caste and creed and, particularly, as "the acknowledged leader of the Hindus in India" (Srinivasan 1961: 137), Bajirao's attempt to keep Mastani as his Muslim wife in his *ghar* was "an intolerable violation of caste purity, religious precepts, social status of the family and public morals" (Vanina 1999: 107). In one of the most powerful sequences of *BM*, we see to what extent the Brahmins were willing to go in order to uphold the sanctity of their (leader's) *ghar*. This sequence comes in the midst of a song, "Gajanana," which was the first audio track released and whose release, in turn, served as a rather interesting event, particularly in relation to the larger metatext I have in mind.

"Gajanana"

The song sequence begins after Mastani and her son, Shamsher Bahadur, have been situated in a part of Bajirao's house known as Mastani Mahal (Mastani's house). The sequence commences with the sound of a conch shell being blown even as Kashi descends from her own quarters with a *pooja* (prayer) tray in her hands. Suddenly a Hindu priest, Shiva Bhatt, appears before Kashi, explaining that, during the *aarti* ceremony dedicated to Lord Ganesha (revered as the remover of obstacles), there will be an invasion of Mastani's quarters and her assassination will take place. He then adds, "Save her if you can," before departing just as quickly. After momentarily pausing, Kashi makes her way to the hall where the *pooja* is taking place, pushing open the door to clouds of red powder hovering in the air above the worshippers as the sound of the music increases. A transition takes us to Mastani bursting through a door in her mahal, running with her son in her arms even as she bends to avoid the sword of an assailant, grabbing another's sword in the meantime and slashing at yet another. The camera cuts back to Kashi, slowly making her way through the *pooja* chamber, tray in hand, then reverts to Mastani, child in hand, facing two more masked assailants. The camera again returns to the Hindu revelers at their *pooja*, throwing up clouds of red powder and roaring along with the song, while Bajirao stands in the center, moving his *pooja* tray in circles before the stone idol, or *murti*, of Ganesha. We again return via an abrupt cut to Mastani, now facing more assassins, holding her son in one arm and lashing out with a *talwar*, or sword, in her other hand. Meanwhile a nervous Kashi now approaches Bajirao and hesitantly stands beside him. Even as the song picks up—the voices chanting "Hare Ram, Hare Ram, Hare Krishna, Hare Ram"—Kashi turns to gaze at Bajirao with a worried look on her face, even as he turns to look at her and the camera, in turn, reverts to Mastani, still fighting desperately, now surrounded by even more men trying to kill her and her son.

Nowhere more than in this *aarti* song sequence is the scathing critique of fundamentalist Hindus apparent. In juxtaposing shots of Hindus praying to their god with images of Hindu soldiers sent to kill the Muslim Mastani and her son, Bhansali's "Gajanana" sequence evokes numerous similar images, for example, scenes depicting the Hindu–Muslim riots in Bombay in *Slumdog Millionaire* (2008), in which the young Muslim protagonists' mother is attacked by marauding Hindus who descend upon their Muslim victims. It is precisely through the vivid juxtapositions of Hindus praying with Hindus striking blows at Mastani, holding her child tightly to her breast, that the images of such earlier religious strife are invoked. Such images also invoke accounts of the riots in Gujarat during Modi's tenure, during which Babu Bajrangi, extremist leader of the Hindu fundamentalist group Bajrang Dal, was "personally hacking to death helpless Muslim workers," aided, in turn, by "a lady doctor and the proprietor of a maternity clinic who was handing out swords to Hindu rioters" (Marino 2014: 113).[8] Even more recently, during Modi's ascension to the post of prime minister, a Hindutva firebrand, Pravin Togadia, "urged Hindus to enter Muslim houses in predominantly Hindu neighborhoods to compel residents to move," following which two dozen families in Gurgaon were "forced to abandon their homes when some of them were beaten" (Manor 2015: 749).[9]

What makes the "Gajanana" sequence even more interesting, particularly in relation to the (silently evoked) metatext I have in mind, is the manner in which Bhansali launched the song. Released at the Chhatrapati Shivaji Sports Complex in Pune two days prior to the Ganesh Chaturthi festival in September of 2015, Bhansali assembled over 5,000 students from across the country to create the biggest human formation of a mosaic image of Lord Ganesha (YouTube 2015). The resulting image, which was over 195 feet in size, is said to have created a Guinness World Record (ibid.). Thus Bhansali utilizes the very elements in launching the (audio) song—Hindus paying homage to Ganesha—that the final (picturized) version of the song, with its interpolated juxtapositions, critiques (Conveniently the cutaway shots to Mastani were not shown at the time of the song's release, during the Ganesh Chaturthi, a juxtaposition that may indeed have struck some of the 5,000 participants as more than slightly scandalous, conflating as it does the barbarity unleashed by the film's Hindu fundamentalists with their religious precepts). Describing the release of the (audio-only) song at this launch event, the Indian commentator claims, "The song is spiritual, uplifting and signifies the massiveness of the movie" (YouTube 2015). Indeed. What it can also be said to signify is the metatextual critique of Hindu fundamentalism, achieved by first separating and then uniting sound and image tracks.

Like Kashi standing beside Bajirao at the Ganesha *pooja*, Bhansali strategically utilizes silence—in this case, regarding the way in which he planned to use the "Gajanana" song—to his benefit. And like Modi, who has both been assailed for his "failure to confront intolerance by fellow Hindu nationalists" (Barstow and Raj 2015) and claimed that his "silence has more power than speech" (qtd in Marino 2014: 267), Kashi's silence before her husband speaks volumes about both the imminent peril facing Mastani and her own ambivalence regarding this.[10] Bajirao correctly interprets the silent look Kashi gives him in the midst of the *pooja* and makes his way to Mastani in the nick of time. However, to return to the notion of the Hindu *ghar*, this sequence also opens the door to a metatextual critique of India's conception of itself as a secular democracy, with equal protection (and love) for all of its citizens, regardless of their faith. This fundamental assumption has come under increasing scrutiny during Modi's tenure as prime minister (even as it did during his time as chief minister in Gujarat) due, in part, to acts of violence perpetrated by Hindus against Muslims, for example, the killing of Mohammed Ikhlaq in September 2015 by a Hindu mob that suspected he had killed a cow and eaten its meat, as well as, crucially, to Modi's failure to condemn such actions in a timely fashion (Barstow and Raj 2015).[11] In *BM*, Bajirao tries to house a Hindu and a Muslim under the same roof, yet is repeatedly thwarted in this endeavor, as is vividly on display in the "Gajanana" sequence. Try as they may, neither Mastani nor Bajirao can convince Kashi that, despite taking Mastani as his wife, the Peshwa continues to love his first wife. In other words, love for a Muslim is seen as betrayal by the Hindu, even as the Muslim is deemed unfit as a partner in a legitimate relationship. Radhabai and Bajirao's brother seem willing to accept Mastani, provided she remain housed separately, in the concubine's quarters. To place her inside the Peshwa's house is, in the Brahmins' eyes, to tarnish the very notion of the *ghar*; hence the need for Kashi's son, Nana Saheb, to order his troops to eliminate the unwanted intruder and her son, his own half-brother.[12]

Navigating a Minefield

BM was both a critical and commercial success, with the film winning nine awards at the 2016 Filmfare Awards, including for Best Picture and Best Director. Yet, crucial to this success, I argue, is Bhansali's simultaneous focus on and avoidance of the broader politics surrounding and informing the relationship of his titular characters. *BM*'s conclusion, which features apocalyptic imagery accompanying the demise of Bajirao and Mastani, exemplifies this approach. Though he saves Mastani from her Hindu assassins, Bajirao is unable to overcome the resistance of the chief Hindu priest, the Panditrao, to his union with Mastani.[13] It is this fact—Bajirao's weakness in the wake of the Brahmin orthodoxy—that can be considered extraordinary, given that Bajirao was, at the time, "the most powerful man in the empire" (Panikkar 1961: xiii). In the Hindu priests' refusal to sanctify his relationship with Mastani, we see both the limits of Bajirao's power and the powerful influence wielded by the religious orthodoxy at the time. It is precisely this element of the film—illustrating Bajirao's inability to overcome "the power of organized Hinduism" (ibid.)—that again opens up *BM* to the contemporary metatext I am suggesting. Just as the Hindu priests refused to legitimize Bajirao's relationship with Mastani, Hindu nationalist groups such as the BJP and Shiv Sena frequently exert their influence on Bollywood today, as was the case with the protests surrounding the opening of *BM*, in which Bhansali's effigy was burned. Just as the Peshwa Bajirao was forced to walk to Canossa, the Badshah of Bollywood, SRK, was forced to walk back his statements regarding the rising intolerance in India in the face of attacks by BJP leaders and threats from various groups to boycott his recently released film (*Hindustan Times* 2015).[14]

As a Bollywood filmmaker, Bhansali would undoubtedly be aware of these forces and, as demonstrated by his launch of the "Gajanana" song, the ensuing need to carefully navigate such a minefield. Ravi Vasudevan has noted the earlier controversy surrounding Mani Ratnam's *Bombay* (1995), which directly explored Hindu–Muslim strife following the riots of 1992–3 and (thus) suffered not only from protests but censorship and an attempt to ban the film.[15] While at least one critic noted that *BM*'s "Hindu–Muslim love angle could have been done with more depth and layer" (Joshi 2015), one wonders what type of response the film would have received had Bhansali further articulated what is arguably already a rather critical depiction of "the dark sides of eighteenth-century Maharashtrian and Indian society" (Vanina 1999: 110–11). Unlike *Bombay* which, as Vasudevan notes, includes features that "significantly distinguish it from mainstream convention," including "its proximity to the events it depicts" (2001: 194), *BM* is simultaneously more mainstream than *Bombay* precisely because of its (historical) story frame's distancing effect and its ensuing indirection in leveling critique. The power of *BM*'s indirect approach to the growing activism from conservative Hindu nationalists that has accompanied Modi's ascendancy can best be seen when comparing *BM* to the contemporary film *Bajrangi Bhaijaan* (2015, hereafter *BB*), which features Salman Khan as a muscular Brahmin who helps a mute Pakistani girl, stranded in India, return to her homeland. While both *BM* and *BB* are "about" Hindus' relations with Muslims, and both were box office successes, *BM* eschews both the populist rhetoric informing *BB* and the latter film's idealized portrayal of its titular Hindu character (played by a Muslim actor). Similarly, while both films utilize song and dance to tell their stories, *BB*'s "Chicken song" features its lead actors dancing like chickens as a way of exploring the difference between Hindus and Muslims (the latter, unlike the Brahmin hero, eat chicken). Such a humorous approach stands in stark contrast to the view of Hindu–Muslim relations on display in the "Gajanana" song sequence in *BM*; while both songs depict Hindus acting like animals, only one representation can be said to approximate savagery.

Given its eschewal of the blatantly aspirational rhetoric on display in *BB*, which concludes with the Brahmin hero not only safely returning the mute

Pakistani girl to her homeland but, in the process, giving her her voice, it is rather puzzling that one Western critic faulted *BM* for lacking "a touch of humor" (Saltz 2015). It is not particularly difficult to grasp why, unlike with the screenings of *BM* in Pune, no member of the BJP or any other Hindu nationalist party demonstrated against *BB*—who, indeed, could provide a better image of the ideal Indian than a muscular Brahmin who befriends a poor Muslim and helps her go back to Pakistan? Yet, it is precisely by refusing such sanguine (and separatist) depictions of Hindu–Muslim relations and setting the story in the past that *BM* paradoxically becomes more relevant to the contemporary situation in India today. Before passing away in 2012, Bal Thackeray, the founder of Shiv Sena, was reportedly exhorting people to "shun the Western-inspired Valentine's Day and its public admission of love," which he found "alien to Indian culture," warning that "cultural squads would be dispatched to halt celebrations" (Varughese 2003: 53).[16] Instead, Thackeray suggested that young Indians looking for an alternative to Valentine's Day take inspiration from "Indian legends of great lovers like Heer-Ranjha, Laila-Majnu and Bajirao-Mastani" (*Times of India* 2006). In light of *BM*'s suggestive metatext and, again, in a catachrestic vein, one hopes his followers might (re) consider his advice. As Ira Bhaskar and Richard Allen note in their discussion of another contemporary Bollywood historical film featuring Hindu and Muslim protagonists, Ashutosh Gowariker's *Jodhaa Akbar* (2008), "History is always written and rewritten from the point of the present" (2009: 168). Via the metatextual reading I have taken, one can similarly argue that *BM* makes available a synchronic parallel between the plight of its doomed couple and the tensions defining Hindu–Muslim relations in the era of Modi, thus demonstrating "the sustained capacity of the Historical genre to address pressing issues of the contemporary" (Bhaskar and Allen 2009: 168).[17] In the following discussion, we will see how Bhansali's approach shifts in his subsequent film, *Padmaavat*, from metatext to fascist aesthetics.

* * *

Padmaavat is a lavish retelling of the legendary tale of the Rajput queen Padmavati, based on the sixteenth century narrative by Malik Muhammad Jayasi. The filmic narrative, set in the early fourteenth century, relays the story of the Rajput queen so renowned for her beauty that Alauddin Khilji, the Sultan of Delhi, launches multiple attacks on the Chittor fort where she resides in an attempt to possess her, ultimately leading the queen and the other Rajput women in the fort to perform *jauhar*, or mass self-immolation, in order to escape his clutches. In recounting this tale, Bhansali hews to the historic, Manichaean dichotomization of Hindu and Muslim, presenting (Hindu) Rajputs as entirely noble figures and Khilji and his (Muslim) followers as essentially barbaric. Additionally, and despite an initial disclaimer disavowing support for the practice, Bhansali's film glorifies Padmavati's act of self-immolation, framing it as the Rajput's greatest victory against the marauding Muslim sultan. Employing Susan Sontag's and Frank Tomasulo's theorizations of the cinema of Leni Riefenstahl, I want to examine how Bhansali, who was ironically attacked by Rajput groups during the shooting of the film, has glorified their purported history via his fascist aesthetics. Such an approach, I argue, rearticulates history as myth and presents it as a form of theater. Bhansali's fascist aesthetics, which include a preoccupation with control, extravagance and uniformity, also glamorize death and dismiss realism in favor of aesthetic excess and romantic idealism. I want to closely examine how Bhansali's use of such aesthetics in his film reenacts the Manichaean framing of Hindu–Muslim relations, employing the trope of "history" as a way of paradoxically reaffirming contemporary chauvinistic formulations of the (Hindu) nation. In the process, I will argue, *Padmaavat* can be seen as lending support to the ideology of contemporary fundamentalist Hindu forces.

As noted at the outset, the always fraught relations between Hindus and Muslims in India were further exacerbated since the election in 2014 of Narendra Modi to the post of prime minister and this exacerbation has, in turn, led to a dramatic increase in activism from right-wing Hindu nationalist groups in India advocating Hindutva, including not only Modi's own BJP Party but also aligned organizations such as the Shiv Sena and, particularly in the case of *Padmaavat*, the Karni Sena, a Rajput caste organization. Such "communal violence"—"overwhelmingly against Muslims and commonly under the narrative of 'Muslim aggression'" (Ohm 2011: 125)—has grown increasingly virulent, including not only the killing of Mohammed Ikhlaq but also the assassination of the scholar and critic of Hindu nationalists, M. M. Kalburgi, on his doorstep, also in 2015; the killing of journalist Gauri Lankesh, who was also accused by right-wing Hindu groups of insulting Hinduism and who was murdered with the same gun used to kill Kalburgi (Abi-Habib 2018); and, in 2018, the rape and killing of an eight-year-old Muslim girl by Hindu men in a Hindu temple (Gettleman 2018). Such acts are further fueled by the rhetoric of Hindu-right politicians, including firebrands like the chief minister of Uttar Pradesh (UP) Yogi Adityanath who, along with praising Donald Trump's proposed ban on Muslims, has said, "[I]f one Hindu girl marries a Muslim man, then we will take 100 Muslim girls in return" (qtd in Safi 2017). It is precisely in such a context that we must situate Bhansali's *Padmaavat* and its use of fascist aesthetics.

The Making of *Padma(a)vat(i)*

While filming in Jaipur in January 2017, Bhansali and his film crew were physically assaulted by members of the Karni Sena that felt the director, in purportedly depicting a romantic relationship between the Hindu Padmavati and the Muslim Khilji, was deviating from the historical accuracy of this legend, particularly via the alleged inclusion of a dream sequence featuring the two leads (Singh 2017). Bhansali's film crew was again attacked in March of 2017, this time in Kolhapur, Maharashtra, by scores of local, right-wing Hindu protestors who burned down the set (Hebbar 2017). Even after completing

FIGURE 1.1 *Hindutva groups burn effigy of Sanjay Leela Bhansali in 2017. Image courtesy of: Shilpa Thakur / Pacific Press Media Production Corp. / Alamy Stock Photo.*

filming, the release of Bhansali's film was repeatedly held up due to a range of issues raised by Hindutva groups like the Karni Sena, including claims of historical inaccuracy. Simultaneously, such groups and affiliated individuals began leveling direct threats against both Bhansali and Padukone (who plays Padmavati), whose effigies were burned at several protests (Figure 1.1).

Leaders of the Karni Sena as well as elected officials affiliated with the BJP publicly called for the beheading of both Bhansali and Padukone and one leader of the Karni Sena, Mahipal Singh Makrana, even threatened to chop off Padukone's nose (*Hindustan Times* 2017). Such groups also threatened to burn down any theatre that screened the film, with one BJP leader, T. Raja Singh, even offering to provide bail for any person who did so (*Hindustan Times* 2017). Leaders of the Akhil Bharatiya Kshatriya Mahasabha (ABKM), whose members burned over 100 effigies of Padukone, threatened to burn the actress alive and offered a reward for any individual who did so (*Hindustan Times* 2017).

Even as such attacks were being leveled against Bhansali and Padukone, as well as any theatre that planned to screen the film, the theatrical release of the film, originally scheduled for early December of 2017, was delayed as members of the Central Board of Film Certification (CBFC) requested the inclusion of additional disclaimers regarding the film, a change to its title—from *Padmavati* to *Padmaavat*—as well as numerous alterations to the film, including the digital covering up of Padukone's midriff in the "Ghoomar" song (Reuters 2017).[18] After the implementation of these requested "modifications," including the change of the film title, the film was finally cleared by the censor board and its release rescheduled for early 2018. Nevertheless, several Indian states moved to ban the screening of the film, including Rajasthan, Gujarat, Madhya Pradesh and Haryana (*Indian Express* 2018a). Despite not being shown in these states, upon its eventual release, the film went on to become one of the highest grossing Indian films of all times (ibid., 2018b). Even members of the Karni Sena, upon watching the film, reversed their earlier objections to it, claiming the film contained no objectionable scenes between Khilji and Padmavati and, furthermore, that it "glorifies the valour and sacrifice of [the] Rajput" (*The Hindu* 2018). This group also said it would help release the film in states where they had previously assisted in having it banned (ibid.). While it "remains unknown whether Bhansali's original screenplay changed in the course of production to accommodate or acquiesce to the protestors" (Qureshi 2018: 49), the released film, as we shall see in the ensuing section, embraces fascist aesthetics which, furthermore, were already apparent in Bhansali's previous work.

Fascist Aesthetics

Even prior to *Padmaavat*, Bhansali was known for his "opulent, extravagant spectacle" (Creekmur 2007: 186); "style," as Varsha Panjwani notes, "is very important to Bhansali" (2017: 124). Indeed, the release of Bhansali's earlier film, *Hum Dil De Chuke Sanam* (1999), marked "the beginnings of a new, visually 'excessive' style of filmmaking" (Wright 2015: 2). Further, Bhansali's "unique aesthetics" (ibid., 165) in many ways "demands to be studied as apart from Bollywood's" (Panjwani 2017: 111), a point which will be explored in greater detail in the ensuing section. For the time being, and as a prelude to the discussion of fascist aesthetics, it is worth noting, as Panjwani does, that "style is not separate from content but rather a part of it" (ibid.); what becomes particularly relevant to this discussion is "how elements of film style [...] become potent ideological tools in the hands of Bhansali" (ibid., 112).[19] Another equally important caveat worth making at the outset of this discussion is that, despite the public endorsements Bhansali may have issued for Modi,[20] one would be remiss to merely rely upon the words of the auteur for "proof" of his ideological affinities with a particular agenda. Such a point is similarly made at the outset of Frank Tomasulo's discussion of Leni Riefenstahl's *Triumph of the Will* (1935, hereafter *Triumph*), when he notes the overdetermined nature of much of the discourse surrounding the German auteur, which generally becomes fixated on "the hoary question of whether or not [she] was a Nazi, supported the National Socialists, or had an affair with Adolph Hitler" (2014: 81). Following Tomasulo, I would like to refocus the discussion here on *Padmaavat* by "examining the *text* of the film, its cinematic imagery and 'political' content, and the psychological *context* in which it was made" (Tomasulo 2014: 81, emphases in original). Before doing so, however, I would first like to review the underpinnings of a fascist aesthetic, in order to better observe how such an aesthetic emerges in Bhansali's film.

In a landmark essay on the work of Riefenstahl, Susan Sontag notes that the director "denied that any of her work was propaganda"; rather, she quotes the director as saying, "It is *history—pure history*" (1980: 82, emphasis in original).[21] Such truth claims by the director—again bracketed by the above critique of auteur theory—are worth bearing in mind when one considers the particularly contentious role that history had played in the *Padma(a)vat(i)* controversy, and in the subsequent "modifications" Bhansali made to his film. Sontag goes on to note a key tenet of fascist aesthetics, namely, that "history becomes theater" (ibid., 83), with elements of the former carefully constructed to incline towards ritual patterns and beautiful spectacle. As Tomasulo notes, "the spectacle of reality *became* reality" (2014: 84, emphasis in original).[22] Such careful and large-scale construction and choreography are key elements of a fascist aesthetic, along with, more generally, "a preoccupation with situations of control, submissive behavior, extravagant effort, and the endurance of pain" (Sontag 1980: 91). "The fascist dramaturgy," as Sontag goes on to note, "centers on the orgiastic transactions between mighty forces and their puppets, uniformly gathered and shown in ever swelling numbers"; fascist art "glorifies surrender" and "glamorizes death" (ibid.).[23] One can see all of these elements on display (and at work) in *Padmaavat* and, in the following pages, I would like to carefully examine how they emerge within the text of this film as well as how these elements may, in turn, illuminate the context in which the film was made.

Following two disclaimers, the first asserting no claims of historical authenticity and the next disavowing the practice of *sati*, *Padmaavat* proper begins with embers flying all over the screen as the title appears. As in *Triumph*, "the musical accompaniment to this opening sequence is serene and peaceful" (Tomasulo 2014: 86) and yet, as one perhaps only eventually realizes, these are the embers flying from the mass act of self-immolation, or *jauhar*, performed at the film's finale by the title figure and her female followers (and their female children). In other words, the very first images of the film—embers flitting like fireflies across the black screen accompanied by serene music—are aestheticized, characterized by one critic as a "gorgeous" start (Qureshi 2018: 46). Another way of putting it is that the film's second disclaimer (the one repudiating support for *sati* or *jauhar*) is immediately belied by the film's stylized depiction of this act (in absentia). In a similar fashion, both in terms

FIGURE 1.2 *The ritualized uniformity of the "Ghoomar" sequence in* Padmaavat *(2018). Source: Screenshot from* Padmaavat, *directed by Sanjay Leela Bhansali, 2018. Viacom 18 Motion Pictures. All rights reserved.*

of aesthetics and foreshadowing and, indeed, conflating these two elements, the film's first song, "Ghoomar," like Hitler's serenade in *Triumph*, is "a torchlit procession ... accentuated both by the dramatic backlighting ... and by the camera's mobility" (Tomasulo 2014: 88). All of the scores of women performing in this sequence—Padmavati and her consorts—dance with pots of fire on their heads in uniform motion, providing an aestheticized foreshadowing of the film's culminating *jauhar* (which, as will be discussed below, is also presented as a ritualized, aestheticized performance) (Figure 1.2).

Here one sees a precise instance of what Sontag describes in her discussion of *Triumph*: "overpopulated wide shots of massed figures alternating with close-ups that isolate a single passion, a single perfect submission: [...] people in uniforms group[ing] and regroup[ing], as if they were seeking the perfect choreography to express their fealty," whether to their dancing queen, the director's fascist aesthetic or to the king, Ratan Singh (Shahid Kapoor), the "benign Super-Spectator" under whose "still gaze" they perform (1980: 87).[24]

This first song's ritual patterns are reinvoked throughout the ensuing film, whether in depicting the duty-bound (Hindu) Rajputs or their Muslim counterparts. Epic battle sequences present huge assemblies of Muslim troops, led by Khilji (Ranveer Singh), and an equally impressive array of stalwart Rajputs defending their Chittor fort in stunning widescreen shots whose perfect symmetry is enhanced by computer-generated imagery (CGI) of violence and submission—"the orgiastic transactions between mighty forces and their puppets, uniformly garbed" (Sontag 1980: 91). The choreography of both these battle and ensuing song sequences "alternates between ceaseless motion and a congealed, static, 'virile' posing" (ibid.). Similarly, the contrast between the marauding Muslims, with their black flags, and the noble Rajputs, garbed in saffron, emphasizes the Manichaean structure underlying such a depiction and "help[s] to forge a common national identity" (Tomasulo 2014: 90), pitting "invader" against "defender."[25] Like Hitler, Ratan Singh is photographed as "erect and ramrod straight," presenting himself as "the national phallus" whose posture itself can be seen as physiologically upholding the will of his people (ibid., 93, 97). Such physical posturing is supplemented by Singh's and Padmavati's repeated exhortations of Rajput valor—all that is good and noble is described as falling under the purview of the Rajputs while, continuing the Manichaean logic at play here, Khilji and his Muslim followers are seen as representing all that is base and immoral, with their leader's posture, in turn, frequently simulating that of the perpetually crouched and brutal black buck of *The Birth of a Nation* (1915), Gus, who also seeks to ravish an unattainable woman.

While it may seem as if Khilji and his Muslim troops are the ones who glorify death, the film's ultimate celebration—indeed, glamorization—of death comes with its culminating and drawn out *jauhar* scene. In accordance with fascist aesthetics this sequence, taking up roughly the last ten minutes of the film, is heavily ritualized and eroticized, transforming "sexual energy into a 'spiritual' force, for the benefit of the community" (Sontag 1980: 93). The film

FIGURE 1.3 *Moving in perfect synchronicity towards* jauhar *in* Padmaavat *(2018). Source: Screenshot from* Padmaavat, *directed by Sanjay Leela Bhansali, 2018. Viacom 18 Motion Pictures. All rights reserved.*

depicts Singh's and Padmavati's elaborate preparations—for war, for *jauhar*—via a sequence set to music in which war and impending death are events looked forward to, indeed, almost serenely desired. Padmavati frames the impending battle as a holy war, one between forces of good and evil, conjuring up Hindu myths in the process. But more than Padmavati it is Bhansali who frames this sequence in accordance with a fascist aesthetic, presenting the ritualized performance of the women preparing for their collective act of self-immolation in a long, drawn out process, lighting the enormous pyre, praying, and walking in perfect, synchronized movements around the fort's inner courtyard, even as Khilji as his troops battle their way in under their ISIS-like black Muslim flags (Figure 1.3).

As was the case with Riefenstahl's *Olympia* (1938), Bhansali furthers the fascist aesthetic here by employing slow-motion photography which allows viewers to view this drawn out sequence as "an enactment of timeless forms and intensities" which valorize "form, linearity, symmetry" (Koepnick 2008: 68)—and death. Somber music featuring female voices wordlessly humming accompanies these slow-motion images as the women, led by Padmavati, approach the pyre in an orderly fashion, with the film "embrac[ing] the special effect of slow motion" in order to present this death march as a "seemingly eternal for[m] of beauty" (ibid.). Yet, this slow motion procession, pictured as "a monumental parade of the triumphant" (ibid., 69) and one which the film depicts as "Chittor's greatest victory," also presents *jauhar* as an act of sublimation, in which a latent sexual energy is invested in this ritual self-immolation.[26] Here one sees an instance of the "ideal eroticism" *à la* the fascist ideal, in which "the erotic (that is, women) is always present as a temptation, with the most admirable response being a heroic repression of the sexual impulse" via, paradoxically, a form of "aesthetic excess" (Sontag 1980: 93). As reviewers have noted, the film's "fealty to spectacle" is increasingly "tethered to violence and death" (Saltz 2018); "never," as one acknowledges, has "mass suicide look[ed] this pretty on screen" (Dutt 2018).

In this predilection (as in Nazi art) for "mythological patterns," Bhansali's film, despite its use of CGI and other contemporary visual technologies, is "clearly anti-modernist in style" and offers a compelling instance of the fascist function of art, namely, to provide "the visible and palpable surface of a fascist ideology which was hard to grapple" (Schmid 2005: 133, 135). Bhansali's "baroque cinematic extravaganz[a]" (Dutt 2018) reverts to the past (drawing upon and, in the process, valorizing, Hindu myth) as a way of paradoxically grappling with the contemporary (fascist) moment. This is precisely why the second of Bhansali's opening disclaimers, repudiating *jauhar*, rings false but, more importantly, why such aesthetics become "potent ideological tools" in Bhansali's hands (Panjwani 2017: 111). As Ulrich Schmid notes, "The look, the design and the rituals of fascism are not its secondary attributes, but its very essence"; "fascism," in other words, is, to a considerable extent, "a phenomenon of style" (2005: 138). This, in turn, is why it is impossible to disentangle *Padmaavat*'s form from its content and why attempts to do so will only lead to bafflement or an impasse. The film's "undeniable beauty" does not "mas[k] its toxic message" (Qureshi 2018: 50) so much as deliver it. That is to say, the film's beauty *is* its toxicity; its "lush portrayal of *sati*" (ibid., 46) is precisely what makes it toxic. Furthermore, to claim that "like a Trojan horse, Bhansali's films weren't always so inflammatory" (ibid., 50) is to overlook how the filmmaker's earlier films always held the potential within them to become so inflammatory, due to their similar embrace of fascist aesthetics. The ideology of such films, rather than "easily forgotten in favor of their undeniable surface pleasures" (ibid., 50), is perhaps unwittingly embraced, just as their surface aesthetics are. To claim, however, that a cinema such as that of Bhansali "conceals its production process" and, further, to frame such concealment as a way of "explain[ing] its capacity to deceive" (ibid.) is too easy. *Padmaavat* doesn't "conceal" anything—it lays bare its fascist aesthetic (i.e., its fascism), wearing it/ displaying it proudly on its sleeve. To say such an aesthetic deceives its audience would be disingenuous and disallow the (disturbing) possibility that audiences, rather than being deceived, appreciated the film precisely for what it is: a fascist work of art, speaking to the masses and invoking, indeed, oozing, Hindutva.[27]

Bollywood Aesthetics

If fascist aesthetics are based on "the containment of vital forces" (Sontag 1980: 93)—via which, for instance, Padmavati's free will is located in self-immolation—then Bollywood aesthetics are based on the dispersal and mixing/ hybridization of vital elements, what is commonly referred to as *masala* and via which movements are anything but confined. This is precisely what, for the most part, is missing in *Padmaavat* and why, as Panjwani notes, Bhansali's style "demands to be studied as apart from Bollywood's" (2017: 111). Exhibit A here would have to be Shahid Kapoor, who plays Ratan Singh and is generally known as one of Bollywood's best male dancers. In *Padmaavat*, Bhansali disallows Kapoor from engaging in a single dance sequence, keeping him "ramrod straight" (Tomasulo

2014: 93) throughout the film. "The fascist hero," as Schmid notes, "is not portrayed as an individual character with a differentiated psyche, but as a prototypic figure" (2005: 139). This is precisely why Bhansali prevents Kapoor from dancing, as doing so would lend his character individuality and difference, for example, the type of bifurcation frequently on display in Bollywood films (even including, to some extent, Bhansali's previous films, for example, *Devdas*). Such containment is unfortunately not just limited to Kapoor's Ratan Singh but also to Padukone's Padmavati who, as noted in the discussion of the "Ghoomar" song, is forced to perform demurely with her midriff digitally covered. In this pair of staid performances, one is presented with a vivid instance of the aesthetic style Bhansali forgoes (in favor of fascist aesthetics) and one that Indian audiences would be all too familiar with, particularly with regard to these two. Even in a film as "different" (i.e., not hewing to typical Bollywood conventions) as Vishal Bhardwaj's *Haider* (2014), the director's adaptation of *Hamlet* set amidst the Kashmiri independence struggles of the 1990s, Kapoor is allowed to show off his dancing prowess (Figure 1.4). This is precisely what goes missing

FIGURE 1.4 *Shahid Kapoor showing off his dancing skills in* Haider *(2014). Source: Screenshot from* Haider, *directed by Vishal Bhardwaj, 2014. UTV Motion Pictures. All rights reserved.*

in *Padmaavat*, as the young actor who trained with Shiamak Davar's dance academy is forced to remain seated on his throne—"the containment of vital forces," indeed.

In a similar vein Padukone, known not only for her dancing skills but her lissome frame, frequently appears in rather suggestive song and dance sequences in typical Bollywood films, for example, in Farah Khan's *Happy New Year* (2014), where her first appearance, in keeping with a longstanding Bollywood convention, is via an "item number," the aptly titled "Lovely" (Figure 1.5).

Directly related to such displays and key to the Bollywood aesthetic is what Sumita Chakravarty calls "impersonation":

> Concentrated within this metaphor are the notions of changeability and metamorphosis, tension and contradiction, recognition and alienation, surface and depth, dualities that have long plagued the Indian psyche and constitute the self-questionings of Indian nationhood. Indian cinema, caught in the cross-currents of this national dialogue and contributing to it,

FIGURE 1.5 *Deepika Padukone displaying her midriff in* Happy New Year *(2014). Source: Screenshot from* Happy New Year, *directed by Farah Khan, 2014. Yash Raj Films. All rights reserved.*

has made impersonation its distinctive signature. [...] Impersonation subsumes a process of externalization, the play of/on surfaces, the disavowal of fixed identity.

1993: 4

This is precisely what one sees in typical Bollwood fare, particularly via song and dance sequences: the ability of individuals to (literally) "step out" of character, briefly, suddenly inhabiting another self and, with it, another figurative identity. This is also precisely what the Indian audience expects with(in) a typical Bollywood film; yet, Bhansali, despite his "extravagant spectacle" (Creekmur 2007: 186), is not a typical Bollywood filmmaker. Were he to have utilized Bollywood aesthetics, his film, rather than "resisting the aesthetics of impurity that link the feminine to sexuality" (Ravetto 2001: 176), would not only have allowed his actors to dance but imbue their performances "with lewd sexual content, sexual innuendoes, erotic gestures, and vulgarity which, as Adorno expounds, 'express the failure of sublimation'" (ibid.). Instead of such content, frequently on display in Bollywood songs featuring Kapoor and Padukone, including the Farah Khan-choreographed "Lovely," in which Padukone engages in pole dancing, winks, and sultry direct address, all while clad in a rather skimpy costume, *Padmaavat* provides, on the one hand, a chaste and digitally censored performance and, on the other, a somber, slow-motion death march in which sexuality, if not digitally altered, nonetheless remains sublimated.[28]

Conclusion

In his review of *Padmaavat*, film critic Bilal Qureshi almost plaintively asks, "How and when had one of my favorite filmmakers become the handmaiden of such problematic imagery?" (2018: 47). While, to some extent, all artists evolve (or devolve), the presence of fascist aesthetics in Bhansali's cinema can be traced back to even his earlier films, albeit not as overtly, tempered as they were to varying degrees by the Bollywood aesthetic, for example, in *Hum Dil De Chuke Sanam*, *Devdas* and *Goliyon Ki Rasleela Ram-Leela*. Indeed, in this latter film, when the male protagonist, Ram (played by Ranveer Singh), "bursts upon the screen for the first time, he sings a song and launches into a ludicrous (but rivetingly so) dance number with hundreds of extras" (Panjwani 2017: 120). Even in *Bajirao Mastani* (*BM*), the Bhansali film directly preceding *Padmaavat* and also a historical drama, the character of Bajirao is allowed to ecstatically move in a fast-paced number that shows off his dancing skills, despite being the Peshwa, or prime minister, of the Maratha state. Previously, then, one could say Bhansali's cinematic form overwhelmed the content of his films with its excess yet, like most postmodern works of art, remained "empty pastiche," devoid of political content. *Padmaavat*, however, employs its excessive aesthetics as a way of augmenting its political content. Similarly, while his earlier work, like most Bollywood fare, was "anchored in pleasure and utopian fantasies" (Wright 2015: 151), *Padmaavat*'s pleasure is decidedly—one could even say hyperbolically—rooted in dystopian fantasy. And it is precisely this combination of (excessive) form and (dystopian) content that makes the film so problematic, that is to say, more so than Bhansali's previous films, where such a confluence was never truly achieved.[29]

To some extent, the answer to Qureshi's question lies in his own implicit dichotomization of Bhansali and Bollywood, a distinction that has only increased over time and is particularly apparent with *Padmaavat*. Accompanying this split—and the increasing emergence of a fascist aesthetic in his work—is a disturbing confluence between Bhansali's cinema and the BJP's polarizing politics, one that has only increased in the age of Modi. Yet, Qureshi and others overlook the presence, albeit latent, of a fascist aesthetic in the auteur's earlier works when wondering "how something so brutal could be made so very beautiful" (2018: 48). Whether in *Devdas*, *BM* or in *Padmaavat*,

Bhansali's "attempt to construct an ideal rather than actual past" also speaks to his willingness—indeed, his insistence—in employing fascist aesthetics to create "an opulent, extravagant spectacle" (Creekmur 2007: 186). Such an aesthetic, in other words, with its rigid adherence to symmetry, preoccupation with control, visual extravagance and "thunderous beats at every emotional high or low" is inherently brutal, "constantly threaten[ing] to overwhelm what might be understood as the story of internally tormented characters" (ibid.) and, in the process, turning "people into things" (Sontag 1980: 91), albeit glamorous and finely chiseled (and/or digitally covered) things.

Such "thingification," in turn, becomes relevant to the ensuing question of "how … a fascist film position[s] its viewers" (Tomasulo 2014: 82). By emphasizing "patriotic themes that convey a renewed sense of national identity and unity following a period of … instability" (ibid., 84), by evoking "the contrast between the clean and the impure, the incorruptible and the defiled," and by glorifying surrender and glamorizing death, *Padmaavat* paradoxically provides its viewers with the means to a collective catharsis, even as "history becomes theater" (Sontag 1980: 88, 83). Rana Dasgupta, in his book, *Capital*, examines the psychological residue of Partition on the psyches of Indians in the twenty-first century, surmising that a "process of purification and eradication" was required, in which (Hindu) Indians severed any remaining kinship with their Muslim brethren; any vestige of "Islam they carried within themselves" had to be annihilated (2014: 191). Simultaneously, because "the events of the partition of British India remain, for the most part, locked in silence," the ensuing trauma became repressed and, "like DDT in the food chain, became more concentrated over time" (ibid., 194). It is precisely in such a way that India has arguably become "a nation composed of frustrated individuals who repress their hostility" and, thus, "behaves in a pathological manner"; "such a people," Tomasulo observes, "easily fall victim to the demagogic propaganda of mystical fascism" (2014: 97). It is precisely such "complex and overdetermined extra-cinematic subjective factors of history" that play "such a vital role in positioning viewers long before they even enter a movie theatre" (ibid., 100), whether in 1930s Germany or in India today, as the controversies and violence surrounding the making of *Padma(a)vat(i)* have demonstrated. While some fans of Bhansali may shake their heads and wonder what happened to their favorite filmmaker as they emerge from the perfectly choreographed doom of *Padmaavat*, and while the filmmaker, like Riefenstahl before him, may issue wide-eyed denials, a film like *Padmaavat*, with its problematic confluence of style and ideology, allows (Hindu) spectators to "experience [their] own destruction as an aesthetic pleasure" (Benjamin 2019: 195) even as it "negates the possibility of the filmmaker's having an aesthetic conception independent of propaganda" (Sontag 1980: 79).

2

Modi's Ad Man: Akshay Kumar

Bollywood actor Akshay Kumar has had a prolific career, completing over 130 films in the thirty years since his debut, in 1991, with *Saugandh*. Over that period, his star text has continually evolved, from action hero to comic performer and now, in his fifties, to "enlightened nationalist hero" (Dore 2021). It is particularly this later phase of Kumar's career that is of interest here, as a case study of the broader Hindtuva-ization of Bollywood. In the past six years (2017–22), Kumar has made a number of films that either directly correspond to BJP projects or more generally align with a Hindutva ideology. As media scholar Sreya Mitra notes, "Kumar's nationalistic narratives have been consistently successful" (2021: 289). These include not only films but also ads for BJP projects, such as the Swachh Bharat Abhiyan, or Clean India Mission, as well as an hour-long filmed interview in 2019 with Prime Minister Modi. In this chapter, I begin by examining what particular elements of Kumar's star text make him appealing to the BJP, before engaging in close readings of five of his most recent films—*Toilet: Ek Prem Katha* (2017, hereafter *Toilet*), *Mission Mangal* (2019), *Kesari* (2019), *Sooryavanshi* (2021), and *Ram Setu* (2022). My discussions of these films will be supplemented by considerations of some of Kumar's extra-filmic collaborations with Modi and the BJP, including the aforementioned public service announcement, or PSA, he filmed for the

Swachh Bharat mission, and his filmed interview with Modi. In the process, my aim here is to chart how Kumar has in many ways become the poster boy for the BJP and its Hindutva platform today, as well as how this reflects a particularly compelling instance of the broader "Modi-fication" of Bollywood.

Kumar's Star Text

Film scholar Richard Dyer has noted key elements of an actor's star text in his canonical study of stardom (1998 [1979]). A character, as Dyer notes, is "a construct from the very many different signs deployed by a film" (1998: 106). These elements, which include audience foreknowledge, name and appearance, inform broader "sign-clusters" and, in turn, Dyer's notion of stardom as "structured polysemy," that is, "the multiple but finite meanings and effects that a star image signifies" (ibid., 107, 63). In his analysis of the structured polysemy of the star image, Dyer is particularly concerned with the numerous ways in which the star image is "used in the construction of a character in a film," which includes its selective use, perfect fit and problematic fit (ibid., 126–9). We will develop a better understanding of how these various uses of stardom are deployed in Kumar's career, however, to begin, I would like to identify some of the key elements informing Kumar's star text within a contemporary Bollywood ecumene, that is, one increasingly informed by a Hindutva ideology. As film critic Bhavya Dore (2021) has observed, "The Hindu-nationalist establishment finds Kumar useful due to a constellation of factors," including "people's image of him as a Hindu alternative to the three big Muslim superstars," Aamir Khan, Salman Khan and Shah Rukh Khan. Kumar's star text is also shaped by more of a rustic *desi*, or native, quality than, for instance, the more cosmopolitan star text of fellow Hindu box-office star Hrithik Roshan. This rustic *desi* quality manifests itself in a variety of elements informing Kumar's star text, most particularly, his manner of speaking.[1] Additionally, as noted at the outset, Kumar has been an incredibly successful star in each of the distinct phases of his career, whether in "testosterone-fueled action dramas," or "slapstick comedies and ensemble films," or, more recently, in films "spewing patriotic fervour" (Mitra 2021: 289). These elements—Kumar's Hindu identity, the particularly rustic, or "earthy," quality he exudes, as well as his elasticity in terms of filmic roles and the ensuing success he has achieved in each of these—all make Kumar particularly effective as a "poster boy" for a variety of Hindutva themes. We will see how all of these traits are effectively utilized in the first film to be examined here, *Toilet*.

Toilet: Ek PSA

Released in 2017 in collaboration with the BJP's Swachh Bharat Abhiyan, or Clean India Mission, *Toilet* stars Kumar as a middle-aged, middle-class Brahmin, Keshav Sharma, living in a small town in Uttar Pradesh, who becomes involved with a (significantly) younger Brahmin woman, Jaya, played by Bhumi Pednekar.[2] Keshav lives with his younger brother and their father, an orthodox Brahmin pandit, in a house with no toilet, per the father's belief that having one in the home would violate his Brahminical sense of cleanliness. After Keshav and Jaya are married and return to Keshav's house, she is shocked to discover it contains no toilet and that she is expected to join the other women of the village to defecate in the open fields in the early morning hours. After a series of (failed) attempts to find patchwork solutions to the problem, Jaya returns to her parents' home in a neighboring town, informing Keshav that she will not return until he installs a toilet. The film, based on a true story, was also directly linked to the Clean India Mission.[3] Rather than engaging with some of the actual obstacles preventing the end of open defecation, however, *Toilet* frames such resistance as stemming more from ignorance and lack of access to toilets. This ignorance—as embodied by Keshav's father and other members of their village—in turn, allows Keshav to enlighten his benighted community through the emergence of what media scholar Pallavi Rao aptly labels a "Brahmin savior syndrome" (2019: 80). Framed as an idealized "male feminist," Keshav fights his community's resistance to toilets not by addressing issues of rural health, sanitation and hygiene but through "rigorous applications of the Brahminical logics of ritual purity and cleanliness" (ibid.).[4]

The "problematic of open defecation" that *Toilet* sets up, in other words, suggests a "superficial reading of the issue" (Rao 2019: 89). Such a superficial reading is also what allows Kumar to emerge as the (male Brahmin) savior in the film. In such an iteration, all the problem of open defecation ultimately requires is Akshay Kumar making convincing speeches to India's rural populations, explaining how the use of a toilet actually corresponds with Brahminical scripture. Such a facile approach also corresponds with Modi's campaign promise of "Toilet first, temple later," which, following his election in 2014, has only been accompanied by "the hyperbole of improved infrastructure without any push for social change addressing caste labour" (ibid.). As Rao and others have observed, one of the key barriers to the installation of toilets is the issue of caste-based labor practices. As sociologist Diane Coffey and economist Dean Spears note, "Villagers reject affordable latrines because their pits must eventually be emptied by hand," and such labor within the caste mode of production has always been imposed upon Dalits (qtd in Rao 2019: 89). Since Dalits "have been abandoning any profession deemed ritually impure within the caste hierarchy for employment that offers dignity and class mobility," finding laborers to complete this work has proved difficult, with Brahmins and other upper castes remaining reluctant to perform such labor themselves (Rao 2019: 89).

Yet, *Toilet* fails to engage with these (caste-related) issues, instead framing the problem as more attitudinal and one easily surmounted by the right person, namely, Keshav Sharma, whose "universalized provincial male subjectivity" is, in turn, "amplified by Akshay Kumar's star presence" (Rao 2019: 83). Keshav "continually delivers his dialogues with a verbal flourish peppered with rhymes, alliterations and poetic constructions" (ibid., 82), which, in turn, helped make the film an enormous popular success. Yet, several of the film's premises, including the alleged reason for the lack of toilets, seem implausible. Key among these is the construction of Jaya's character. Though framed as a "college topper," and constantly shown accessing information on her iPhone, Jaya chooses to marry a significantly older man with no formal education beyond high school. Furthermore, despite her education, determination and access to information, she remains reliant upon Keshav to solve the problem. Yet, this implausibility is precisely what allows Keshav to become the (Brahmin) savior and idealized "male feminist" (ibid., 80). Keshav's subsequent critique of (Hindu) religious traditions embraced by members of the village *panchayat*, or council, is similarly deceptive, functioning as a strawman in many ways, as Keshav ultimately relies upon this same religious logic to convince others to accept toilets, thus recuperating these principles in the process.

Along with Kumar's star turn as the country bumpkin who ends up schooling his fellow villagers with acts of rhetorical jujitsu and *jugaad*, another reason for the film's tremendous success was due to its alignment with the BJP government's Swachh Bharat mission, which resulted in the film receiving tax breaks in a number of BJP-led states, including India's most populous state (where the film is set), Uttar Pradesh (Dore 2021).[5] Additionally, the film benefited from a direct endorsement from Modi, who tweeted to his 50 million followers that the film was "a good effort to further the message of cleanliness" (qtd in Rao 2019: 81). Yet, as Rao goes on to note, the "intersection between a central government policy, tax exemption by BJP-led states, the film's representational politics and overarching central message ... thus raises some critical questions about ideological constructions of cinema, state and nation and their discursive relationships" (ibid.). Key among these is how *Toilet* in many ways provides ideological cover for the BJP's (failed) enterprise. Rao notes that "sociology and ethnographic research already suggests that the 'Swachh Bharat Abhiyan' mission ... has misdiagnosed both the problem and the solution to open defecation" (ibid., 92). While the Modi-led campaign pledged to "end open defecation by 2019," this promise, as anthropologist Lynn Meskell observes, "has, by all accounts, failed" (2021: 152–3).[6] Nevertheless, or perhaps precisely by not addressing the key (caste-labor) issues underlying the cause of open defecation, the film has been an incredible success and, in a double entendre worth noting, *Toilet* thus "becomes a mouthpiece for the Modi government's rhetoric" (Rao 2019: 90).

It is precisely this synergy, this alignment with state policy, that marks *Toilet* as a significantly new type of Bollywood venture. While previous films may have also received tax exemptions due to their (socially / nationally focused) content, *Toilet* aligns not so much with a viable plan for implementing successful change as it does with the manufacture of the illusion of such change being seamlessly developed. And while one may argue that, at the very least, by providing an "entertaining" and "light-hearted" take on the issue of open defecation, the film is effective in raising public awareness of this social problem, one could likewise argue that it is precisely these elements of the film—that is, its superficial engagement with the issue, drawing upon the star quality of Kumar—that make the film a disservice to the cause it was ostensibly made to aid (Meskell 2021: 152; Rao 2019: 92). By pandering to "India's middle-class stereotypes of caste, labour and rurality," *Toilet*, rather than raising awareness of the deeper problems that remain unaddressed at the bottom of the pit, functions as an empty gesture which only carries rhetorical weight, thanks in large part to Kumar's star presence and its utilization to paradoxically skirt the deeper (caste- and labor-based) issues at hand. In such a way, however, the film simultaneously becomes a PR coup for the BJP, precisely because the actual mission has been such a resounding failure (Meskell 2021: 153). One can thus trace a direct and inversely proportional relation between the film's success (and, in turn, the "success" of the Clean India mission as a public

FIGURE 2.1 *Akshay explains the value of shit in Swachh Bharat PSA, 2018.* Source: Screenshot from "Twin Pit Technology Campaign," available online: https://www.youtube.com/watch?v=dFpF2RK-gO4 (accessed May 5, 2023). PIB India.

relations exercise), on the one hand, and the "inevitable victimi[zation of] the poor and vulnerable, the Dalits, the so-called illegal encroachers, or those from non-Hindu communities," on the other (ibid., 165). The film's effectiveness as BJP propaganda is further demonstrated by the short public service announcement (PSA) Kumar and Pednekar filmed for the Swachh Bharat mission following the release (and success) of the film. In this advertisement, which draws upon the duo's roles and relationship in *Toilet*, Kumar advocates for the use of a twin-pit latrine, explaining to his dubious neighbor how it works (Figure 2.1).

Kumar explains that the twin-pit technology will allow for the creation of manure which, in turn, can be used as fertilizer, which he proceeds to demonstrate, flinging the accumulated manure from one of his twin pits joyfully into his garden (Figure 2.2).

Though Kumar here lifts the manure with his own hands and performs the subsequent labor of fertilizing his garden with a grin, it remains unclear

FIGURE 2.2 *Akshay joyfully flings fertilizer in Swachh Bharat PSA, 2018. Source: Screenshot from "Twin Pit Technology Campaign," available online: https://www.youtube.com/watch?v=dFpF2RK-gO4 (accessed May 5, 2023). PIB India.*

whether others would be as willing to perform such work—and cultivate their gardens—themselves.[7] Yet again, precisely due to this lack of clarity, the ad and the related film function as effective propaganda for the government's (failed) mission.

Mission Mangal: *Desi* Science

One sees a further alignment of Kumar's star text with BJP schemes and nationalist ideology in his ensuing project, *Mission Mangal* (2019). Here, Kumar plays Rakesh Dhawan, a bespectacled scientist and mission director at the Indian Space Research Organization (ISRO), assigned "a mission nobody really wants," namely, an expedition to Mars (Sen 2020b). One also witnesses the elasticity of Kumar's star text, as his character and appearance are superficially quite different from that of country bumpkin Keshav in *Toilet*. Here, Kumar's Rakesh speaks English with ease, displaying a cosmopolitan fluency also reflected by his sartorial style. Yet, his outward appearance and form of direct speech are frequently belied by what Dyer refers to as a character's indirect speech, or "what a character betrays about him/herself" (1998: 112). We are privy to such "betrayals" of his cosmopolitan veneer in Rakesh's frequent muttering and humming of old Hindi songs which, as forms of indirect speech, "we are more inclined to trust," due in part to our perception of the "truth" of Rakesh's personality being determined by what we "take to be the truth about the person of the star playing the part" (ibid.: 112, 125). As Dyer has observed, along with "audience foreknowledge, the star's name and her/his appearance," the "sound of her/his voice," "the lines s/he is given to say," and "how the lines are said," all contribute to an actor's performance style and, in turn, to our understanding of his character (ibid., 126, 134). The frequent muttering, singing of old Hindi film songs and other asides all convey the "truth" of (Kumar-as-)Rakesh, belying his veneer of polished space scientist. These forms of indirect speech are also highlighted by the speech of another character, the non-resident Indian (NRI) scientist Rupert (Dalip Tahil), who has just returned from the US where he was working for NASA. Rupert's speech is primarily in English and even his Hindi is inflected with a slight foreign accent, furthered by his staunchly pro-Western (and anti-Indian) views. Rupert functions as an effective foil to Rakesh, not only in outlook but as manifested through their respective speech acts.

This vocal contrast, in turn, functions as a microcosm of the film's broader framing of a nationalist narrative, and as an endorsement of another government mission, the "Make in India" initiative, launched by Modi in 2014 and geared towards creating and encouraging companies to develop, manufacture and assemble products made in India (Choudhury 2014). As with *Toilet*, *Mission Mangal*'s endorsement of this government scheme informs the film's cadences and is particularly reflected in Kumar's speech patterns, forms of address and the ensuing contrast with Rupert's mode of speaking. An instance of such indirect speech reflecting the film's nationalist ethos comes early in the film when, following a failed mission launch, Kumar walks out of the central space command, humming an old Hindi song and casually eating a *laddu* (Indian sweet) while speaking to reporters. When one asks him why he is eating a *laddu* at this moment, Kumar replies, in his typical rustic deadpan style, "Who says you can't eat a *laddu* in a difficult time?" These forms of indirect speech confirm Kumar's star text and provide the audience with the "truth" of Rakesh's character, read as it is through Kumar's manner of speaking, as a *pukka desi wallah*, that is to say, a true Indian. Such affirmation of true Indianness is further developed through the film's foregrounding of *jugaad*, a colloquial term conveying the "ability to come up with creative solutions that enable one to fulfill one's aspirations in contexts of scarce resources" (Mankekar 2013: 28). As anthropologist Purnima Mankekar argues, *jugaad* entails not only "a business strategy or even a strategic plan of action" but also a mindset (ibid., 33). It is precisely such a mindset that encapsulates the nationalist ethos of the film and corresponds with Modi's "Make in India" initiative.

After Rakesh is provided scant resources for the Mars mission, his assembled team of (primarily young and female) scientists engage in various iterations of *jugaad* in order to achieve success. One particularly compelling instance of this occurs when scientist Tara Shinde (Vidya Balan) comes up with a plan for developing a low-cost rocket and satellite from frying *puris* (whole-wheat bread) without a flame, an act she demonstrates at ISRO headquarters while Rupert sputters in disbelief. *Pukka desis* Rakesh and Tara frequently deploy such instances of nativist *jugaad*, to which a flabbergasted Rupert responds on cue, pooh-poohing their approach as "*puri* science" and asking (in English), "Why do you want the world to laugh at us?" Such a question and its particular articulation by this particular (NRI) character, in turn, allow Kumar-as-Rakesh to respond in a mode aligned with his star text—"Sir," Rakesh says to his boss, "Aaj hum duniya ke liye tailender, kal opening batsman ban sak te hai. Let's not take singles, let's hit a sixer."[8] This line and the manner in which it is delivered simultaneously epitomize the spirit of *jugaad*—coming up with a compelling analogy on the fly and expressing it through a colloquial mix of Hindi and English—even as they allow Kumar-as-Rakesh to introduce "irreverence and humor" to the plot, "as if to make sure the film never becomes 'too smart'" (Masand 2019). Such iterations are further underscored (as quintessentially *desi*) by Rupert who, in turn, incredulously responds (again in English), "This is great, first it was *puris*, now it's cricket." Thus, as Dyer has noted, both the speech of the central character (Rakesh) and the speech of others (Rupert in this case) help "indicate a personality trait of that character" (1998: 112) as well as the overall film.[9] These contrasting speech acts also bring the film's nationalist message into sharp relief even as, by portraying *jugaad* as "intrinsic to Indian culture," they also reinforce essentialist conceptions of "Indian culture" (Mankekar 2013: 34–5). And, as Mankekar goes on to note, such essentializing of "Indian culture," in turn, reinforces "nationalist assumptions about India" (ibid., 35). This is precisely why, as Dore observes, *Mission Mangal*'s "positive messages around Indianness" mix "seamlessly" with government propaganda, for instance, the Make in India scheme (2021: 10).

Like *Toilet*, which was made in conjunction with the Clean India mission, *Mission Mangal* received tax exemptions and went on to become a box office hit (Dore 2021). Like *Toilet*, *Mission Mangal* is also emblematic of the ecosystem created by the Modi government in which "producing content the government likes has big rewards" (ibid.). Perhaps the most compelling instance of such synergy between the BJP and the film comes at its conclusion when, following the successful launch of the Mars orbiter, we first hear and then see Modi speaking in praise of the mission. Again, as with Kumar, whose "image seems to have been manufactured along the lines on which Modi has sought to construct his own" (ibid.), the manner in which Modi speaks—his colloquial turns of phrase and the sentiments informing them—reaffirms the particular notion of *jugaad* as quintessentially Indian. As the film ends with the song "Shabaashiya" (Congratulations) triumphantly playing on the soundtrack, Modi addresses an offscreen audience whose loud cheers can be heard as he

FIGURE 2.3 *Modi hails (cheap) success of Mars mission in* Mission Mangal *(2019). Source: Screenshot from* Mission Mangal, *directed by Jagan Shakti. 2019. Fox Star Studios. All rights reserved.*

concludes: "Hollywood ke film banana ke jitna budget hota hai, ussee kam budget main Mars ponch gaye!"[10] (Figure 2.3).

Here, as with Kumar-as-Rakesh employing cricket analogies to make a case for India's space mission, we see (and hear) how Modi engages with the rhetoric and ideology of *jugaad* and how this is hailed as quintessentially Indian. Technically, though Modi's (self-)congratulatory address seems to imply that he was responsible for its success, the Mars mission depicted in the film was announced in 2012 by then Prime Minister Manmohan Singh and launched in 2013 (Masand 2019), details that are conveniently elided by the film and its (self) congratulatory concluding speech by the current prime minister. Thus, as film critic Raja Sen observes, "we applaud a Prime Minister who had very little to do with supporting the mission" (2020b). Yet, Modi's imprimatur on the film (and, by proxy, on its mission), which engages in a form of hagiographical revisionist history, nevertheless reifies the symbiosis between such enterprises—not only the actual Mars mission but *Mission Mangal*—and the Modi regime. Thus, from toilets to Mars, the mission seems clear and revolves around the key star in the contemporary Indian firmament: Planet Modi, like Mars, the saffron planet, named after the god of war.

One witnesses an even more compelling instance of such a mission—to buttress Modi—in Kumar's filmed interview with the prime minister, aired just prior to the release of *Mission Mangal* and during the 2019 election cycle when Modi was seeking reelection. Billed as a "non-political" interview and shot in the prime minister's official residence "in true cinematic style," this hour-long interview stands in stark contrast to Modi's refusal to take part in a single actual press conference or news interview since assuming the position of prime minister (Mitra 2021: 282). Alternately sitting on Modi's marble veranda, walking through his lush garden, and sitting down for tea amidst the distant sounds of peacocks on an immaculately manicured lawn, a "visibly bashful and fawning Kumar" asks Modi a series of banal questions including whether he likes to eat mangoes and, if so, how (Mitra 2021: 288) (Figure 2.4).

Precisely because this hagiographical interview was framed as being "non-political," it effectively functions as a "cleverly disguised PR exercise to bolster Narendra Modi's public image" (Mitra 2021: 283). Yet, even its "clever disguise" is as fundamentally transparent as the camera crew who are frequently seen on the sidelines moving equipment and setting up subsequent shots, even as

FIGURE 2.4 *Fawning Kumar asks Modi about his fashion style in BJP video (YouTube, 2019). Source: Screenshot from "PM Shri Narendra Modi in conversation with Akshay Kumar," available online: https://www.youtube.com/watch?v=rPIT6-PL050 (accessed May 5, 2023). Bharatiya Janata Party.*

Kumar and Modi continue conversing as if unaware of their presence. Here we witness both Kumar's willingness to participate in such "cleverly disguised" (though transparent) PR exercises and the ensuing synergy between film and politics, in which Kumar's star text as a *pukka desi* plays no small part. Here we see not only a blurring of Kumar's and Modi's image constructions (and the ensuing consolidation of both as "enlightened nationalist hero[es]") but of Bollywood and the BJP, and the willingness, indeed, eagerness, of both to take part in such collaborations (Dore 2021). In the ensuing discussion of *Kesari*, we will see how Kumar, in his current capacity as "the poster boy for Indian patriotism" (qtd in Mitra 2021: 289) has further transitioned from the "soft Hindutva" of films like *Toilet* and *Mission Mangal*, with their related BJP tie-ins and interviews, to "harder" forms of Hindutva.

Kesari: Saffronizing Bollywood

Kesari can be seen as part of the broader saffronization of history, in this case, of the Battle of Saragarhi in 1897, in which twenty-one members of the 36th Sikh regiment held off thousands of Pashtuns attacking the fort before their ultimate demise. The film was another blockbuster for Kumar, who plays the leader of the Sikh regiment, Ishar Singh, generating over 200 crore in box office revenues (Tieri 2021: 362). Following a lengthy (219-word) disclaimer, the film includes a statement that it is "dedicated to all the martyrs," accompanied by a banner stating "homage and support to India's Bravehearts, Ministry of Home Affairs, Government of India," and, in smaller print below, "This website is an initiative to pay homage to the bravehearts who laid down their lives in the line of duty. Using this platform individuals can contribute directly into the bank accounts of the bravehearts' kin." It is unclear whether such a statement amounts to an official government sanction of the film or whether it functions, as with *Toilet*, as another form of synergy between Bollywood and the BJP. In either case, it seems to constitute a doubly monetized endeavor, per the listed platform (to which viewers can contribute directly) accompanying—indeed, introducing—the film. The film also begins by thanking "Gurinderpal Singh Josan (Researchers, M.A. History)," which again reflects the increasing importance assigned to historicity by such films (Merivirta 2016).

Following its disclaimer and dedication, the film itself commences with the sound of Kumar speaking. This again attests to the significance of the sound of Kumar's voice to his performance style. Even as the screen remains black, Kumar's voice commences with a colloquial explanation of the broader border conflict informing the story. As the first image appears, we see Kumar, sporting a particularly long beard and oversized turban, providing his casual synopsis to his Sikh colleague, explaining that the British is the husband; the ruler of Afghanistan, his wife; with the Pathans of the region functioning as the magistrate. Kumar goes on to explain that the wife wants to continue her Russian affair and divorce her husband but only the magistrate can grant the divorce. When his colleague asks, "So who are we then?" Kumar replies in his typical deadpan manner, "The wedding guests, here to dance to their tunes." Following these rustic and humorous opening images (and sounds) of the Sikh soldiers, the film presents the initial images of the (Muslim) Pathans, who are dragging a young woman to be stoned to death. These competing opening images—of Kumar and the Sikhs, on the one hand, and of the Pathans, on the other—stand in stark contrast to one another and their juxtaposition in the film's opening minutes works to further endear viewers to Kumar and his colleague, who seem eminently more human in their colloquial exchange than the (silent, savage) Pathans.

South Asian studies scholar Silvia Tieri has analyzed *Kesari*'s trailer and how it endeavors to "socialize the viewer into a specific historical and political discourse that celebrates Sikh martiality" while "promoting Islamophobia and anti-secularism" (2021: 359). Tieri's analysis of the trailer can be applied more broadly to the film as a whole, as both arguably endeavor to socialize the viewer in this manner. Like its trailer, the film includes many creative licenses with regard to the history it purports to recount (e.g., turning "thousands" of Pashtuns attacking the fort into "10,000 or more") and it is precisely in such a way that it can be said to function as a saffronized version of history, replete with attendant saffronized aesthetics. These also include, as Tieri notes, "hyper-realistic renditions of violence" (ibid., 360), which shall be examined in more detail below. Such an approach to "history," with its attendant "socialization" of the viewer, calls to mind Sanjay Leela Bhansali's *Padmaavat* (2018), which similarly frames Rajputs as valorous warriors and Muslim Afghans as marauding evildoers.[11] Tieri's question concerning *Kesari*'s trailer can also be applied to the overall film, namely, how does it engage the viewer / consumer to "buy" the film's content as well as "the worldview embedded into" it (2021: 360)? To address this question, I would like to build on Tieri's analysis to examine how the film's formal elements are employed to "sell" its (saffronized) worldview, or what Tieri subsequently refers to as its "(pseudo)facts" (ibid., 363).

Kesari's framing of characters provides a compelling instance of how events are depicted to accord with such a saffronized worldview. As per the opening sequences, the film frequently presents the twenty-one Sikh soldiers in close-ups, while the Pathans are typically relegated to long shots. This alternating proximity to or distance from the respective subjects helps to create familiarity and thus empathy for the Sikh soldiers, who acquire individuality, even as the Pathans remain "dehumanized and anonymous" (Tieri 2021: 363). Similarly, the film's alternating choreographic patterns frame the Sikh soldiers as rational and disciplined while the Pathans are framed as hordes devoid of "any apparent strategy" (ibid.). Chromatism becomes another way of distinguishing between the two groups, with the eponymous *kesari* (saffron) color associated with the valiant Sikhs. As Tieri rightly observes, this color is associated with "political Hinduism" and is embodied in the film through a variety of symbols, including Kumar's war turban and his flaming, "kesari-hot sword" (ibid., 364). All of this saffronization, pitted as it is against the anonymized Pathan hordes with their green (Muslim) flags, creates a colorized Manicheanism, or what Tieri labels a "Hindutva meta-discourse" (ibid., 372), which also carries religious undertones, framing the struggle as one between noble, kesari-clad Sikhs and evil Muslim invaders. *Kesari*'s multiple "creative licenses" also aid in furthering this saffronized worldview, including Kumar's heroic decision at the outset to singlehandedly save the poor Afghan woman from being stoned by the Pathans; or Kumar ordering his Sikh regiment to help rebuild a mosque for the local Muslims, an event which, as Tieri notes, has no historical record (ibid., 367). Such elements function as effective propaganda and help define Kumar and his Sikh cohort as the moral heroes of the film, upholding and embodying the valorous "Sikh archetype of adogmatic humanism, equality, and mutual respect" (ibid.).

Another key motif of the film that furthers such Manichaean framing is the "fort under siege." As in many past films, including *Padmaavat* and *The Birth of a Nation* (1915), *Kesari* presents the siege of the Saragarhi fort as "the siege of a civilized nation at the hands of barbaric destroyers" (Tieri 2021: 369). Like the "helpless white minority" in Griffith's silent film being attacked by savage black soldiers, or the Rajputs in their Chittor fort facing an onslaught from marauding Afghans in *Padmaavat*, the twenty-one Sikh soldiers bravely standing up to the thousands (upon thousands) of swarming Pathans effectively frames them as victims who, in turn, deserve our sympathy. This motif can also be extended to, and adopted by, a contemporary discourse of victimization increasingly invoked by Hindus in India, in which this overwhelming majority in Indian society paradoxically sees itself as coming under increasing attack from the "foreign," "invading" forces of Islam.[12] When the Saragarhi fort is attacked, Kumar addresses his twenty-one Sikh troops, telling them he will fight but not for the British. Reappearing with an oversized saffron turban on his head, Kumar asks his troops if they know why he is wearing such a turban, then explains that *kesari* is the color of bravery and sacrifice (Figure 2.5). In

FIGURE 2.5 *Fully saffronized Kumar in* Kesari *(2019), directed by Anurag Singh.*
Source: Directed by Anurag Singh © Dharma Productions / Hari Om Entertainment / Azure Entertainment 2019. All Rights Reserved. Image Courtesy of: Collection Christophel / Alamy Stock Photo.

subsequently explaining to the other Sikh soldiers that he is fighting for his guru and for his turban (a speech which, in turn, effectively rouses the troops), we see how *Kesari* reframes a colonial-era military battle into a religious / holy war.[13]

Such reframing, in turn, furthers the film's "Hindutva meta-discourse" (Tieri 2021: 372). This is underscored by Kumar commencing the fort's defense by saying a brief prayer, adjusting his oversized saffron *pagdi* (turban) and removing all the British military insignia from his uniform, holding only a sword made orange from being placed in a fire. Extrapolating from the "fort under siege" motif, Tieri argues that Kumar and his sepoys can be read as representing the modern Indian state and, by merging two levels of meaning—the moral and the political—the film presents "the moral and religiously tolerant state" challenged by "amoral and religiously intolerant invaders (India's Muslims)" (ibid.). Kumar's invocation of his *kesari* turban as the cause for which he is fighting is, as Tieri notes, sufficiently fluid for the chromatic connotations to oscillate between Sikhs specifically and (non-Muslim) Indianness more generally (ibid.). These fluid connotations and ensuing saffronized discourse "converge to constitute a meta-allegory—India and the Muslims," or, indeed, India *versus* the Muslims (ibid.). The ensuing battle, which takes up the last hour of the film, is quite savage, with Kumar's concluding, singlehanded rampage, in particular, aestheticized via slow motion, heightened sound effects, cinematography and song. One witnesses a particularly compelling instance of the film's "hyper-realistic renditions of violence" (ibid., 360) as Kumar falls in slow motion and is slashed and stabbed repeatedly while a plaintive song sung by a young woman plays on the soundtrack. This is followed by a form of male *jauhar* as the last remaining Sikh solider, having barricaded himself in one of the fort's towers which the encroaching horde sets on fire, emerges in flames and advances towards the Pathans with a determined look on his face as he repeatedly screams "One shall be forever blessed who says God is the ultimate truth!" and then detonates a bomb, killing himself as well as a number of the Pathans.

Such aestheticization of hyper-violence continues even in the aftermath of the battle, as the camera pans over all the dead bodies while a final song, "Yeh Mitti" (This Soil), plaintively plays on the soundtrack. As the film concludes, a series of statements appear onscreen, explaining that two *gurudwaras* (Sikh temples), one in Amritsar, one in Ferozepur, were built in memory of the "martyrs" and are visited by "thousands of devotees, even today." All of these elements—highly choreographed and aestheticized battle sequences, chromatic motifs promulgating the bravery of the saffron-turbaned Kumar and his fellow soldiers, the endless (and forever distanced) hordes of attacking Pathans, as well as the ensuing language of the concluding statement, invoking "martyrs" and "devotees"—contribute to the film's "Hindutva meta-discourse," even as *Kesari*, in turn, "aligns with consolidated trends" in which such films are presented as "normative nationalist texts" (Tieri 2021: 377–8).[14] Thus, even as its production design and costumes, along with the locations, "transport us back to the late nineteenth century," the film's "religious tint" and reframing of the battle as a holy war "place it firmly in the present," with Kumar's Ishar Singh becoming the "mirror image" of the jihad-waging Muslim cleric leading the Pathans to battle (Ramnath 2019). We shall see, in the ensuing discussion of Kumar's subsequent blockbuster, *Sooryavanshi*, how such a Hindutva meta-discourse is transplanted to the present era, where it is similarly deployed to reshape recent history. However *Kesari* helps us trace a noteworthy shift in the ongoing evolution of Kumar's star text and the increasing gravitational pull of Hindutva upon it. An effective way of charting Kumar's voyage from semi-saffronized / soft Hindutva scientist to fully saffronized Sikh avatar is via the synecdochic images of his head in these films' respective posters (Figures 2.5–2.6).

In the *Mangal* poster, a soaring rocket bifurcates Kumar's head in profile, his face juxtaposed with the semicircle of the (encroaching) saffron planet. In *Kesari*'s poster, meanwhile, Kumar's head is entirely covered by the (oversized) saffron turban. A figurative reading of these promotional images allows us to chart corresponding shifts in Kumar's characters' *soch*, or thought, as well as in

FIGURE 2.6 *Encroaching saffronization of Kumar's* soch *in* Mission Mangal *(2019), directed by Jagan Shakti. Source: © Fox STAR Studios 2019. All rights reserved. Image courtesy of: Everett Collection Inc / Alamy Stock Photo.*

Kumar's star text. From (pseudo) *desi* scientist making in India, to the "(pseudo) facts" of a Sikh warrior killing scores of invading Muslims in defense of his religion (Tieri 2021: 363), one sees the actor's already elastic star text stretched even further in the service of a revisionist, Hindutva-ized history. To intermix the connotative imagery of these posters, one could say Hindutva's orbit trajectory, rather than bifurcating Kumar's *soch*, now encircles his *kesari pagdi*, the new center of gravity, as it were.[15]

Sooryavanshi: Erasing Ayodhya and Not Giving a Damn

At first glance, *Sooryavanshi* seems very much like the typical, big-budget Bollywood *masala* film. Directed by Rohit Shetty and the fourth installment in his *Cop Universe* series, the film stars Kumar along with a host of other big names and includes cameos from the actors who appeared in the previous films of the series.[16] The film's disclaimer in fact insists that it be read as such— "the film," it states, "must therefore, be viewed as purely a non-commenting source of harmless entertainment not designed to hurt or disdain any individual or any community." Following this disclaimer/ command, the film, like *Kesari*, contains a dedication, in this case, to "our real heroes Mumbai Police, Anti Terrorism Squad, Armed Forces and Central Agency Officers for their relentless service towards the nation." The film itself, which features Kumar in the titular role as a tough cop, begins on "12th March 1993 Bombay," when we see his parents blown up in a bomb blast. This is followed by documentary footage of actual bomb blasts, while a voiceover describes these events as "the first terrorist attack of this kind in India." As the opening credits continue to roll, the voiceover goes on to state that one of the terrorists responsible (for the 1993 bomb blasts in Bombay) received training from Pakistan's Inter-Services Intelligence (ISI) and one of them, Bilal Ahmed, fled to Pakistan-occupied Kashmir (PoK) following the attacks. The voiceover goes on to narrate subsequent events, including the Kargil War, fought between India and Pakistan in 1999, as the credits continue to appear onscreen. We then see the film's villains—Muslim terrorists—planning their next moves in 2007. Bilal tells the others they will all go to India on two-day visas to watch the Pakistan-India cricket match but will then remain in India, in different cities, where employment and housing will be provided by their terrorist network associate. The voiceover then states, as the camera pans over these men's faces in close-up shots, "They [these Muslim terrorists] were everywhere around us. They could've been anyone. Maybe the watchman at your building or an employee in your office," while the men continue to stare directly into the camera, that is, directly at the viewer. We are then presented with a series of images of subsequent damage, presumably caused by subsequent terrorist attacks, including at the Taj Hotel in Bombay. It is only after all of this that the film title appears onscreen; in other words, the first seven minutes of the film provide a decidedly skewed overview of recent history, which makes no reference to the destruction of the Babri Masjid in Ayodhya, which preceded and arguably served as the key flashpoint for the ensuing violence in Bombay, nor to the targeted killing of Muslims in the subsequent riots that followed.[17] This is how *Sooryavanshi* begins, this is how it situates or, to employ Tieri's term, "socializes," its viewers (2021: 359).

The film then moves to "Mumbai present day" at the Anti-Terrorism Squad headquarters, where the sleeper units' coordinator, Riyaaz Hafeez, has been located in Jaisalmer. Following a cut to the Rajasthani city, Kumar emerges from a helicopter as a male voice loudly and repeatedly intones his name on the soundtrack ("Soooo-rya-vanshi!"). Kumar is framed here as the "badass cop," whose character name is repeated multiple times as he descends in slow motion from the helicopter (like the sun god of his namesake), then enters a black SUV and roars off with his team. Like *Kesari*, *Sooryavanshi* alternates between such heightened moments of intense action and banal comedy, which ensues in the SUV as Kumar bungles his colleagues' names and engages in light banter in his typical, rustic *desi* palaver. The film quickly returns to action, however, when Kumar and his team attempt to apprehend Riyaaz Hafeez, while Kumar's character's name is again repeated on the soundtrack. During the subsequent interrogation of Hafeez back at the Anti-Terrorism headquarters in Bombay, Kumar observes that Hafeez has been living incognito as "Rajbir Rathod" and has married "an Indian girl, Jyoti Gupta." What is left unsaid but understood here is that both Hafeez's sleeper identity and the woman he has married are Hindu, thus rehashing another familiar, Islamophobic trope of Hindutva groups, namely, "love jihad," the idea that Muslim men target Hindu women for conversion to Islam by means of seduction. Coupled with the film's opening shots of sleeper agents gazing directly into the camera as the voiceover intones, "They could've been anyone," the film blatantly insinuates that any Muslim man living in India could potentially be a member of a sleeper terrorist unit who is engaging in love jihad, as in the case of Hafeez.

When Kumar and his crew catch up with Bilal Ahmed, who has returned briefly to Bombay to visit his mother's grave, and face off with him in his hotel room, where he holds a gun to his head, threatening suicide, Kumar tells Ahmed, "This is your country, too." Yet, Ahmed says no, then asks Kumar, "Have you ever seen your house on fire?" "They," he says, burned his children, wife and father alive.[18] Kumar notes that he also lost his parents in "those blasts," but adds that that is in the past and that we need to forget it and move on (a sentiment clearly belied by the film, which continues to revisit this past, albeit in a truncated and problematic way). Ahmed replies that he wants to see India burn and then shoots himself. Ahmed's comment before he dies, coupled with brief (2–3-second) flashbacks of a house on fire, are the only (oblique) reference to the additional (anti-Muslim) violence preceding the Bombay bomb blasts in March of 1993. Yet, here, too, Hindus are never directly indicted or even named, much less the (Hindu) authorities who either tacitly or explicitly condoned the anti-Muslim violence including and accompanying the attack on the Babri

Masjid—Ahmed merely says, "Uun logon" (those people). Such an abridged history is repeated just before the film's interval, when Kumar tells his police colleague that "Mumbai and its people have suffered a lot," and recites a litany of events—"Pehle 1993 serial bomb blast, phir 2002 Ghatkopar bus blast, 2006 mein, train blast, aur phir Taj 26/11."[19] Again, Ayodhya and other subsequent attacks (by Hindus) on Muslims are elided in this account which, again, starts with the 1993 bomb blasts. Coming just before the interval, this abridged account, selectively mentioning certain atrocities and leaving out others (particularly those in which Muslims were targeted), reiterates the film's distorted history and again works to "socialize" the viewer to its skewed version of events. As Indian journalist Rana Ayyub (2021) has observed, "The film makes a point of repeating attacks carried out by Muslims, ignoring the numerous episodes of violence carried out by Hindu radicals."[20]

It is in the film's second half that we see a further development of this problematic historiography. Sooryavanshi goes to arrest a local Muslim suspected of being part of the Muslim sleeper cell plot, and explains to the assembled Muslims that Indian law does not discriminate on the basis of religion. He continues to sermonize to the arrested Muslim, Usmani, back at police headquarters[21] but then summons Usmani's wife and daughter to the station, where he pretends to have them beaten in an adjoining room in an effort to pressure Usmani to talk. These scenes—of the purported torture of Usmani's wife and daughter, which Usmani believes to be real—are "played for laughs and hoots," with Sooryavanshi admonishing the female police officer providing the (fake) screams for sounding too erotic (Girish 2021). Usmani, believing his wife and daughter are actually being tortured by the police, relents and leads Kumar's unit to where the sleeper cells are preparing their bombs. These Muslim sleeper agents are all shown praying together, begging the question one film critic poses, namely, "Do only terrorists pray?" (Menon 2021).[22] After Hafeez is shown killing the Hindu wife of a fellow Muslim sleeper agent after she discovers their plot (while her husband does nothing to

FIGURE 2.7 *Muslims safely placing Ganesha statue before their mosque in* Sooryavanshi *(2021). Source: Screenshot from* Sooryavanshi, *directed by Rohit Shetty. 2021. Reliance Entertainment. All rights reserved.*

stop her killing), and following the arrival of Simmba (Ranveer Singh), the titular super cop from Shetty's previous film, Sooryavanshi and his team spread out across Bombay, trying to find and disarm all the bombs that have been planted by the sleeper agents. We then see the police ordering people to evacuate a temple and, as the song "Chodo kal ke baatein" plays on the soundtrack, we watch as a group of Muslims helps move a statue of Ganesha from the temple, where a bomb was found, to a safe location (Figure 2.7).[23]

As we see the Muslim men moving the statue to safety in slow motion, the song's refrain continually repeats, "Hum Hindustani, Hum Hindustani" (We are Hindustani, we are Hindustani, i.e., Indian). This sentiment—the song title's command to "forget yesterday's issues"—is rather rich, given that the film excises many of the key "baatein" from "kal" in its repeated and truncated history. Nevertheless, the response of at least one Indian film critic to this scene was "a lump in the throat" (Tuteja 2021). A more understandable reaction might be a gasp, given the sheer audacity of the propaganda on display in this sequence, particularly when coupled with the film's abridged history of communal tensions.

Following the arrival of Ajay Devgn as fellow bad ass cop Singham, this Hindu police trident (Sooryavanshi, Simmba, Singham) proceed to beat up a seemingly never-ending number of Muslim terrorists (as with the Pathans in *Kesari*, they seem to keep surfacing everywhere). Unlike *Kesari*, however, *Sooryavanshi* ends in triumph, with the trio standing over the three remaining terrorists who sit unarmed before them. As one of the terrorists verbally taunts them, Kumar says, in his typical deadpan voice, "Let's get this over with," and the three super Hindu cops shoot dead the three unarmed and seated terrorists at point-blank range.[24] The film then concludes with an item number during its end credits, featuring the lead trio accompanied by policemen and women in uniform with guns, all dancing aggressively as they lip-synch the song's lyrics:

> The party has just started, it will only get better
> Music is on, it will continue to play
> We are celebrating, we'll continue to celebrate
> Come what may, nothing's gonna stop us
> I don't care a damn, to hell with you.

This song, with which the film literally ends, is essentially a celebration of extrajudicial killings (by Hindus, of Muslims) and provides a rather compelling and crystallized instance of the film's overall ideology. Adding to a film "rife with gleeful scenes of police brutality" (Girish 2021), this end credits song and dance sequence, featuring policemen in uniform, celebrates not only such brutality but, just as disturbingly, the complete impunity felt by the police in committing such acts. The song's second stanza includes these lyrics:

> We'll crush anyone who messes with us
> We're brave soldiers, nothing scares us
> Come what may, nothing will stop us
> I don't care a damn, it's time to party.

Thus, even as the Muslim sleeper agents (who are everywhere and could be anyone) are exterminated, their love jihads exposed, and order restored, with Muslims helping to move Hindu statues to safety as the soundtrack urges them to forget yesterday's issues, Hindutva order is restored in a cinematic world in which the destruction of the Babri Masjid is forgotten and the extrajudicial killing of Muslims not only justified but, indeed, celebrated. One wonders what the viewer, socialized into this Hindutva cine-verse, makes of such a resolution. In the words of the film critic who admitted having a lump in his throat during the "Chodo kal ke baatein" sequence, "*Sooryavanshi* works, and how" (Tuteja 2021). This is precisely the key issue—how this blockbuster film works, how it employs the star text of Kumar and his fellow super (Hindu) cops, as well as over-the-top action and song sequences, to sell a narrative that calls to mind "Nazi Germany, where Hitler cultivated a film industry that paid obeisance to him and made propaganda films against Jews" (Ayyub 2021). Even more worrying than such blatant distortions of history and pandering to Islamophobic tropes, is the sentiment expressed by the police in the film's concluding song, namely, of not giving a damn. This is perhaps why, as Ayyub (2021) notes, the film's ensuing success at the box office should worry us all. As the film's opening disclaimer insists, it must be viewed as "purely a non-commenting source of harmless entertainment." Indeed.

Ram Setu: Immersive Hindutva

The final Akshay Kumar film I would like to discuss in this chapter engages in a different form of Hindutva historiography than *Sooryavanshi*, which is more concerned with recent events, but one that is no less problematic. This film, *Ram Setu*, also provides a further instance of the ongoing evolution of Kumar's star text, which continues to be utilized in myriad ways to serve a Hindutva agenda. Departing from his "bad ass" look as the titular cop in *Sooryvanshi*,

Kumar (again) plays a scientist in *Ram Setu*, in this case, an atheist archaeologist. If *Toilet* and *Mission Mangal* try to sell BJP initiatives to viewers, and *Kesari* and *Sooryavanshi* attempt to proselytize viewers to their respective Hindutvaized historical accounts, *Ram Setu* provides a different type of conversion narrative, one in which Kumar's character's own conversion plays a key role. The film also illuminates the ongoing utilization of "History" that Merivirta (2016) has previously described, as a way of reframing contemporary religious debates. Relatedly, the film begins with a lengthy disclaimer whose final line states, "References to certain facts and events in the film are duly supported and based on known published literature/books/material such as 'Dating the Era of Lord Ram' by Pushkar Bhatnagar, which has been verified with reference to such facts and/or events depicted in the film." Kumar's character, Dr. Aryan Kulshreshtra, is recruited by a scheming businessman, Indrakant (Nassar), to verify that the Ram Setu, a chain of natural limestone shoals between India and Sri Lanka, was not manmade, so he can demolish part of it to allow for the passage of larger ships. The businessman enlists Kumar for this task in order to counter Hindus protesting against his plans who, in turn, believe the bridge was built by the Hindu deity Ram, in order to reach Sri Lanka and liberate his wife, Sita, from the clutches of Ravana, as per the account given by the Hindu religious text, the *Ramayan*.

Kumar's look as Dr. Aryan is a departure from his typical filmic appearance. Sporting longer, unruly hair, salt and pepper beard and spectacles, Kumar as Dr. Aryan again extends the parameters of his star text, as he approximates the look of an Indiana Jones-esque rugged archaeologist. Nevertheless, as we have seen throughout the films discussed in this chapter, certain elements, in particular, Kumar's voice and the deadpan manner in which he delivers his lines, remain the same, thus retaining what could be considered a defining element of his star text. Early on in the film, Aryan makes his viewpoint regarding religion clear in precisely such a voice, stating that "religion only divides, culture unites." The atheist Dr. Aryan is thus perfect for the scheming businessman's plans to confirm that the Ram Setu is indeed a natural formation. The film takes place in 2007, which is also significant, as this was during the reign of the Congress party, which the BJP has consistently attacked as the party of secularists who, it is implied, are beholden to big businessmen like Indrakant intent upon eradicating key elements of Hindu history such as the Ram Setu.[25] With the clock ticking down to a Supreme Court hearing on the matter, Dr. Aryan is dispatched to Rameswaram, on the southeastern edge of India, to investigate the Ram Setu. Upon arriving and flying over the structure in a helicopter, he is amazed at the sight, as arguably the viewer is, given the broad aerial perspective provided. Here and in subsequent shots when Aryan descends below the water to take a closer look at the formation we are provided with wide angle shots that work to immerse the viewer (and Aryan) in the broad imagescape of the Ram Setu. Indeed, when he first glimpses the formation underwater, Aryan exclaims, "This looks like an engineering marvel!" while a Hindu chant, "Om nama Shivaya" (Salutation to the auspicious one) plays repeatedly on the soundtrack.

Here, and in accompanying scenes, the film engages in what can be described as "IMAX Hindutva," that is, an immersive form of Hindutva that relies upon IMAX-like visual aesthetics to generate amazement at these (religiously inflected) underwater images. As in this initial underwater sequence, the use of accompanying Hindu chanting on the soundtrack helps generate a Hindutva-ized aura aimed at conveying a sense of religiously inflected wonder at this sight. Just as the IMAX image "astonishes with its vibrant colors and fine details," and is particularly designed to attract what media scholar Charles Acland calls "the tourist gaze," IMAX Hindutva works to astonish viewers and formulate what could be called the Hindutva gaze, in which naturally occurring phenomena are reinscribed with(in) a religious aura designed to generate religiously inflected awe (1998: 429).[26] As with IMAX, the "total encompassing of the field of vision" by these underwater shots results in the only point of orientation being that provided by the film (ibid., 430). In this sense, to continue building on and redeploying the immersive IMAX experience, these underwater sequences are designed to "create the experience of being there, or getting there, for spectators" (ibid., 431). With Kumar's Dr. Aryan as our guide, we are submerged in a blue hued hyper-realism aimed at generating "an illusion of material presence" (ibid., 431). Such simulated aura, or "fauxra," attempts to immerse the viewer in a Hindutva-ized seascape and, as is the case with Aryan, generate "belief" in the attendant myths associated with such formations. We will return to this point shortly but suffice to say that the viewer may very well share Aryan's sense of wonder as he emerges from his underwater voyage, carrying a floating rock that apparently came from the bridge formation as he appears to walk on water (Figure 2.8).

This sense of visual wonderment seems to shake Aryan's earlier conviction that the Ram Setu is a natural formation and he proceeds to make a series of fallacious arguments in order to "prove" the Ram Setu was manmade. For instance, Aryan claims that, if rocks from the Ram Setu are 7,000 years old,

FIGURE 2.8 *Aryan appearing to walk on water in* Ram Setu *(2022). Source: Screenshot from* Ram Setu, *directed by Ashishek Sharma. 2022. Zee Studios. All rights reserved.*

then that means the Ram Setu is 7,000 years old which, in turn, means that it must have been manmade as the era of Ram has also been dated to 7,000 years ago.[27] After a series of additional adventures, Kumar arrives at the Supreme Court, where he makes the case for the existence of Ram, again deploying a series of syllogisms. The court renders its decision: until the government can prove that Ram did not exist, the Ram Setu cannot be destroyed. As repeated intonations of "Jai jai jai" play on the soundtrack, signifying (Hindu) victory, Aryan and his colleagues emerge from the court in slow motion, where they are greeted with cheers and applause by the assembled crowd. Thus, we witness what one critic labels "the intention of the film," which, furthermore, "is laid out for everyone to see," namely, "the conversion of the secular, science-minded Aryan into a believer" (Gupta 2022). It is precisely for this reason that *Ram Setu* has been characterized as "propagandist cinema" in which Bollywood and Kumar "openly pande[r] to majoritarian elements in the audience and to the present government," deploying arguments that are "nothing but a slightly polished, insidious version of the propaganda floating around on WhatsApp and Twitter" (Vetticad 2022).[28] The source material for the film, Bhatnagar's "Dating the Era of Lord Ram," referenced in the film's lengthy disclaimer, is itself a "pseudo-scientific study," in which the writer attempts to date the era of Lord Ram "on the basis of planetary positions described in Valmiki's Ramayan" (Ramnath 2022; Kumar 2022). As with the "(pseudo)facts" of *Kesari*, we see how such pseudo-science is used to reaffirm Hindu myth and, in the process, critique those who do not believe in Ram.

In the process, *Ram Setu* can be seen as (engaging in) a form of immersive Hindutva in a variety of ways. To begin with, the film approximates an IMAX aesthetic to create an immersive experience for the viewer, in which the spectacularly depicted images of the Ram Setu are used to historicize myth. As political scientist Christophe Jaffrelot has observed, satellite photographs taken by NASA of the Ram Setu formation were similarly used by Hindu nationalists to argue for the existence of Ram (2008: 11). After members of the

Sangh Parivar stated that "pictures taken by NASA from space show the remains of what appears to be an age old man-made bridge," and that "the discovery of Shri Ram Setu by NASA confirms that Hindu scriptures and belief are correct," NASA had to "clarify repeatedly" that these photographs had been "misinterpreted by the Sangh Parivar" (ibid.). Yet, as Jaffrelot notes, such clarification matters little to Hindu nationalists who "mix Sanskrit and 'scientific' sources" to validate their belief (ibid.). The film also engages in this form of proselytizing via its protagonist, Dr. Aryan, who becomes immersed (via his immersive underwater experiences) in Hindutva historicity, eschewing his earlier atheism for belief in Ram and, via a series of syllogistic arguments, a corresponding belief that the Ram Setu was manmade. This conversion is also echoed by Kumar in a brief video issued prior to the film's release, in which he announces that he will be donating money to the construction of a Ram temple in Ayodhya at the site of the demolished Babri Masjid.[29] As Dore (2021) notes, in the video Kumar "narrates a story about the building of the Ram Setu" and, in the process, "the video seemed like a simultaneous promotion for two ventures: Kumar's upcoming film, and the government's Ram Temple project." Here, again, we see Kumar's willingness to collaborate on BJP projects and utilize this synergy to simultaneously promote both his film and the underlying Hindutva ideology informing it. As in the case of *Toilet*, "the film and the government's messaging seemed to have blurred into one" (Dore 2021).

Though *Ram Setu* was not a commercial success, it nevertheless demonstrates Kumar's flexibility and his pliancy, willing to bend again and again to the BJP agenda. Whether collaborating directly with BJP schemes like the Clean India mission or Make in India, or directly invoking Hindutva ideology as in *Kesari*, *Sooryavanshi* or *Ram Setu*, Kumar has made his willingness to serve as Modi's ad man clear, just as one could simultaneously argue that the continued use of his star text for such films illuminates just how crucial such star presence is to "shaping political discourse" and, by turn, "Brand Modi" (Dore 2021). If critics and observers label such films as "dangerous" (Vetticad 2022) or their ensuing success as worrying (Ayyub 2021), then the complicity they expose, whether of certain Bollywood players like Kumar or of the viewing public more generally with the Hindutva agenda of the BJP, is equally of concern. While the films discussed here make a point to hammer home the significance of certain events, whether they be bomb blasts affecting certain communities or the destruction of certain monuments, about others, they have very little to say.[30] And, as is the case with Modi, such silences speak volumes.

3

Modi's *Bhakt*: Kangana Ranaut

The case of Kangana Ranaut provides another compelling instance of the Hindutva-ization of Bollywood. An outsider to the film industry, Ranaut's film debut came in 2006 with *Gangster: A Love Story*. This was followed by *Fashion* (2008), for which she won the first of multiple national awards, in this case, for Best Supporting Actress in her turn as a model on the decline. Ranaut went on to star in a number of successful Bollywood and *hatke* (offbeat) features in the 2010s, including *Tanu Weds Manu* (2011), *Queen* (2014), and *Tanu Weds Manu Returns* (2015). The subsequent years, however, witnessed a turn in Ranaut's star trajectory, with the young actress increasingly attacking members of the industry on social media as well as increasingly aligning herself with the BJP and Prime Minister Modi. This increased aggressiveness on social media and newfound political alignment corresponded with a decline in the success of her subsequent filmic ventures, with the majority of the films she has made since *Tanu Weds Manu Returns* declared box office failures.[1] At the same time, Ranaut enjoys a wide following on social media, which has "increased by the year," with 7.8 million followers on Facebook, 9.6 million followers on Instagram and over 3 million followers on Twitter (Konikkara 2022). Yet, as journalist Aathira Konikkara (ibid.) notes, this huge social media following "no longer seems to translate to actual success for her recent films," the majority of which, as noted, have been flops. Ranaut has, nevertheless, gained fame in becoming "Modi's most strident supporter" online (ibid.), frequently attacking anyone deemed to be a critic of either the Prime Minister or of the BJP's Hindutva platform. In 2021, the stridency of her online statements led to her being permanently suspended from Twitter; yet, like Trump, she had her Twitter account reactivated in January 2023. Ranaut also stepped into the role of director, replacing Krish Jagarlamudi behind the camera on her 2019 historical epic, *Manikarnika: The Queen of Jhansi* (hereafter, *Manikarnika*), in which she also plays the lead role of the nineteenth century queen who took part in the 1857 uprising against the British. All of this is to say that there are many contradictions in Ranaut's star text and these contradictions themselves become key components of it. As film theorist John Ellis has observed, "There is always a temptation to think of a 'star image' as some kind of fixed repository of fixed meanings" (1982: 92). Yet, Ranaut's career is replete with several contradictions, including, among others, being a three-time winner of the National Film Award for Best Actress, yet permanently suspended by Twitter (until 2023); a Bollywood star, yet a perennial outsider in the industry; a successful actor now turned director but one who has not had a box office hit in nearly a decade; the broader oscillations between her filmic voice and persona and her social media presence; and her role as Modi's *bhakt*, or devotee and, alternately, her limited direct interaction with him (compared, e.g., to Akshay Kumar's collaborations and public interactions with the Prime Minister—cf. Chapter 2). In this chapter, I intend to examine not only these contradictory elements of Ranaut's star text and how they paradoxically inform her star persona but also, more broadly, how Ranaut has increasingly become aligned with Modi and the BJP, both on- and offscreen, most prominently through her directorial debut, *Manikarnika*, but also through her ongoing social media activity on behalf of the man who, in her view, gave India its true independence upon assuming the office of Prime Minister in 2014.[2]

The Multiple Iterations of Kangana Ranaut

As noted, Ranaut's Bollywood debut came in 2006 with *Gangster*, in which she played the role of an ill-fated bar dancer who becomes involved with a gangster. Journalist Piyasree Dasgupta has described her subsequent career trajectory—"from 'vulnerable' (*Gangster*) to confident (*Queen, Tanu Weds Manu*) to unapologetically self-loving (*Simran, Judgmentall Hai Kya*)"—and this trajectory in many ways corresponds with her increasing presence on social media (2020). As with Akshay Kumar, I am particularly interested in Ranaut's voice or, more precisely, her voices which, as Richard Dyer has observed, indicate the personality of the star both directly and indirectly (1998: 112). Like Kumar, Ranaut, while fluent in English, has what has been called an "earthy accent," which distinguishes her from the "polished English-speaking elite circles" of the film industry, including "film industry children" who have attended "top schools in the country and abroad" (Menon 2020).[3] Ranaut's speaking voice, as expressed in her films, also has a shrill quality at times that paradoxically seems to emphasize her vulnerability; as one film critic has noted, "When she's in a state of fury, her eyes tear up and her voice gets tremulous and rises a few notches" (Palat 2019). Simultaneously, reflecting the elasticity of the star's voice, Ranaut's frankness in interviews and her willingness to critique elements of the industry that largely go unaddressed, including nepotism, were seen as "refreshing" (Konikkara 2022). Rananut also tends to revert to speaking in Hindi, both in interviews and in films, in moments of crisis, including in the more cosmopolitan *Fashion*, and these moments accord with what Dyer describes as indirect speech, that is, "what a character betrays about him/herself," and what, in turn, we are more inclined to believe as representing the "truth about the person of the star playing the part" (1998: 112, 125). Such a tremulous, Hindi-speaking voice belies the affected, English-inflected palaver Ranaut and her on-screen characters opt for at times and, cohering with her status as industry outsider, conveys a sense of vulnerability behind her persona.

Ranaut's online voice, meanwhile, while shrill, is far from vulnerable, even as she paradoxically frames herself as the frequent victim of sinister plots by Bollywood insiders. The voice reflected in Ranaut's social media posts, including on Twitter and Instagram, is frequently aggressive and bullying and, correlating with instances of her indirect speaking voice, often employs a rather crude lexicon. Such a lexicon is particularly on display in Ranaut's frequent attacks against women online, which seem to create yet another fissure in her start text, between Ranaut as "feminist icon" and as the frequent heckler of women on social media. Such attacks include, for instance, referring to other actresses and female performers as "soft-porn stars," "porn singers," "porn stars," "fools," and "dummies." The nature of her online speech, particularly when directed against women, in other words, rearticulates the notion of her "frankness" as misogynistic. This tendency also seems to correspond with her increasing online alignment with Modi and the BJP. Along with deploying ad hominem attacks against fellow female industry outsiders, including Swara Bhaskar, Richa Chaddha, and Taapsee Pannu, whose only achievement, Ranaut tweeted, was to be "a sasti copy" (a cheap copy) (qtd in Zain 2023: 250), Ranaut has also increasingly leveled online attacks against perceived critics of the Modi regime. It was following Pannu's announcement of support for farmers who were protesting against the Modi government in 2021 that Ranaut leveled her attacks against the actress as well as other perceived critics of Modi, including pop singer Rihanna, who had also tweeted in support of the protesting Indian farmers and whom Ranaut, in turn, labeled a "porn singer" (DNA 2021). Corresponding with Ranaut's increasing affinity with the BJP, she has amplified these types of personal attacks by labeling critics of the government "terrorists," including not only the protesting farmers but a member of Canada's Parliament, Jagmeet Singh, who had discussed Rihanna's tweet (ibid.).[4]

Here, then, we see not only the disjuncture between the timbre of Ranaut's onscreen voice and her online voice but her willingness to attack people (and particularly women) who "don't fall in line" with the BJP platform, itself a "well-oiled strategy" of the BJP (Dasgupta 2020). In the process Ranaut has "morphed into the perfect right-wing poster girl" in a way that other supporters of the BJP, including Akshay Kumar, would avoid doing (ibid.).[5] Interestingly, even as Ranaut has been further ostracized within the Bollywood industry for making such online attacks, she is perceived by members of the everyday public as being an activist icon who is "fearless and uninhibited," and "doesn't shy away from saying the ugly truth" (qtd in Jain et al. 2021: 9). Here we see alternating receptions of Ranaut's controversial speech acts, with some seeing her as "refreshing" and "uninhibited," while others perhaps see her as increasingly unhinged in her increasingly strident online support for Modi and the BJP. As Konikkara notes, "Her vitriol against other actors, as well as those outside the industry, became sharper, often descending into petty name-calling" which, in turn, has earned her the moniker "mad queen of Bollywood" (2022). Yet, as Konikkara goes on to point out, "more troubling" has been her role in advancing the Hindu Right's agenda (ibid.). Whether such attacks demonstrate that Ranaut has "mastered the media game" (Rao 2020: 216) is an open question but, along with leading to her being banned on Twitter, this escalation and corresponding decrease of comportment becomes an apt way of tracing the shift in her star construction, from "cutting myth-buster" to increasingly unhinged "mad queen of Bollywood" and, in turn, from film industry outsider to Modi's *bhakt*.[6] The increased stridency of her online avatar is correspondingly reflected in the trajectory of her onscreen performances, moving as she has from quirky *hatke* films like *Queen* and *Tanu Weds Manu* to overt paeans to Hindu nationalism like *Manikarninka*. Yet, as Konikkara has noted, this rightward shift has not resulted in box office success. Ranaut's increasing alignment with the BJP, both in her filmic and social media endeavors, also reshapes another key component previously informing her star text—that of not being a conformist (Rao 2020: 215). While her earlier iterations, both on and offscreen, helped to frame her as a "myth-buster," she has increasingly conformed to the Hindutva platform of the BJP and, in turn, actively worked to propagate its corresponding myths and ideologies. These shifts, and corresponding alliances, in Ranaut's star text indeed "make it impossible to separate the actor from the outspoken woman in the public domain," as one discourse increasingly "infiltrates" the other (ibid., 217). Such a blurring of Ranaut's extra-filmic persona with her onscreen persona is particularly on display in her directorial debut, *Manikarnika*, which in many (troubling) ways aligns itself with a contemporary Hindutva ethos, as we shall see in our ensuing discussion of the film.

The Multiple Iterations of the Rani of Jhansi

The Rani (Queen) of Jhansi is one of the most iconic figures in Indian history. Historian Sunil Khilnani describes her as "the most famous female figure of the uprising of 1857," the period which saw one of the first large-scale mobilizations by Indians against the British East India Company (2016: 170). According to legend, the Rani, originally known as Manikarnika, fought valiantly against the British to defend the Jhansi fort and, by proxy, her kingdom, which the British sought to annex per their Doctrine of Lapse, following the deaths of the Rani's infant son and her husband, Gangadhar Rao, the erstwhile Raja of Jhansi.[7] After the British laid siege to the fort, the Rani executed her "legendary jump," allegedly leaping from the rampart of the fort atop her horse with her adopted son Damodar strapped to her back, a "sheer plunge of about fifteen metres" (ibid., 166). As Khilnani goes on to note, it is "hard to imagine anyone human surviving" such a jump (ibid.). Nevertheless, the Rani apparently did (even if her horse did not) and took part in one final battle against the British at Gwalior, the capital of the adjoining state, Madhya Pradesh, during which she was killed. The Rani's legend lives on, however—as Khilnani notes, *Time* magazine recently named her, along with Michelle

Obama, as one of history's "Top 10 Bad-Ass Wives," and the subtitle of Khilnani's own chapter on the Rani is "Bad-ass Queen" (ibid.). Multiple stories and films have been made about the Rani of Jhansi and before analyzing Ranaut's recent adaptation and in order to more fully appreciate how it deviates from earlier iterations, I would first like to examine some of the earlier filmic adaptations of the Rani's life story, beginning with Sohrab Modi's *Jhansi Ki Rani* (1953).

As South Asian studies scholar Harleen Singh observes in her book on this legendary figure, Manikarnika came from a family of Maharashtrian Brahmins who served the Peshwa, or ruler, Baji Rao II (2014: 12). Most Indian historical accounts give her date of birth as 1835 which, as Singh notes, would have made her seven at the time of her marriage to the Raja of Jhansi, Gangadhar Rao who, in turn, was between 30 and 50 years of age at the time of the wedding (ibid.).[8] Modi's film adaptation, allegedly the first Technicolor Indian film,[9] does not skirt from this issue of age (and attendant age gap) but indeed addresses it head on. Director Modi (no relation to the current prime minister) also stars in the film as the Rani's mentor, Rajguru, who first discovers her as a young child and, impressed by her courage, embarks upon the idea to have her marry the Raja of Jhansi. In what Singh describes as "a deft handling of the film's most uneasy moment," the marriage of the child Manu, as she was colloquially known, to the significantly older Gangadhar Rao is "negotiated through the prism of national service" (ibid., 125). When Manu's father objects, noting that Gangadhar is "over fifty years old and Manu is hardly nine," Rajguru replies that Manu's wedding is not for pleasure but for the nation (Figure 3.1).

As Singh goes on to note, it is Rajguru who "moulds" Rani into a queen and Manu's father and then her husband, Gangadhar, who "have final say over her life" (2014: 124), in other words, she is thoroughly ensconced within a patriarchal structure. Through a subsequent "montage of scenes," Modi's film depicts the young Manu "transfor[med] into a beautiful woman," while engaging in sword play (Singh 2014: 125).[10] The grown-up Rani, now played by

FIGURE 3.1 *Child bride Manu with much older Gangadhar Rao in* Jhansi Ki Rani *(1953). Source: Screenshot from* Jhansi Ki Rani, *directed by Sohrab Modi. 1953. Minerva Movietone. All rights reserved.*

the director's wife, Mehtab, thus "replaces" the child Manu in what amounts to another "deft handling" by the filmmaker. This grown-up goes on to fight the British in a number of battle scenes choreographed with the aid of the Indian Ministry of Defence, as an opening statement proclaims. Though we do not witness the Rani's famous horseback leap, the film depicts her ultimate death, first being wounded on the battlefield and then collapsing on her horse, which takes her to the hut of her childhood friend, Shankar, where she dies while gazing at the setting sun and calling out, "Azaadi" (Freedom). Shankar then prepares her corpse for cremation (Figure 3.2) and, following this, leaves the hut which he proceeds to set on fire. As fire engulfs the hut, we hear Mohammed Rafi's plaintive voice on the soundtrack singing "Azaadi ki yehi aag hai" (This is the Fire of Freedom), as Shankar steps back and bows reverently to the burning hut.

Singh describes this as a "final and complicated obeisance to traditional notions of Indian womanhood" and one she furthermore labels a "particularly elastic rendering," as it "allows for a compromise between the progressive and

FIGURE 3.2 *Shankar prepares Rani's corpse for cremation in* Jhansi Ki Rani *(1953). Source: Screenshot from* Jhansi Ki Rani, *directed by Sohrab Modi. 1953. Minerva Movietone. All rights reserved.*

regressive mode of representation" (2014: 128). The Rani, in other words, does not perform *sati* (female self-immolation upon her husband's funeral pyre) yet, in Singh's view, she "continue[s] to uphold the *sat* (the truth) of the *sati* by eventually immolating herself" (ibid.). To be precise, however, the Rani does not "immolate[e] herself"—her corpse is cremated by Shankar. Yet, the image of the burning hut (in which her corpse lies) may indeed allude to the "regressive" act of *sati* in its connotation, per Singh's reading, of the Rani's goodness and devotion to her (wifely / Hindu) duty.

A subsequent filmic adaptation, *Jhanis Ki Rani Laxmibai* (2012, hereafter *Laxmibai*) further fleshes out several of these themes. Directed by Rajesh Mittal, this version is decidedly a "B movie," in terms of its production credits and cast. Nevertheless, *Laxmibai* similarly depicts its titular heroine as a young girl at the outset and, as in Modi's film, features a sudden transformation of the Rani from young girl to mature woman via corresponding editing. This version also illuminates how certain potentially outdated elements of this tale continue to be deployed and mediated in the twenty-first century, including in particular the young age of Manu when she is married and the corresponding age gap between her and Gangadhar.[11] As in Modi's film, the young Manu undergoes a transformation from young girl to grown woman during a sequence in which she engages in sword practice. While the earlier film employed a lap dissolve, *Laxmibai* merely deploys an abrupt cut, with the young Rani leaping, with sword in hand, in one shot, then descending in the following shot, one second later, as the fully grown Rani. Like the earlier *Jhansi Ki Rani*, this film version also includes Manu's father expressing initial shock at the prospect of the marriage. When first informed of this decision by the Raja and his spiritual advisor, Manu's father stammers, "Ye-yeh kaise ho sak ta hai? Aap-aap-aap kya kehere hai?" (H-how can this happen? Wh-wh-what are you saying?) Manu's father goes on to note that the Raja is "forty or forty-five," and his daughter, only "eight to ten years old." Again, the Hindu priest assures Manu's father that the marriage is not one of pleasure but for Jhansi, that is to say, for its defense. Thus, while the invocation of the greater (national) good is again summoned to paper over this uneasy moment, it is arguably not handled as deftly in this B-movie as it is in Modi's earlier film.

Yet, *Laxmibai* works even more expeditiously to efface this age gap by utilizing Bollywood conventions. From the film's first song, accompanying the young Manu learning to fight with a sword, only to quickly cut to a suddenly mature Rani, to the third song, which comes approximately fifteen minutes later and features Gangadhar, still looking very much the same age, now accompanied by the grown-up Rani while a group of singers performs a song, the broader age gap and the problematic framing/ elision of this in the name of the greater (Hindu) good is itself elided via recourse to the quintessential Bollywood element, the song sequence.[12] Thus, the initial shock manifested by young Manu's father at the idea of such a marriage turns out to be a strawman and the larger problematic, enfolded as it is within the broader patriarchal Hindutva discourse of female duty, is elided via narrative ellipsis further enhanced by song. Is it any surprise that the film's following song, soon after, features the Rani as a happy new mother? Or that the ensuing song features her leading a prayer at a Hindu temple? It would be interesting to reframe such a problematic in terms of film scholar Corey Creekmur's (2005) discussion of what he labels the "maturation dissolve" of young male protagonists frequently featured in Bollywood films. What such moments suggest, according to Creekmur, is "a direct causal—and conscious—chain between the suffering of youth and the acts of adulthood" (ibid., 850). Such a link is elided entirely in the case of the Rani of Jhansi and, rather than a "maturation dissolve," what we get in the 2012 *Laxmibai* is a maturation cut, in which the ensuing trauma of being a child bride married to a significantly older man is also excised from the film, again, in the name of a broader patriarchal Hindutva ethos. We will see in our ensuing discussion of Ranaut's *Manikarnika* how such a problematic elision is itself elided in favor of a more seamless (and hence palatable) depiction of this union and, in turn, of Hindutva patriarchy.

Kangana Ranaut's *Manikarnika*

Ranaut took over directing *Manikarnika* after the original director, Krish Jagarlamudi, was removed. The reasons for his removal remain contested however; according to Konikkara (2022), he was removed after Ranaut "complained about other actors being given more prominent roles and the production resembling 'a Bhojpuri film.'" Upon taking over as director, Ranaut reshot several parts of the film, in which she also stars as the titular Hindu heroine (ibid.). Asked about making the film, Ranaut replied that she was "doing a biopic on Rani Laxmibai of Jhansi," and that "you cannot take too much liberties [*sic*] when you make a biopic" (qtd in Pillai 2018). It is worth noting, before delving into the many "liberties" the film takes, how Ranaut's own extra-filmic star text operates in tandem with the character traits of the ("bad-ass") Rani of Jhansi—as scholars Prashant Maurya and Nagendra

Kumar note, "The film propels the idea that [Manikarnika] emerges as the 'modern woman' who defies the effeminate instincts associated with women, like timidness and tenderness, and appears as a 'virangana' (a female warrior)" (2020: 253). Ranaut, as noted in the first section of this chapter, has become notorious as a social media warrior of sorts, with attributes such as "incendiary," "volcanic," "tsunami-like," "combative," "unconstrained," and "uninhibited" associated with her public persona (ibid., 216–17). These extra-filmic character traits accord with the "virangana" role attributed to the Rani of Jhansi and function as an instance of what Dyer describes as a "perfect fit," that is, when "all the aspects of a star's image fit with all the traits of a character" (1998: 129).

Ranaut's *Manikarnika*[13] engages in a number of interesting deviations from both the recorded history of the Rani of Jhansi and its previous filmic depictions. In the process, the film can be seen as engaging in what literary scholar Sneha Kar Chaudhuri describes as "the presentification of history" (2019: 183). Such an approach attempts to "focalize" contemporary ideas such as *gauraksha* (cow protection), Hindutva, and patriotism which are "central" to contemporary BJP discourses (Maurya and Kumar 2020: 253).[14] Indeed, one of the first "cinematic liberties" taken by *Manikarnika* is with regard to the title character's age, or apparent age, when she becomes the Rani of Jhansi. Unlike the earlier filmic depictions (*Jhansi Ki Rani* and *Laxmibai*), *Manikarnika* does not begin by depicting the title character "as a child prodigy" (ibid., 251); rather, the film commences with a grown-up Manikarnika, played, in turn, by Ranaut. Though, according to the film's timeline (in conjunction with the recorded history of this figure), Manikarnika is fourteen when she marries the Raja of Jhansi, Ranaut clearly does not appear to be a teenager. Here we see the first instance of how the film projects "contemporary attitudes" upon "past historical situations" (Chaudhuri 2019: 182). It is safe to assume that the issue of child brides, particularly one as young as the Rani of Jhansi was when she was married, would be unpalatable to twenty-first century audiences or, at the very least, not in keeping with "contemporary attitudes" regarding such arrangements. Such a "cinematic liberty" with regard to the lead character's age and appearance is furthered by casting an actor only ten years older than Ranaut to play the role of Gangadhar Rao, thus lessening the significant (and hence problematic) age gap between Manu and the Raja.[15] To paraphrase Singh (2014), the film's most uneasy moment is thus deftly handled by having Ranaut play the young Manu, that is, by dissolving the actual age gap between the couple at the time of marriage. While not as overtly related to contemporary Hindutva movements, by glossing over the actual disparity in age *Manikarnika* helps de-problematize the arranged Hindu marriage of a girl to a man more than four times older than her. Such "cinematic liberty" was doubtless sought to alleviate concerns contemporary audiences may have regarding this contentious issue rather than for "dramatization purposes," for which nothing could arguably be more effective than casting an actor who actually approximates the age of Manu when she became the Rani.

The film's additional deviations from, or "presentifications" of, history are more overtly aligned with contemporary Hindutva discourses and movements, including its depiction of the Rani of Jhansi as a *gauraksha*, or cow protector and, more broadly, as an agent of Hindutva. Early on in the film, after arriving in Jhansi, marrying the Raja and being installed as the new Rani, Ranaut rides to the rescue of a baby calf that has been cruelly abducted from a Dalit village woman. When she arrives at the British compound, the British troops exclaim, "You can't come here—can't you read bloody English?" Ranaut as the Rani dismounts and, approaching the troops, proclaims in English, "I can read English, it's a mere language. Just words. Words without culture have no meaning." She then continues to admonish the British troops in Hindi, telling them to "respect the people and their feelings," further noting that the English language could never be the Indians' mother tongue, as a mother tongue is akin to a mother and there can only be one mother. In this scene we witness the endorsements of a variety of contemporary hot-button Hindutva issues, including cow protection, "one of the key ingredients of the right-wing idea of nationalism" (Maurya and Kumar 2020: 254), as well as the idea of Hindi as the (sole) official language of India, another goal pushed for by the BJP today. Ranaut's manner of expressing this idea is itself relevant: though beginning in English, she limits her speech in this language to less than twenty words before reverting to Hindi. When she returns to the village, holding the baby calf in her arms, Ranaut as the Rani appears not only as a savior of the animal but, more broadly, as "a symbol of Hindutva" (ibid.). Such an idea is not only "explicitly expressed" in the film but arguably understood by a contemporary Indian audience in relation to the contemporary *gauraksha* movement, whose vigilantes have frequently made headlines in their violent attacks on people (usually Muslims and Dalits) suspected of killing cows (ibid., 253).[16]

Another instance of this "historical" drama aligning with contemporary Hinduvta politics comes in the midst of the battle against the British, who position one of their cannons next to a Hindu temple in order to deter the Indians from firing at them. Ranaut as the Rani rushes out atop her horse, singlehandedly leading an attack against the British and successfully destroying their cannon before returning to the fort unscathed. Here and, more broadly, with the "fort under siege" motif, one again sees how particular tropes are Hindutva-ized, that is, their dramatic intensity aligned with and augmented by a discourse that not only equates the protection of Hindu symbols and places of worship with the protection of the nation but frames the ensuing battle as a religious struggle. Ranaut as the Rani wears a saffron sari when she leads her troops to battle and they similarly hold giant saffron flags as they charge. Such "saffronization" of battle aligns with contemporary trends on display in other recent "historical" films which similarly reframe earlier conflicts in accordance with contemporary, religiously inflected discourses.[17] Such instances become emblematic of what scholar Rudrani Gangopadhyay calls the "Historical Epic 2.0," namely, the contemporary avatar of the popular historical Indian film which operates as an instrument for "resurrecting the Hindutva wave and its paternalistic discourse" (2023: 104). Such a "re-telling" attempts to "evoke in the public imagination an origin story for Hindutva politics," and "re-shape historiographies for the average cinema-going audience" (ibid.). An even more problematic instance of such "re-telling" and "re-shaping" emerges with yet another "cinematic liberty" taken by the film and one furthermore utilized to paradoxically promulgate the notion of the film as having a feminist ethos. I am referring to Manikarnika's concluding *jauhar*.

After Ranaut as Rani, wearing her saffron sari, singlehandedly and graphically kills over thirty British soldiers who have breached the Jhansi fort, she makes her famous leap from the ramparts atop her horse with her adopted son tied to her back, landing successfully before riding away.[18] Arriving at Kalpi, where she joins other Indian freedom fighters and is informed by one of them that the British have reduced Jhansi to a "graveyard," Ranaut as the Rani proclaims, "We will fight and reawaken Chhatrapati Shivaji's dream of self-rule—a unified India!" Her words are in turn, greeted by raucous repetitions of a Hindu war cry, "Har har mahadev!" Again we see how the battle and its aim are framed in religious terms—the dream of a unified (Hindu) nation and the religiously inflected battle cry that greets it are further instances of a Hindutva discourse.[19] After Ranaut as Rani takes over the fort at Gwalior, removing the Gwalior king from his throne after his troops rally behind her, she states that she will "be the flame of freedom that will burn in every Indian's heart," and the film, in turn, proceeds to the final battle scene, where she instructs her troops to "fight like warriors, descendants of Krishna." Shouting "Azaadi" (Freedom), she and her troops charge at the British, with many falling to their death. Ranaut as Rani again singlehandedly slices and dices several British troops in increasingly graphic shots, courtesy of computer-generated imagery (CGI), which also frequently bails her out of impending danger and is used to heighten her martial prowess. Nevertheless, even as she again shouts her Hindutva war cry, she is finally shot, in slow motion, and falls to the ground. Seeing the British commander, Sir Hugh Rose, approaching on his horse, however, Ranaut as the Rani rises and, gazing steadfastly at him, proceeds to walk into a literal line of fire on the battlefield, whereupon her sari catches on fire. As Rose watches helplessly atop his horse, Ranaut as the Rani extends her arms and lifts her head upwards in a beatific grin as she is consumed by fire (Figure 3.3).

As she burns, the camera pulls up, framing her in an increasingly widening shot that ultimately reveals the Rani at the center of a giant "Om" symbol in Devanagari script (Figure 3.4).

FIGURE 3.3 *Beatific Rani engaging in* jauhar *in* Manikarnika *(2019).* Source: Screenshot from Manikarnika, *directed by Kangana Ranaut and Krish Jagarlamudi. 2019. Zee Studios. All rights reserved.*

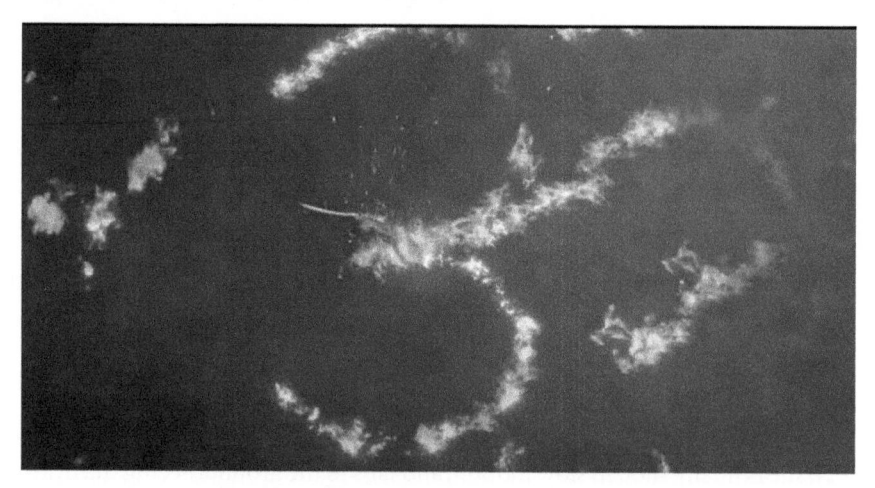

FIGURE 3.4 *Becoming one with the Absolute in* Manikarnika *(2019).* Source: Screenshot from Manikarnika, *directed by Kangana Ranaut and Krish Jagarlamudi. 2019. Zee Studios. All rights reserved.*

This is accompanied by a singing voice on the soundtrack which intones, "Main rahoon ya na rahoon, Bharat yeh rehena chayein" (Whether or not I remain, Bharat [India] must remain).

Here we see a particularly insidious instance of "cinematic liberty" taken with the history of the Rani of Jhansi, one that, following Singh's (2014) analysis of the earlier film, is regressive in nature. One can also trace the shift in Hindutva ideology via the corresponding aesthetics of this tale's adaptations, from the plaintive, subdued ending of *Jhansi Ki Rani*, coming six years after India's independence, featuring the Rani quietly dying even as she utters "Azaadi" one last time as she glimpses the setting sun and whose corpse is subsequently and humbly cremated by her childhood friend, to the over-the-top, CGI-enhanced visualization/celebration of *jauhar* and its conflation with the Hindu nation in *Manikarnika*, released five years after its director and star claimed India truly received its independence. What we witness here is a continuation and intensification of a fascist aesthetic—the glorification of self-immolation—stemming back to Sanjay Leela Bhansali's *Padmaavat* (2018), one just as, if not more, troubling with regard to its gendered constructions of "honor" and "sacrifice" within a patriarchal order.[20] Here, unlike even Padmavati, who solemnly approaches her *jauhar*, the film exudes in glamorous shots of a smiling Manikarnika who blissfully embraces her self-immolation even as the camera blissfully embraces this image, before pulling back to reveal it as part of a larger image—a type of dystopic Busby Berkeley configuration. This is a vivid instance of what film scholars Swapna Gopinath and Rutuja Deshmukh describe as "the faux-historical," fetishized in accordance with a Hindutva-ized discourse that celebrates such sacrifice (2023: 11).

Even more troubling is the reading of such a moment—*jauhar*—as feminist empowerment. While Maurya and Kumar describe this moment as a "significant cinematic appropriation," they also label it "dignified," and go on to claim that "the filmmaker [Ranaut] has enhanced the level of sacrifice made by her to save her Jhansi" (2020: 254). Yet, it is important to note that such "sacrifice" and subsequent reaffirmation of (female) "dignity" occur within and in accordance with a patriarchal code of honor. While, for these two (male, Indian) authors such a depiction "arouse[s] the feeling of profound respect for Rani" (ibid., 255), it arguably does not "arouse" such feelings in others, for whom such a scene may instead evoke the same kind of revulsion the concluding *jauhar* of *Padmaavat* does, if not more, given Ranaut's blissful embrace of her self-immolation. The act, and its subsequent theorization as "dignified," engage in a dangerous (fascist) ideation, in which devotion to the motherland inexorably leads to such (religiously inflected) sacrifice. Yet, Maurya and Kumar are not alone in framing this act in such a manner. Chaudhuri, who also notes that "the Queen gives up her life in the fire," claims the film "succeeds in projecting the Queen of Jhansi as an able symbol of both female empowerment and national resistance" (2019: 186), a sentiment echoed by Maurya and Kumar's assessment that, in committing such an act, the Rani has "exhibited the notion of Indian feminine valour and patriotism" (2020: 255). Yet, there are problems in such a reading of *jauhar* (as empowering). As historian Veena Talwar Oldenburg has observed, the notion of *jauhar* as an act of (feminine) valor is based on the confusion stemming from the transliteration of this word into the Arabic script, in which "the meanings of the Persian *jauhar*—a gem, jewel, pearl; essence, merit, virtue, worth—are most ironically (and mistakenly) imputed to the rite of Rajput suicide" (1994: 164). Thanks to such confusion, the act of *jauhar* comes to "savor of valor rather than of desperation" (ibid.). Postcolonial scholar Gayatri Chakravorty Spivak has similarly noted "the profound irony in locating the woman's free will in self-immolation" (1999: 299).

Here, we come upon an even more intriguing issue: how did an act associated with Rajput tradition find its way into a tale about a non-Rajput Rani? As historian Lindsey Harlan observes, "the Rani of Jhansi was not a Rajput but a Brahmin and was married to a Maratha" (1992: 195). At the same time Ranaut has "long asserted her proud Rajput identity," including in issuing threats to the Karni Sena, a chauvinist Rajput group that had threatened to protest against her film (Konnikara 2022).²¹ Perhaps it is Ranaut (as director) who has projected "her" "cultural tradition" onto "her" character, a process of overwriting the Rani with a patriarchal Rajput code of honor (itself based upon a misunderstood transliteration) in an attempt to once again reinscribe this figure within the (Hindu) national symbolic, that is to say, the "Om" in(to) which Ranaut's Rani is subsumed. Thus, what may, at first glance, appear to be a "revival of an ancient custom," is ultimately "the symptom of a modern pathology rooted in a stubbornly patriarchal society" (Oldenburg 1994: 171). As Spivak has observed, a person engaging in such an act—"the self-immolating woman"—"may have (been imagined to have) thought she was exceeding and transcending the ethical," and this is precisely its danger (1999: 296). "Not all soldiers die unwillingly," Spivak notes (ibid., 297).²²

Also intriguing is that, though *Manikarnika*, like *Padmaavat*, begins with red and orange embers flitting across the black screen (a foreshadowing and ensuing aestheticization of the film's concluding *jauhar*), unlike *Padmaavat*, it includes no mention of *jauhar* in its opening disclaimer.²³ Though *Padmaavat*'s disclaimer is belied by its aesthetic glorification of this act, the Rajput Ranaut seems to feel no need to even nominally disavow such an act and, as noted above, its depiction is arguably even more disturbing in its heroine/ director's blissful celebration of it, which in many ways resembles an advertisement ("Jauhar" by Rani/Ranaut) for both the act and the larger patriarchal Hindu order in which it is literally and symbolically enfolded. Such an aesthetic calls to mind the "Padmavati" collection by the designer company Art Karat (Figure 3.5).

Released in the spring of 2018 (thus coinciding with and building upon the release of *Padmaavat* in January 2018), the company's founder designer, Asha Kamal Modi (again, no relation to the current Prime Minister), claims that this collection "bring[s] out the grandeur of the period" (Art Karat 2018: 3). The question then becomes: what precisely is being promoted here and in *Manikarnika*'s culminating, blissful *jauhar*? Female empowerment? Honor? Valor? Or perhaps just plain old patriarchy, inflected with a particularly odious

FIGURE 3.5 *Art Karat's "Padmavati" jewelry collection (2018). Source: Art Karat. 2018.*

saffron tinge. Such images are not unique and indeed seem to have proliferated in the past few years. Following *Manikarnika* (itself following *Padmaavat*), the film *Samrat Prithviraj* (2022) similarly features its lead heroine joyfully leaping into a *jauhar* pit following a carefully choreographed and highly aestheticized song and dance sequence (Figure 3.6).

Figure 3.6 *The heroine's blissful leap into the* jauhar *pit in* Samrat Prithviraj *(2022). Source: Screenshot from* Samrat Prithviraj, *directed by Chandraprakash Dwivedi. 2022. Yash Raj Films. All rights reserved.*

As in *Manikarnika*, the women in this song sequence—"Yoddha" (Warrior)—wear saffron and sing of their transformation into fearless warriors. As in *Manikarnika*, such self-immolation is framed as heroic, with the heroine's leap aestheticized and drawn out via slow motion shots framing her blissfully jumping into the flaming pit from multiple perspectives.[24]

Though *Samrat Prithiviraj* was not a box office hit, this is the third film in the past five years (2018–22) to feature its leading lady performing *jauhar*, with each representation, in turn, increasingly aestheticized and conflated with Hindutva-ized patriarchal notions of honor, duty and (female) sacrifice. While Ranaut claimed that she was "doing a biopic" and that she therefore "cannot take too much liberties" [*sic*], she also described the action scenes in her film as "mind-blowing" (qtd in Pillai 2018). If one recalls that Ranaut stepped into the director's role because she felt the production was lacking in aesthetic oomph, and went on to reshoot several portions of the film (Konikkara 2022), it becomes difficult not to accord ultimate responsibility for these depictions to her. It becomes all the more troubling when such a depiction is subsequently framed as "empowering" for women; indeed, in Maurya and Kumar's assessment, *Manikarnika* serves as a "booster dose for Indians who have allowed their feelings of patriotism and nationalism to fade" (2020: 257). While Samanth Subramanian, in the conclusion of his recent piece in *The New Yorker*, notes the "accretive psychic weight" of such films (2022), for Maurya and Kumar *Manikarnika* is "successful in rekindling the lost fire among the Indians" (2020: 257). These viewpoints are not mutually exclusive. Indeed, it is precisely through such valorizations that their psychic weight accretes.[25] Though Ranaut's *Manikarnika* was not one of the top box office hits of 2019, it has been heralded for being one of the highest grossing "female-centric" films of the year (*Deccan Chronicle* 2019). Though one critic claims the film "blow[s] historical accuracy to smithereens," she also finds that Ranaut "brings her feminist views into the story" which, the critic goes on to add, "is one of the better points about the film" (Palat 2019). Maurya and Kumar claim the film "gives a strong message to male patriarchs of any society" (2020: 253); one wonders what precisely that message is.[26] Suffice to say, Ranaut's adaptation serves as a compelling instance of both a Hindutva-ized history and the ability to frame such a retelling as a form of feminist empowerment. *Har har Mahadev!*

Kangana Ranaut's *Emergency*

If Ranaut's de facto directorial debut showed her willingness to embrace a patriarchal Hindutva discourse and provide a "booster dose" for Indians (Maurya and Kumar 2020: 257), her second directorial endeavor, the forthcoming *Emergency*, demonstrates a willingness to collude even more closely with the Modi regime. Featuring Ranaut as Prime Minister Indira Gandhi, *Emergency* (2024), like *Manikarnika*, is not the first Hindi film to address this issue or this figure, who notoriously declared a twenty-month state of emergency from June 1975–January 1977. This period witnessed numerous human rights violations, curtailments of freedoms, arbitrary jailing of political opponents, and press censorship. Gandhi's younger son, Sanjay, became particularly notorious for his five point plan, which included, among other elements, a mass sterilization campaign and slum clearance. Members of the BJP were among those arrested, including future prime ministers Morarji Desai and Atul Bihari Vajpayee and, in many ways, the period of Emergency also functions as "an origin story for Hindutva politics" (Gangopadhyay 2023: 104), one which gave "great social standing" to the BJP and other "radical Hindu groups," for their opposition to Gandhi's autocratic rule (Dasgupta 2014: 329). As with *Manikarnika*, in analyzing the forthcoming *Emergency*, Ranaut's "own political alignment with the ruling party" is "doubtlessly relevant here" (Gangopadhyay 2023: 111). While the earlier film *Aandhi* (1975), featuring Suchitra Sen as a female politician, was briefly banned during the Emergency due to perceived parallels between its female protagonist, Aarti Devi, and Indira Gandhi, in the current Modi regime the only political content that is allowed, according to one screenwriter, "is anything that demonises the Congress" (qtd in Konikkara 2022). With "Modi's most strident supporter" occupying both the director's chair and the role of Indira Gandhi, the Congress Party has already expressed concerns about the film and how it (or, rather, Ranaut) will portray Gandhi (Das Gupta 2022). The vice president of the Madhya Pradesh Congress Media Department, Sangeeta Sharma, referring to Ranaut as a "BJP agent," has reportedly demanded to watch the film before its release (*Times of India* 2022a). While *Aandhi* is not "a 'biopic' that purports to be based on Indira Gandhi's life" (Prasad 1998: 180), it remains unclear whether Ranaut's *Emergency* is intended to be a biopic (as she claimed *Manikarnika* was) or a "political drama" (*Times of India* 2022a) or, indeed, some admixture of the two, as in the case of *Manikarnika*.[27]

Along with *Aandhi*, there are two more recent Hindi films that have provided depictions of Indira Gandhi, *Indu Sarkar* (2017) and *Bell Bottom* (2021). The former, directed by Madhur Bhandarkar, chronicles the period of Emergency but predominantly focuses on Sanjay Gandhi rather than on his mother, who only appears for one minute near the very end of the film, when she wordlessly accepts a portfolio from an aide, who assures her and Sanjay that they will have the necessary votes to win if Gandhi calls for fresh elections. We then see the Prime Minister being driven away in her car, where she wordlessly adjusts her spectacles and generally maintains a grim forbearance. The subsequent *Bell Bottom* meanwhile is set during Gandhi's return to power in the early 1980s and provides a dramatization of the Indian government's attempt to deal with an Air India plane hijacking. While Bollywood star Lara Dutta effectively portrays Gandhi in this latter film, it is set after the period of Emergency and makes no mention of it. Given Ranaut's decision to play Indira Gandhi, one can assume *Emergency* will primarily focus on her character (rather than, as in *Indu Sarkar*, on Sanjay Gandhi) and the film's first look, released in mid-2022 on YouTube and already viewed more than 10 million times, bears this out.

The sequence, approximately one-and-a-half minutes in length, begins with a caption stating "Washington, D.C., 1971," as a phone rings and a seated Indian man reading a newspaper gets up to answer it, as somber mood music plays. The phone call is from Henry Kissinger, calling on behalf of President Nixon, and the Indian man goes to inform Gandhi. We first see her from a high angle wide shot in a Xanadu-esque room where large paintings of Abraham Lincoln and wounded civilians cover the high walls. Her back is turned to the camera and the approaching aide in three-quarter profile as she stands in a sari, looking at the contents of a portfolio she holds. As the aide approaches, the camera slowly descends, cutting to the man, now framed from behind in a low angle shot. This is followed by a cut to her point of view as we see what she is reading—a letter she has addressed to someone regarding Bangladesh, with her name and signature at the bottom. As the man informs her that Kissinger is asking whether Nixon can greet her as "Madam" when he calls, the camera cuts to an extreme close-up of her eyes behind her reading glasses, which pause from reading when Nixon's name is mentioned. As triumphant horns play on the soundtrack the camera cuts to a medium close-up as she turns, her mouth and lips moving soundlessly as she continues to look down at her portfolio, before finally saying "Teek hai" (Alright). This is followed by a cut to the aide, who replies, "Ji" (Yes), and begins turning to leave. "Ek minute," (One minute) she then says and, as the aids turns, there is a cut to her in medium close-up as she removes her reading glasses and finally looks up at the man, the white streak in her hair now visible, and says, in Hindi, "Tell the American president that everyone in my office calls me sir, not madam," as she gazes directly at the man (and the camera) with pursed lips. The image then cuts, with the sound of clapping thunder, to the word "EMERGENCY," which appears onscreen as we hear her voice, as if speaking on the radio, stating that there is nothing to worry about, followed by "A Film By Kangana Ranaut," appearing onscreen as the triumphant and slightly ominous mood music continues to play.[28]

Based on this first look, Ranaut's *Emergency* appears to be both political drama and biopic. Ranaut effectively captures Gandhi's soft, lilting cadences and slightly high-pitched manner of speaking with her own voice which, as critics have noted, becomes "tremulous and rises a few notches" in moments of emotional intensity (Palat 2019: 3). Here we see an instance of what Dyer calls a "perfect fit" between star image (or, in this case, star voice) and character construction (1998: 127). Yet, Ranaut's overall approach to the subject matter, tinted as it is by her loudly proclaimed political affiliations, in turn, creates a "problematic fit" with the character (ibid., 129). As Dyer observes, the "selective use of a star's image is problematic for a film, in that it cannot guarantee that the particular aspects of a star's image it selects will be those that interest the audience" (ibid., 127). Here we see Ranaut's dilemma in casting herself as Gandhi: unlike *Manikarnika*, in which her offscreen (and online) attributes meshed perfectly with the warrior queen of Jhansi, such a discrepancy creates "a clash between two complex sign-clusters, the star as image and the character as otherwise constructed" (ibid., 130). Such a disjunction, Dyer notes, runs the risk of becoming "contradictory to the point of incoherence," that is, of her being "simultaneously polar opposites" (ibid.). As noted earlier, Ranaut's star image has shifted in recent years, accompanying, it seems, her increasing proximity to the BJP and Modi. Now, as in *Manikarnika*, earlier elements that informed her star text, such as those on display in films like *Queen* and *Tanu Weds Manu*, have diminished in favor of a more martial star image. With *Emergency* Ranaut deviates even further from her earlier persona, now essentially inhabiting the role of a figure her political perspective frames as a focus of critique. To paraphrase Dyer (ibid.), will audiences buy it?

In recent social media posts Ranaut has commented on wrapping up the shooting of *Emergency* and how exhausting of an ordeal the entire process was. Claiming that she had to mortgage her own property in order to complete the film (*Daily Star* 2023), Ranaut lashed out at what she labeled the "Bollywood mafia," for apparently attempting to block her film's forthcoming release, originally scheduled to coincide with the Hindu festival of Dussehra on October 20 (*Indian Express* 2023).[29] Following her most recent tirade against the industry, Ranaut declared that she will now only announce the release date for *Emergency*, as well as its official trailer, one month in advance (ibid.). Will the film be a success? As the Entertainment Desk of the *Indian Express* noted, "Kangana needs a win," particularly as her most recent film, *Dhaakad*, was "the most notorious box office bomb of the pandemic era" (ibid.).[30] Here, we vividly see the disjuncture of the twin dynamics informing Ranaut's star text: a young female star now making (and starring in) her own films and one who has increasingly eschewed earlier elements informing her star text that brought her early success, as she has increasingly tethered her boat to the BJP. *Emergency* deploys the biopic to retell recent, traumatic Indian history, a period inextricably linked to the gestation of the BJP, deployed here to provide another "origin story for Hindutva politics" (Gangopadhyay 2023: 104) and another instance of the "presentification of history" (Chaudhuri 2019: 183), one that simultaneously retells the story of this period and uses this retelling to paradoxically deflect parallels between these two authoritarian moments. Yet, just as people speak of "Indira Gandhi's cult of the self" (Dasgupta 2014: 328), there also exists today "the cult of Modi" (Guha 2022), in which Ranaut plays an outsized role. Historian Ramachandra Guha (2022) has recently noted how the formation of such a cult around the sitting Prime Minister has been accompanied by subsequent erosions of all the fundamental aspects that constitute a democracy.[31] Though he does not include the role of film in this erosion, given the outsized role that film plays in India (a point Guha himself has previously acknowledged), it stands to reason that the industry's cooptation to a certain degree by the Modi regime serves as another compelling instance of such capitulation. Even as critics of the Modi government have "compared its tenure to the Emergency because of diminishing press freedoms, backsliding democracy, and rising religious intolerance" (Das Gupta 2022), Ranaut's film arrives just ahead of scheduled national elections, prepared to displace such critiques back onto the earlier Congress regime, deflecting critiques of the "cult of Modi" with a redeployed "cult of Indira."

Writing about what she calls "the *Bhakt* paradigm," historian Lindsey Harlan describes how Mira Bai, known as the Hindu god Krishna's *bhakt*, only sang "songs of devotion" to him and, in the process, gained "widespread fame as a *bhakt*" (1992: 205, 207). Even as her behavior "depart[ed] from conventional norms," Harlan notes, "an overwhelming number of women mentioned Mira as a woman they admired" (ibid., 208). At the same time, as political leader B. R. Ambedkar observed in his final speech to the Constitutional Assembly in 1949, "In India, bhakti, or what may be called the path of devotion or hero worship, plays a part in its politics unequalled in magnitude [...] Bhakti in religion may be the road to the salvation of a soul. But in politics, bhakti, or hero worship, is a sure road to degradation and to eventual dictatorship" (qtd in Guha 2022). Like Mira Bai, Ranaut seems more than willing to dance to Modi's tune and to eviscerate one demagogue in order to buttress the political fortunes of another. Will she succeed? And more importantly, if Ranaut's

Emergency does turn out to be a success, what will its success bode for the future of India? Even as some in Bollywood shake their heads in disbelief every time the "mad queen" issues yet another tweet, there are others who acknowledge that "Ranaut may have her flaws" but believe that she is "fearless and uninhibited, and doesn't shy away from saying the ugly truth" (qtd in Jain et al. 2021: 9). It is precisely and paradoxically for these reasons that Ranaut, even as she departs from "conventional norms," remains "a convenient outlier" in the broader propaganda machinery of the BJP, reshaping those very norms so that they align with the agenda of the Hindutva right (Harlan 1992: 208; Dasgupta 2020). Will *Emergency* be the super hit that resurrects Ranaut's career and once again rehabilitates the BJP, itself under increasing fire for engaging in the techniques of Emergency? Or will yet another Emergency be required?

4

The Kashmiri Pandit: Anupam Kher

The case of Anupam Kher provides yet another interesting instance of collusion by a Bollywood actor with the agenda of Prime Minister Modi's Bharatiya Janata Party (BJP). Kher is a consummate actor, with nearly 500 films to his credit, including a number of English-language films, beginning with Gurinder Chadha's *Bend in Like Beckham* (2002). In this and subsequent performances, both in Bollywood and other popular cinemas, Kher often plays the father of the protagonist or otherwise appears in such avuncular roles.[1] Prior to such roles, Kher became known for his comic propensity, earning Filmfare Awards for Best Comedian in films such as Subhash Ghai's blockbuster *Ram Lakhan* (1989). Kher is married to fellow Bollywood actor Kirron Kher, who is a Member of Parliament (MP) from the ruling BJP. Kher himself is an outspoken supporter of Prime Minister Modi—as film critic Kaveree Bamzai observes, Kher "routinely retweets" Modi's various accomplishments and, like Kangana Ranaut, enjoys a wide following on social media, where he has emerged as "the right wing's most vocal cultural ambassador on Twitter with 12.9 million followers" (2019). Over a nearly forty-year career Kher has played a variety of roles and arguably has a more diffuse star text than any other actor in India. For the purposes of this chapter, however, I would like to examine two of his most recent performances, as former Prime Minister Manmohan Singh in *The*

Accidental Prime Minister (2019, hereafter *Accidental PM*), and as a Kashmiri Pandit in the even more recent blockbuster, *The Kashmir Files* (2022), for which he has received a Filmfare nomination for Best Actor. Both of these films, in their differing ways, align with a BJP agenda of, on the one hand, maligning the opposition Congress Party and, on the other, highlighting (and embellishing) the plight of Kashmiri Pandits during the late 1980s and early 1990s. Kher himself comes from a Kashmiri Pandit family and has invoked his identity as a Kashmiri Pandit exile in multiple instances to raise awareness of this group's plight. Such advocacy for upper caste Hindus from Kashmir has taken place against the backdrop of Modi unilaterally revoking Article 370, which provided Kashmir with semi-autonomy, soon after his reelection in 2019. Kher, in his self-appointed role as advocate for Kashmiri Pandits, has pushed for the removal of Article 370 for several years, which has similarly been a longstanding aim of the BJP, arguing for the resettlement of Kashmiri Pandits in the Kashmir Valley, whose population is predominantly Muslim (Sharma 2015). Kher has also previously criticized Bollywood performers who returned awards to protest growing intolerance in India (ibid.) and compared students protesting against BJP policies to "pests," likening the arrest of student leaders at Jawaharlal Nehru University (JNU) to "pest control" (Bamzai 2019).[2] In this chapter, I want to examine how Kher's recent performances, both as the former Congress PM Manmohan Singh and as a Kashmiri Pandit, not only align with but further key elements of the BJP platform. In such a way, Kher, despite or due to his diffuse star text, becomes a key ally of the BJP and its ideology and a key player in legitimizing important components of its agenda.

No Accident: *The Accidental Prime Minister*

Based on Sanjaya Baru's book of the same name, *Accidental PM* examines the two-term tenure of Congress PM Manmohan Singh (2004–14). Told from the point of view of Baru (played in the film by Bollywood actor Akshaye Khanna), who served as media advisor to Singh during his first term, the film essentially portrays Singh as a puppet of the ruling Gandhi family, headed by the Italian-born widow of former prime minister Rajiv Gandhi, Sonia Gandhi, and her son, Rahul Gandhi. While Baru claims "the Manmohan Singh of UPA-1 was not the 'puppet PM' that he came to be seen as in UPA-2," he also notes the "complex relationship" between Singh and the Congress party president (Sonia Gandhi) as well as the ensuing public perception that Singh negotiated this relationship through "unquestioning submissiveness" to the Gandhi family whose matriarch, in turn, "needed to bury the controversy over her Italian birth" and retain control of the Congress party "till her son or daughter was old enough to take charge" (2014: xii, xiii, 3). One sees all of this in the ensuing film which begins with a disclaimer stating that the film is a "cinematic adaptation" of Baru's book, "meant solely for the purpose of entertainment" and, furthermore, that "nothing in the film is intended to defame any person," or to "disgrace, offend or hurt any ... beliefs or feelings of any person ... and/or a political party in any manner, whatsoever." The film commences with the Congress-led United Progressive Alliance (UPA)'s victory in the 2004 elections, in which they defeated the BJP-led National Democratic Alliance (NDA). Following brief documentary footage of street celebrations and people saying they want Sonia to be their leader, we see the front pages of various newspapers, all of which feature Sonia's image. We then see Sonia (played by German actress Suzanne Bernert) and her entourage emerge and approach a podium with several microphones.[3] Speaking in accented Hindi which closely resembles Gandhi's speaking voice, both in terms of accent and the cadences of her speech, Sonia (Bernert) says an announcement will be made the following day. We then see documentary footage of various female BJP leaders, including Sushma Swaraj and Uma Bharti, who speak out against the foreign born Sonia becoming prime minister, with the latter claiming Sonia "had to accept [Indian] citizenship due to constitutional compulsion and not because she wanted to."[4]

We also see footage of the right-wing Shiv Sena leader Bal Thackeray stating, "We do not want a foreigner as our PM," adding, "And I won't let it happen." Following this opening montage, we see the Gandhi family engaged in discussion, with Sonia seated quietly, appearing nervous, while Rahul (Arjun Mathur) tells her, in Italian, that he is giving her twenty-four hours to "think about this," after which he will "do what he needs to do."

The following day Sonia again approaches the podium, announcing her polite refusal of the PM post. We then see party leaders privately conferring before approaching Sonia, who announces that she has decided Dr. Manmohan Singh will be prime minister. It is at this point, approximately ten minutes into the film, that we first see Singh (Kher), who approaches a full-length mirror and buttons his vest, wearing a blue turban.[5] Then, as the camera remains on him looking at his reflection, we hear him speaking to the nation and reading the oath of office. Kher's voice (as Singh), which has alternately been described by critics as "feeble," "reedy, thin, shaky," is soft and high-pitched and in some ways calls to mind his earlier, avuncular, English-speaking roles (Mishra 2019; Gupta 2019). Here we hear a hyperbolized rendering of the "image problem" that faced Singh—that of his "unquestioning submissiveness"—through Kher's enunciation of the PM's voice (Baru 2014: xiii).[6] In stark contrast to Kher's initial appearance as a submissive Singh, Khanna as Baru confidently walks onscreen and immediately breaks the fourth wall, speaking directly to viewers, to whom he introduces the array of politicians gathered behind him in huddled conversations. "They write the nation's story," Baru says, "and I write their story," then again turning to face the camera as he says, "Hi, Main Sanjay Baru" (I'm Sanjay Baru). In the ensuing sped-up montage, narrated by the all-knowing Baru, we see that it is indeed Sonia, and not Singh, who makes the key decisions. After Singh asks Baru to be his press secretary, with Baru, in turn, requesting that he instead be his media advisor and only accountable to him, we see Baru explain to the slightly befuddled PM how twenty-four hour internet media works. This condescending approach to Singh continues, as we see Singh struggle to speak in Parliament, standing helplessly while others speak and shout, as Baru intones in voiceover, "Everyone was taking advantage of the PM's weakness." We then see Singh practicing a speech, stuttering over words in a halting delivery while Baru listens quietly. "Was it OK?" Singh meekly asks after finishing while Baru turns to the camera and says, "Now what response could I give?"

In this way, the film (based on Baru's book) presents Baru as the effective backstage guide to an otherwise hopelessly inept PM. In direct addresses, Baru notes that, thanks to his effective coaching, people were beginning to notice changes in the PM, including a growing confidence, and were not happy. Despite his growing confidence in addressing others, however, Singh's walking style, as performed by Kher, remains particularly strange and serves as an instance of what Baru, in his book, describes as the "emasculating of the prime minister" (2014: 277). As Singh, Kher walks slowly, with his arms close to his sides and slightly in front, his hands turned diagonally inwards. In tandem with his "feeble" voice, the characterization of Singh through his walking style is an effeminate and simultaneously disempowering one, presenting him not only as weak but as naïve to the ways of the world, forever deferring to Sonia and conjuring up, in many ways, Peter Seller's simple-minded gardener Chance in *Being There* (1979), who is unexpectedly thrust into the political sphere of Washington, DC. Singh's manner of walking, as performed by Kher, also calls to mind C-3PO from *Star Wars* (1977), imbuing his character with a certain mechanistic, or robot-like, quality, which again coheres with the broader portrayal of him as a puppet.[7] An additional filmic antecedent emerges when Singh reads something Baru said to the media regarding the impending nuclear deal with the US. Looking blankly at Baru, he says, "Yeh 'Que sera sera' kya hota hai?" (What is this "Que sera sera"?) Baru and Singh's wife, suppressing laughter, slowly explain both what the term means (Whatever will be, will be) and its filmic referent (Hitchcock's *The Man Who Knew Too Much*) while Singh listens quietly and remains looking confused, much like Louise Beavers'

Mammy character, Delilah, in *Imitation of Life* (1934), to whom Claudette Colbert's character similarly has to explain such simple things.[8]

Accidental PM continues to portray Singh in this weakened vein in the film's second half, which depicts Singh's second term in office (UPA-2, 2009–14). In the process, the film furthers its portrayal of Sonia and Rahul ("The Family") as the true center of power. Though Baru resigns ahead of the 2009 elections, refusing, as he says in voiceover, "to play this political game," he warns Singh, "If you lose [reelection] it will be your fault; if you win, it will be thanks to them [the Family]." Baru also urges Singh to run from the lower house of Parliament, the Lok Sabha, this time, noting that this will give him added legitimacy. Singh, however, meekly replies, "Whatever the Party wants, I will do," in his typically weak, soft-spoken voice. In the ensuing scene Sonia visits him in hospital and, looking down at him in his bed through her glasses, perched on the bridge of her nose, informs him that Rahul will lead the elections this time.[9] In an ensuing scene we see Singh giving a speech on a platform, Sonia seated to his right, giving a scowling look through her glasses at the camera while, superimposed between her and Singh, is the overblown image of an even more scowling Rahul on the Party's backdrop poster (Figure 4.1).

FIGURE 4.1 *Gandhis scowl as Singh speaks in* The Accidental Prime Minister *(2019). Source: Screenshot from* The Accidental Prime Minister, *directed by Vijay Gutte. 2019. Bohra Bros Productions. All rights reserved.*

FIGURE 4.2 *Party members in the Family's hand in* The Accidental Prime Minister *(2019). Source: Screenshot from* The Accidental Prime Minister, *directed by Vijay Gutte. 2019. Bohra Bros Productions. All rights reserved.*

The film then presents an ensuing sequence of speeches by Singh, including one in which he reads from notes as he tremblingly describes the success of the nuclear deal. The framing of the shot highlights that all the seated Party officials are in the "hand" of the Family, with Rahul and Sonia's oversized images on the backdrop poster serving as bookends to the assembled officials, behind whom appears the oversized hand symbol of the Party (Figure 4.2).

Singh, in turn, is positioned on extreme screen left of this wide shot, that is, in opposition to the rest of the assembled Party members (in the Family's hand, as it were) and at the very edge of the dais, a framing that clearly positions him as being "outside the Party," an outsider, someone fighting on his own, without the support of (those who control) the Party. Despite the lackluster support from Party leaders, Singh leads the UPA to reelection in a landslide for which, per Baru's earlier prediction, television pundits immediately give credit to Rahul. As Baru observes in his book, Prithviraj Chavan, a protégé of Singh, claimed, during a televised panel discussion, that "this victory is a vote for Rahul Gandhi. Rahulji's good work helped us win" (2014: 265). This chant,

Baru goes on to note, "became the official mantra," with "every party loyalist" claiming Rahul was "the architect of the 2009 result," thus denying, "in the very hour of victory," due credit to "the man who made it happen," that is to say, Singh (ibid.).

Baru, again speaking in direct address, notes that people were already speculating when Singh would step aside and Rahul would ascend. Indeed, following Singh's meeting with the Pakistani ambassador at a bilateral summit in Egypt later that year, during which Singh agrees to let Pakistan take control of Baluchistan, Sonia tells Singh this is unacceptable to the party. As she continues speaking, saying "Agar aap" (If you), the audio of her speech cuts out, apparently muted by the censor board, even though, as film critic Utkarsh Mishra has noted, it is still audible in the film's trailer (2019). What does she tell Singh in this (muted) moment? "If you make peace with Pakistan, then what will the new Prime Minister do?" As she says this line (itself muted in the film), the camera first tracks toward her, then cuts to a reaction shot of Singh, also framed in close-up, with a painting of Indira Gandhi hanging on the wall behind him, watching Sonia's lips move. The camera then cuts to a long shot of the two, as Sonia imperiously turns away from Singh to gaze out the window as Singh, in turn, turns his head away in puzzled disappointment. As he leaves, still appearing confused, the camera remains focused on the painting of Indira, who, in turn, looks back at the camera with an equally imperious regard (Figure 4.3).

In the process *Accidental PM* makes the dynastic connection (and attendant imperiousness of its female matriarch) quite clear via the inclusion of this painting in the *mise-en-scène*. The image's juxtaposition with the bewildered Singh and the camera remaining fixed on the portrait even after Singh exits the shot, make clear not only who wields the power but unsubtly draws a parallel between the current Congress matriarch and its former matriarch, the current matriarch's mother-in-law, who notoriously declared a state of Emergency and assumed dictatorial powers during her tenure in the 1970s.[10] As Baru, in turn, leaves Singh's office, after urging him to take action to defend his turf and take

FIGURE 4.3 *Spectral presence of Indira Gandhi in* The Accidental Prime Minister *(2019). Source: Screenshot from* The Accidental Prime Minister, *directed by Vijay Gutte. 2019. Bohra Bros Productions. All rights reserved.*

credit for the election, with Singh, in turn, declining to do so, our narrator again turns to us and says, with a condescending smirk on his face, "What a weak man."

In the wake of the ensuing 2G scandal, in which UPA coalition members were accused of selling 2G spectrum licenses at reduced cost, Singh offers his resignation to Sonia, who declines it, asking, with all the current problems, how can Rahul take over now? As the 2G scandal metastasizes, and Singh remains silent, Rahul makes a series of attention-grabbing statements to the press, including, in one scene, ripping up an ordinance proposed by his own party to protect politicians convicted of a crime, claiming, "This is what should be done" with the ordinance.[11] At a subsequent news conference of his own, Singh announces that he does not want a third term as PM and silently walks out. In subsequent documentary footage with which the film concludes, we first see Rahul and then Modi campaigning, with the latter stating that "the era of the mother-son government is over," adding that "not even jail can now save the Congress Party," as the large assembled crowds laugh and applaud. Even as the Congress-led UPA suffers its worst defeat in a general election to the BJP-led

NDA and we see additional documentary footage of a triumphant Modi waving to crowds, the film adds an extra layer of icing to the cake by presenting Singh, in a final scene, looking dejected as he finishes reading Baru's book, even as Baru, reading from his book in voiceover, claims that Singh's biggest mistake was "to sacrifice himself for the family," adding that, for Singh, "the family was more important than the party."

What we see in *Accidental PM* then is not only "the emasculating of the prime minister" (Baru 2014: 277) but, just as significantly, the demonization of the Gandhi family. As film critic Aijaz Ashraf observes, "the film seems designed to remind viewers about the alleged imperious nature of the Gandhis, and simultaneously provide the BJP the opportunity to turn, once again, the dynastic rule into its principal electoral issue" (2018). Indeed, as Ashraf and other critics were quick to note, the timing of the film's release was itself significant, coming just a few months ahead of the 2019 elections. Noting "the enthusiasm" the BJP has taken towards the film, Ashraf mentions that "many suspect … a hidden hand behind the film," a suspicion further fueled by the casting of Kher, "an avid supporter of the BJP," as Singh (ibid.). More than Kher's casting, however, it is his performance as Singh that effectively reminds viewers of the Gandhi family's alleged imperiousness and, via his capitulation, of the broader control this family wields over the Congress Party. Even as Kangana Ranaut's forthcoming biopic about Indira Gandhi, due out in 2024 and also starring Kher, may be said to engage in a similar strategy—releasing a film critical of the Gandhi family just ahead of national elections—Kher's ensuing film demonstrates his broader commitment to the BJP agenda, in this case, with regard to his own ancestral homeland of Kashmir.[12]

Manufacturing Genocide: *The Kashmir Files*

The status of Jammu and Kashmir, India's sole Muslim-majority state, has been a source of contention even prior to India's independence. Since the 1950s, this northern region has been accorded semi-autonomous status under Article 370 of the Indian Constitution, which limited the Indian government's control over the state (Jaffrelot 2021: 360). In August of 2019, however, following its resounding reelection, the BJP under Modi abolished Article 370, which had been a longstanding goal of the party, thereby in essence abrogating the constitution of Jammu and Kashmir (ibid., 361). The subsequently introduced Jammu and Kashmir Reorganization Bill of 2019 essentially transformed Jammu and Kashmir into a union territory. Fearing protests from the local population, the Modi government deployed 175,000 additional troops to the region, itself already "one of the most militarized territories in the world" (ibid., 364). The Modi government also initiated a "complete communications blackout" in the region, blocking both landlines and mobile phones, then launched a series of brutal raids by Indian armed forces in which locals were "rendered sleepless" due to the "nightly raids, harassment, humiliation and torture" (ibid., 365). Though cases of torture were publicized by local media outlets, most New Delhi-based media outlets took "little interest" in them and the government, in turn, "exerted control over journalists," both in the nation's capital and in Jammu and Kashmir, with regard to coverage of the region (ibid.). As political scientist Christophe Jaffrelot observes, the BJP government's new media policy "allowed authorities to decide what news was 'anti-social and anti-national'—and therefore illegal" (ibid.). Even as some landlines and mobile services in the region were restored, social media and high-speed internet remained blocked by the government "for security reasons," which, in turn, had "devastating effects on the economy, health and education" of Kashmiris, particularly during the Covid lockdown (ibid.).

The BJP government also arrested political leaders of opposition parties. According to BJP Home Minister Amit Shah, a total of 4,000 people were arrested (ibid., 367). Yet, as Jaffrelot notes, this number only takes into account "those who had been arrested under the Public Safety Act (PSA)," a "draconian preventive detention law" under which an individual could be arrested and detained to prevent him or her from "acting against 'the security of the state or the maintenance of the public order'" (ibid.). Individuals arrested under the PSA could be held in jail for up to two years before their trial. The total number of arrests, according to a fact-finding mission, was "around 13,000" (ibid.). As the government was required by law to release some prisoners after six months, an Emergency-era practice was (re)introduced by the BJP, wherein those imprisoned could regain their freedom "if they agreed to sign a bond saying that they would neither comment on the abrogation of article 370 nor hold rallies against this decision" (ibid.). For the region's Muslim majority, such draconian actions were reminiscent of "the Dogra rule that prevailed under the Hindu dynasty" that reigned over the province prior to 1947 (ibid., 370). Furthermore the government rescinded Article 35A, which defined "permanent residents" of the state and reserved certain rights for them, including to own land in the state and have access to government jobs (ibid.). In March of 2020 the government replaced this article with a new provision, in which "the children of officers, soldiers and members of the paramilitaries," as well as others who had lived in the region for a period of time, were now "eligible to own land and hold government jobs" (ibid.). All of this, as Jaffrelot observes, was meant to show "the only Muslim-majority state of the union its place" (ibid.).

It was precisely in such a context that *The Kashmir Files* was released. Directed by Vivek Agnihotri and starring Anupam Kher as a Kashmiri Pandit, the film purports to expose the "truth" of what occurred in Kashmir some thirty years prior, during a period of increased repression by Indian security forces which, in turn, led to an increased uprising against these forces (Hussain 2021). The film begins with a lengthy disclaimer which states that it is "based on true incidents as narrated in video-recorded testimonials of the victims and their families of the Kashmir Genocide of 1990. All the events have been further corroborated by experts, administrators, historians, scholarly books and various news reports" and, furthermore "verified by various renowned scholars of the Kashmiri Pandit community." Nevertheless, while "inspired by true events," the disclaimer states that the "film makers have taken cinematic liberty to ... merge many incidents in one fictional timeline" and, furthermore, that "the film doesn't claim accurateness or factuality of historic events." As part of such "merging," the film telescopes the broader exodus of Kashmiri Pandits during this period (1989–90) through the experiences of one particular family, that of Pushkar Nath (Kher), a retired schoolteacher. The film immediately presents the evil cruelty of the local Muslim population, who alternately beat young children who cheer for Indian cricket players and shoot dead members of the police and the local Hindu population, including killing the mother of a young girl who refuses a wedding proposal and is subsequently shot at point-blank range in front of her daughter, upon whose face her mother's blood spatters. Accompanying these opening scenes of violence are cries of "Convert, leave or die!" from local Muslims men and boys who run through the streets waving guns.

Kher emerges within this opening chaos in Srinagar on a tiny scooter, picking up his grandson Shiva and Shiva's friend Abdul. As he proceeds to drive them home, they and we witness additional scenes of violence as well as speakers at a rally, who proclaim that "a new Kashmir will rise!" Meanwhile, back at home, Nath's son hides in a barrel of rice in an attempt to evade local Muslim men who pound on the door. Breaking in and led by the man previously speaking at the rally, Farooq (Chinmay Mandlekar), these men rush upstairs, pushing aside Nath's daughter-in-law, Sharda (Bhasha Sumbli), who insists that her husband is not there. Approaching the barrel of rice, Farooq mutters, "Bloody Indian spy," then unleashes a barrage of gunfire at the barrel. Pushkar, who has returned home with Shiva, is also beaten by Farooq's men and told, "If you want to stay in Kashmir, you have to say 'Allah-hu-Akbar.'" Recognizing Farooq as one of his former students, Pushkar begs for mercy and Farooq agrees but on one condition: scooping up a handful of blood-soaked rice, he extends it towards Sharda, saying, "If you eat this rice." It is at this moment that the film title appears onscreen, accompanied by somber cello music. The film then moves to Kashmir in the present era (2020), where we see Pushkar's old friend Brahma (Mithun Chakraborty) and his wife Laxmi (Mrinal Kulkarni) preparing for the arrival of other old friends as well as Krishna, Pushkar's younger grandson who was just an infant in the opening sequence and who is now returning with his grandfather's ashes. The film alternates between past and present, including brief detours to 2016, when the grown-up Krishna (Darshan Kumar) first attends "ANU," a prestigious university in the nation's capital where he meets Professor Radhika Menon (Pallavi Joshi), who makes impassioned speeches to students at the university, arguing that Kashmir has never been a part of integral India, and pushing for *azaadi*, or freedom, for the region and its people. Over the course of this nearly three-hour film, we move back and forth from the present to the past (1990), as we follow Krishna in his growing enlightenment about the so-called "truth" of Kashmir.

In contrast to Professor Menon, who argues that the whole world acknowledges that India has illegally occupied Kashmir and identifies numerous sites where mass graves of murdered Kashmiri Muslims have been located, Pushkar's old friend Brahma, a retired Indian Administrative Services (IAS) officer, insists in ensuing conversations with Krishna that "when 500,000 Pandits were killed and made to run away, it's not called an exodus but a genocide." Krishna pushes back, insisting that it was not a genocide and that "only 200,000 Pandits fled." He also argues, perhaps as a sign of his tutelage by Professor Menon, that the radicalization of Kashmiri Muslims was inevitable, given their treatment by Indian security forces. Yet, Krishna remains unaware of what happened to his parents and older brother and asks Brahma, "What's the truth?" The film, in turn, responds to this query by taking us back to 1990, where we again see the images of violence with which the film commenced and again hear cries of "Convert, leave or die." One hour in, the film returns to its opening sequence, which plays out again, this time showing Krishna's mother, Sharda, eating the blood-soaked rice that Farooq offers her, along with additional scenes of sadistic violence committed by Kashmiri Muslim militants. We also witness the impunity with which these militants operate, enjoying the protection of local political authorities. When Krishna, in the present, asks Brahma why Kashmiri Pandits did not let the world forget what happened to them, as the Jews did, Brahma replies, "Because no one was ready to listen." Through repeated flashbacks, the film shows up the plight of the Nath family (Pushkar, Sharda, and her two sons, Shiva and Krishna) after they leave their home in the Kashmir Valley. When a government minister arrives at the refugee camp and is told by a local doctor that "5,000 to 6,000 people have died so far" in the camp due to poor conditions, the home minister blandly replies that it is only normal, as it is the first time the Kashmiris have experienced such hot weather. Pushkar holds up a sign demanding the removal of Article 370, which the visiting minister describes as "another matter."

The Nath family eventually relocates to Nadimarg, Kashmir, where Pushkar, showing signs of early dementia, repeatedly makes calls to New Delhi, insisting to speak with the Prime Minister. When Sharda asks the local schoolteacher, an old Muslim man with a long hennaed beard, to also teach science at the school, he smiles and tells her to forget such matters, instead telling her that the situation is grim and that she should marry him—"then," he adds, "all your troubles will disappear." We also see Farooq being interviewed on a local television station, admitting that he has killed twenty to twenty-five people himself and identifying himself as a freedom fighter. When asked why he killed a particular individual, Farooq replies, "Because he worked for the RSS."[13] When subsequently asked whether working for the RSS is a crime, Farooq replies, "Yes," adding that this is a war and, in war, all is fair, even as his sleepy eyelid twitches. The film returns to the present, where we see Pushkar die in hospital while the grown-up Krishna weeps at his bedside. When he announces his plan to return to Kashmir with his grandfather's ashes, Professor Menon urges him to record what he sees there on his phone—how Kashmir is under attack from the state of India—and then to share what he discovers with the rest of the ANU student body when he returns. Professor Menon shares a personal contact with Krishna, telling him to seek this contact out when he arrives in Kashmir. The contact turns out to be none other than Farooq, in whose house hangs a framed photo of him holding the hand of a joyful Professor Menon, which Krishna silently gazes at.[14] Farooq, claiming to be a "new age Gandhi," tells Krishna he knows who killed his mother and brother, adding, "People may have said that I killed them but that's not true. I was his [Pushkar's] student, Sharda was like a sister to me." He goes on to claim that the Indian army killed them, even as his sleepy eyelid opens and closes.

Returning to Brahma's house, Krishna tells his grandfather's old friend that he now knows the truth as well as why they have all hidden it from him. Brahma tells Krishna he has been brainwashed and shows him his assembled "Kashmir Files," several dossiers of local newspaper clippings chronicling the events of the past thirty years. As Krishna skims through these clippings, he comes across one with a headline reading, "Nadimarg Massacre: Gunmen Kill 24 Kashmiri Pandits." Flipping through the subsequent pages, he comes across images of all those killed, which include photos of his mother and brother, which are accompanied by another caption reading, "Terrorists dressed as Indian army kill Kashmiri Pandits." As plaintive cello music ensues, Krishna shuts the file and sobs in anguish. His education now complete, he returns to Delhi to share what he discovered with the rest of the ANU student body at a large rally organized by Professor Menon, where she leads the students in singing a song, "Hum Dekhenge" (We Will See). After being introduced by Radhika, Krishna proceeds to deliver a twelve-minute speech, in which he claims that Kashmiri Pandits were forcibly converted by Islamic tyrants, likening what happened to them to what happened to Jews during the Second World War, claiming that the Pandits' exodus was a genocide and further claiming that a second genocide occurred when "we all took them out of our minds." Krishna insists that the Pandits be allowed to return to Kashmir, then tells the assembled crowd, "Now let's watch something that I have never seen before," adding, "Then you can decide yourself who the true culprit is." The film then returns to Nadimarg, where we see jeeps full of armed men dressed in army fatigues pull up outside the police station. These men enter the station, identifying themselves as the Army and claiming they have received word of an impending attack on Pandits, then asking for the names and locations of all local Pandits. We watch as these men assemble the local Pandits in an open area in the town center, near a saw mill. Pushkar arrives and claims these men are not the Army. He is struck down and, as Sharda comes to his rescue, Farooq, in army fatigues, approaches her from behind, grabbing her and making her turn to face him. The other men then kick Pushkar repeatedly while the others assembled watch quietly and Sharda continues to cry out.

Hearing his grandfather crying in pain, Shiva also runs out to see what is happening and is grabbed by a "solider" as he approaches. Sharda breaks free and runs to him, telling him to flee. Farooq then grabs Sharda and rips the entire back of her blouse off, then holds her by the neck and parades her around before the others, saying, "Today we will show them such horror that never will any infidel think of daring to step on the sacred land of Kashmir again!" The older Muslim teacher then approaches and spits at Sharda. Seeing this, a pregnant woman standing on the side proceeds to vomit. Farooq approaches her, saying, "You're unable to watch?" then shoots her dead at point-blank range. He then turns to the others and says, "Now watch that which you've never seen before." The camera then cuts to the image of the vertical sawblade, with its piercing sound, as we watch Sharda placed face up on a horizontal platform and bisected by the saw, which we see in a medium long shot, her blood-drenched body held in place by the "soldiers." The camera then cuts to a weeping Shiva calling out for his mother, while the "army troops" assemble all the remaining people before an open pit. After one of the men goes down the line counting the number of assembled people (twenty-four), Farooq proceeds to shoot each of them dead at point-blank range, the camera presenting these killings from his point of view so that, as he shoots, it is as if we are shooting these people, who occasionally look up at us as they are about to be shot. After going down the line and shooting what appears to be twenty people (the first four of whom are women), Farooq approaches Shiva, being held by the other men, and has him line up before the pit as well. Then, as his sleepy eyelid opens and closes, he shoots Shiva in the head as well, who also falls into the pit. The remaining people gaze down into the pit and the camera follows their gaze, descending into the pit where it tracks over all the dead bodies as the somber cello music returns and the film concludes with a close-up of the dead Shiva, wide-eyed with blood spattered on his face, remaining fixed on this image for approximately twenty seconds as the cello music continues to play, before the image finally fades to black.

Amplifying the film's opening disclaimer, Agnihotri has insisted that "every frame, every word in my film is truth" (qtd in Kak 2022). Agnihotri's claim, in turn, has been amplified by none other than Prime Minister Modi, who publicly stated that "the film has shown the truth which has been suppressed for years," and urged everyone to watch it (Kak 2022) To echo the question Krishna Pandit perennially poses, however, what is the truth with regard to Kashmir and the period in 1990 depicted in *The Kashmir Files*? To begin with, the Indian government appointed Jagmohan Malhotra, a member of the BJP, to a second term as governor of Jammu and Kashmir at this time (Hussain 2021: 315). As historian Shahla Hussain notes, Jagmohan's administrative policies "aimed to crush resistance in every form" in what he considered the "valley full of scorpions" (ibid.). Even women protesting against Jagmohan's "strong-arm methods" were not spared, with the "army us[ing] rape as a weapon of suppression" (ibid., 315, 317). During one demonstration in Srinagar, Indian security forces "opened fire on unarmed civilians, killing almost sixty protestors, including women and children" (ibid., 315). As Hussain observes, "this was no longer a fight between the insurgents and the security forces, but now pitted the latter against the entire Kashmiri Muslim population" (ibid., 315). The Indian government introduced "draconian laws" which gave the military special powers, including the Jammu and Kashmir Disturbed Area Act of 1990, in which Governor Jagmohan declared the entire Kashmir Valley a "disturbed area," which allowed security forces "the right to shoot any person who, according to them, was indulging in breach of public order" (ibid., 315–16). This act also stated that "legal proceedings could not be instituted against security forces with regard to any action taken by them to maintain law and order" (ibid., 316). In such a context, "the state controlled machinery practiced torture to contain and eliminate organized dissent"; men picked up during raids were "tortured with electric shocks and red-hot iron rods"; and in some cases, people detained were never seen again (ibid.).

As Indian security forces in Kashmir saw every Kashmiri as a "security threat," violence increasingly became "a routine part of people's lives" with "almost every house in the Valley" having "a story of humiliation" to narrate (ibid., 317). The former chief justice of the Jammu and Kashmir High Court, Bahauddin Farooqi, filed a petition demanding the "nullification of proclamations enabling the state administration to assume arbitrary powers of arrest, detention, curfew, and house arrest," and sought to prosecute Governor Jagmohan for "acts of genocide" (ibid., 318).[15] As Hussain notes, the Indian press at the time "remained silent" about human rights violations taking place in Kashmir, with the "nationalist media" dismissing stories of such violations as "mere 'allegations' or 'fabrications' that could not be proved" (ibid., 319). The exodus of the Kashmiri Pandits, in turn, created "alternative versions of Kashmiri history," what Hussain describes as "alternative memories" (ibid., 320, 324). The Pandits' situation was further complicated "by the indifference of Indian political parties," including the 1989-90 National Front government (ibid., 323).[16] Simultaneously, the "extreme intolerance" of Kashmiri Muslims became "a major talking point" for right-wing political groups who, in turn, claimed that the Muslim-dominated Valley was "waging an Islamic movement to secede from Hindu India" (ibid.). Such a perception, in turn, "legitimized India's use of force in Kashmir," even as it delegitimized the demand for *azaadi*, or freedom, labeling it as "Islamic fundamentalism" (ibid., 323). The International People's Tribunal on Human Rights and Justice estimated that, between 1989 and 2009, "India's military and paramilitary forces in Kashmir have perpetrated more than 8,000 involuntary disappearances and 70,000 deaths," including through "extrajudicial or 'fake encounters' executions, custodial brutality and other means" (ibid., 333). Additionally, the prominent Kashmiri civil rights activist Parvez Imraz has documented "1,500 cases of people becoming impotent after their genitals were electrocuted" as well as "hundreds" of other cases involving "the systematic use of sexual violence to humiliate Kashmiris" (ibid.).

The Kashmir Files does not show any of this. Instead, per Brahma's invocation, it claims that, "500,000 Pandits were killed," thus referring to it, not as an "exodus" but as a "genocide." What actually happened? As documentary filmmaker and writer Sanjay Kak observes in a recent piece, "the simplest questions fail to yield reliable answers" (2022). In addressing a litany of related questions—how many Kashmiri Pandits lived in the Valley prior to 1990? How many of them left? How many were killed?—Kak, himself a Kashmiri Pandit, reveals the difficulty of knowing with complete certainty. He also exposes the tendency of the right-wing to consistently overinflate the related figures. Regarding his first question, Kak (2022) notes that "the figures conjured up by the right-wing fluctuate between 500,000 and 700,000, although considered estimates place it at about 170,000." Similarly, with regard to his second question, Kak notes "a recent response by the region's Relief and Rehabilitation Commissioner," which placed the figure at 135,426, though also notes how "the needle again fluctuates between 500,000 and 700,000" during "inflated television debates," during which the number can even "inexplicably go up to a million" (ibid.). Regarding his final question, Kak notes that "in conversations around *The Kashmir Files*, the figure has hovered around 4,000" but points out that "the most recent figures provided by the region's police department" put the number of Kashmir Pandits killed at 89, with earlier official estimates coming to a tally of 270 and the Kashmiri Pandit Sangharsh Samiti, a Kashmir-based citizens group, arriving at a figure of 700 (ibid.). While, as Kak notes, none of these questions "can be answered with any degree of certainty," the difference in respective tallies—between those cited by official commissions, "considered estimates," and Kashmir-based citizens groups, on the one hand, and those thrown out during "inflated television debates," as well as cited by Brahma in *The Kashmir Files*—reveals a gaping chasm, itself perhaps the result of what Hussain describes as "alternative memories" (2021: 324).[17]

Supplementing and indeed enhancing such "alternative memories" is *The Kashmir Files*' brutal and graphic imagery. As Kak (2022) observes, "this is a film that brutalizes its audience with scenes of such extreme violence." The film's protracted, ten-minute ending sequence in Nadimarg is a particular case in point. While some of the individual events depicted did, in fact, occur,[18] as Kak (and the film's own disclaimer) notes, the film "pick[s] a few dreadful events from across a decade and a half ... and telescop[es] them into a gruesome narrative" of a considerably shorter time, further "compressing" these events by "heap[ing] them upon a single fictive family" and "embroider[ing] them with further acts of unspeakable cruelty" (ibid.). Such "merging" of multiple events into "one fictional timeline," amplifies both the unspeakable cruelty of these acts and their horror. To return to Modi's entreaty to people in India to watch the film, and in light of the film's enormous subsequent box office success, we need to come to a better understanding of how such a film—one that "brutalizes its audience" (ibid.)—simultaneously engages its audience.[19] As philosopher Noel Carroll has asked, "Why would anyone *want* to be horrified, or even art-horrified?" (1990: 158, emphasis in original). Typically, "people shun what disgusts them," yet many—"so many, in fact, that we must concede that they are normal, at least in the statistical sense"—nevertheless "seek out horror fictions for the purposes of deriving pleasure from sights and descriptions that customarily repulse them" (ibid.). To ask a deliberately crude question, what type of pleasure does a film like *The Kashmir Files* provide? We may come to a better understanding of this by considering what Carroll describes as "the paradox of horror," that is, how people can be attracted to what they find repulsive (ibid., 160). Building on the earlier work of psychoanalytic theorist Ernest Jones, Carroll posits that such a paradox can be explained via "the ambivalence felt toward the object of horror" which, in turn, stems "from a deeper ambivalence about our most enduring psychosexual desires" (1990: 170). Carroll goes on to note that, "in a gesture of catholicity," such horrific figures can also manifest "repressed anxieties" which "may not be only sexual in nature" (ibid., 171). A horror narrative revolves around "something that defies conceptual schemes" and, furthermore, our desire will not be satisfied "unless the monster defies our conception of nature" (ibid., 181, 185).

Along with the paradox of horror more generally, there are arguably particular cultural elements at play in *The Kashmir Files* which contribute to the simultaneous attraction and repulsion viewers in India may have to the film. As a way of coming to a better understanding of such elements, and particularly in light of Prime Minister Modi's public championing of the film and his exhortations to others to watch it (supplemented by paid holidays and tax breaks), I would like to consider an earlier blockbuster which also received a presidential endorsement, D.W. Griffith's silent epic about the American Civil War and its aftermath, *The Birth of a Nation* (1915, hereafter *Birth*).[20] As film historian Donald Bogle points out, in the process of telescoping the adverse effects of the Civil War on the South through the plight of one "good, decent 'little' family," Griffith's film also introduced the "mythic type" of the "brutal black buck" to (white) American audiences (2007: 10). As in *The Kashmir Files*, which commences with belligerent Kashmiri Muslims perpetuating acts of violence against Hindus, *Birth* depicts black Union soldiers on the street, "shoving whites off the sidewalk" (ibid., 12). Like the whites of *Birth*, the Pandits of *The Kashmir Files* are presented as a "helpless minority." The role of the savage black buck, in turn, is performed by the savage Kashmiri Muslim

Farooq (with his sinister sleepy eye), or what film scholar Krupa Shandilya has described as "the raping Muslim man" (2019).²¹ Like the black bucks of Griffith's film, Farooq is barbaric and "out to raise havoc"; also, to return to Carroll's (1990) psychoanalytic approach to the attraction of horror, "audiences could assume that his physical violence served as an outlet for a man who was sexually repressed" (Bogle 2007: 13).²² Like such bucks, Farooq is presented as "savage, violent and frenzied" as he "lust[s] for white flesh," in this case, of the Kashmiri Pandit widow (ibid, 13–14).²³ Similarly, just as *Birth* was "calculated to work [white] audiences into a frenzy," Kak and others have described how screenings of *The Kashmir Files* have "frequently ended amid sloganeering and speeches," with "brazen calls for violence against all Muslims" (2022). Such calls may be furthered by the film which provides no heroic saviors (as *Birth* does in the form of the Ku Klux Klan) to the menacing terror of its savage and frenzied Muslims. Like *Birth*, *The Kashmir Files* has already triggered a riot and social media is "flooded with videos of members of the audience erupting in rousing hate speeches after seeing the film," frequently including "calls for the slaughter of Muslims and a boycott of Muslim businesses" (Chowdhury 2022).

In his analysis of the paradox of horror, Carroll considers the possibility of "some sort of cathartic explanation" for the pleasures of horror (1990: 246n57). Such an approach, he argues, "sees the aesthetic pleasure of distressful representations" as "a matter of having our negative emotions relieved" (ibid.). Yet, Carroll claims "it would make no sense for me to put my hand in a vise simply for the pleasure of having my pain relieved when the vise is loosened" (ibid.). Carroll further notes that if "the negative emotions relieved are not those engendered by the fiction itself" but rather those built up "over the course of everyday life," then such a cathartic approach "will clearly have no application to art-horror," as "the horror of the sort found in horror fictions has no correlate in ordinary life" (ibid.). This, Carroll adds, "is entailed by the fact that we don't encounter monsters in everyday life" (ibid.). Yet, what of everyday life in India, particularly in Kashmir? Based on the observations of Hussain (2021), Guha

(2007), and Kak (2022), violence became a "routine part of people's lives" there, to the point that, as Hussain notes, the "ongoing trauma has created alternative memories" (2021: 317, 324). Is it possible, in light of this ongoing trauma and the film's hyperbolic rendering of such traumatic incidents, that contemporary (Hindu) Indian viewers, rather than seeking catharsis, seek blood? This is what descriptions and recordings of audience reactions to *The Kashmir Files*' conclusion seem to suggest and why, for instance, its trailer invited public interest litigation (on the grounds that its "inflammatory scenes are bound to cause communal violence") (Kak 2022). This may be compounded by both Agnihotri's and Modi's claims that the film reveals "the truth" of "the terror and atrocities" that occurred in Kashmir and then, too, "during Congress rule," as Modi's home minister Amit Shah has claimed (Raj 2022). As with *Birth*, there appears to be a deliberateness to all of this, not only on the part of the filmmaker and BJP politicians, but of the groups of men whom Kak (2022) describes "show[ing] up at theatres waving the Indian tricolour," or, indeed, shiny steel tridents.[24] It is safe to assume, in other words, that someone coming to a film carrying a trident has already reached a conclusion about it, or is already prepared to respond to it in a particular way. As in the "Two Minutes Hate" described by George Orwell in his dystopic novel, *1984*, being whipped up into a state of frenzy may indeed be part of the pleasure. Yet, the implications for the agency of such viewers are troubling, to say the least.[25]

Film critic Darragh O'Donoghue describes *The Kashmir Files* as playing "like a movie adaptation of a paranoid Anupam tweet" (2023: 7). Indeed, even prior to starring in this film, Kher had publicly invoked his identity as a Kashmiri Pandit to advocate for a number of related causes, including the revocation of Article 370 and the right of return for Pandits to the Kashmir Valley. Kher appeared in a six-minute video released in 2016 on what has become known as "Holocaust Day" in India, a day dedicated to the commemoration of the plight of the Kashmiri Pandits (Raina 2016). In this brief "emotionally charged soliloquy," Kher identifies himself as a Kashmiri

Pandit and goes on to describe how he was "shunted out from my homeland."[26] Kher's subsequent descriptions of what happened to his community in many ways sound like an advance script of *The Kashmir Files*, replete with descriptions of "killings, abductions, rapes," as well as "the slogans from the mosques" ("Convert, leave or die!") and the "murderous intent" of armed (Muslim) militants. At the conclusion of this brief soliloquy, Kher intones, "I am still hopeful today that justice will be done to us" (qtd in Raina 2016). In many ways, the Modi government has subsequently provided the "justice" Kher has been asking for with the repeal of Article 370 and the subsequent military occupation of Kashmir.[27] When the Israeli filmmaker serving as head of the jury at the International Film Festival in Goa, where *The Kashmir Files* was screened, described the film as "a propaganda" and "vulgar movie," Kher, in turn, responded by calling the filmmaker's comments "shameful" on Twitter, adding that "Jews have suffered Holocaust and he comes from that community" (qtd in Schmall and Kumar 2022).

In his most recent avatar as "the self-professed narrator and champion of the Pandit story," then, it appears that Kher has been aided in no small part by both director Agnihotri, whose claims of his film's "truthfulness," in turn, evoke Leni Riefenstahl's infamous description of her "documentary" about the Nazis, *Triumph of the Will* (1935),[28] and Modi who, going one step beyond Woodrow Wilson, has not only publicly endorsed *The Kashmir Files* (as showing "the truth") and exhorted everyone to watch it but has even provided paid holidays for government employees to do so. As with Kher's performance in *Accidental PM*, one witnesses not only a willingness on the actor's part to align his star text with(in) the BJP firmament but the simultaneous willingness—indeed, alacrity—of the BJP to reciprocate. While, for one critic, Kher's "phenomenal rise" in the political esteem of the Hindutva right reminds him of German actor Gustaf Grundgens, played onscreen by Klaus Maria Brandeur in Hungarian filmmaker Istvan Szabo's masterpiece *Mephisto* (1981), who, "in his quest for power and greater glory abandoned his conscience and good judgement to serve Hitler's Nazi Party" (Raina 2016), one paradoxically witnesses Kher and Agnihotri being framed, and framing themselves, as "conscience keeper[s] of the whole nation" (Paranjape 2022). If this is the case, then *The Kashmir Files*, particularly in light of the BJP's recent moves in Kashmir, themselves urged on by supporters like Kher, becomes redolent of nothing so much as a guilty conscience, engaging in historical revisionism as a way of justifying "the brazen Hindu extremism of the present" (Chowdhury 2022).

5

Hope from the Hinterlands? Ayushmann Khurrana

The films of Ayushmann Khurrana provide compelling alternatives to contemporary trends in Bollywood explored in the previous chapters. A relative newcomer to the industry, Khurrana has quickly become known for his variety of unusual roles and his effective performances in such roles, many of which fall outside typical Bollywood parameters. Whether playing a sperm donor in his debut film, *Vicky Donor* (2012), a small-town high school dropout married to an overweight woman in *Dum Laga Ke Haisha* (2015), or a man with erectile dysfunction in *Shubh Mangal Saavdhan* (2017), Khurrana, who initially took part in several reality TV shows, excels in such *hatke*, or offbeat, alternatives to mainstream, big budget Bollywood fare, which tend to focus on the denizens of small towns in the outskirts of India. As media scholar Baidurya Chakrabarti has observed, the past several years have been "very good" for Khurrana, as they have not only "cemented his place as a major bankable male star in contemporary Bollywood" but have also seen "a broad generic template coalescing that defines Khurrana's star persona" (2020: 72). Chakrabarti refers to such a template as "the Ayushmann genre" and notes that, beyond the "two outliers" in Khurrana's career (as of the time of writing), *Andhadun* (2018) and *Article 15* (2019), the majority of Khurrana's films can broadly be described as romantic comedies, with an increasing subset of sex comedies (2020: 72–3). Khurrana has indeed continued to make such sex comedies, many of which have been critical and commercial successes but he has also starred in additional "outlier" films which also address heretofore underexplored themes in the context of popular Hindi cinema.

In this chapter, I would like to examine Khurrana's performances in both of these veins, both as a way of charting his range as an actor and exploring the multiple contemporary issues these films address which have generally not been taken up by Bollywood. These include issues of caste and caste discrimination in Anubhav Sinha's *Article 15*, homosexuality and homophobia in *Shubh Mangal Zyada Saavdhan* (2020), and the fraught political tensions of Northeast India in his subsequent collaboration with Sinha, *Anek* (2022). My aim here is to examine both the elasticity of Khurrana's star text, his willingness to take on a variety of challenging roles, as well as how, in the process, his films provide alternatives to some of the more dominant trends in Bollywood today, including the growing Hindutva-ization of the Bollysphere, as explored in earlier chapters. I am particularly interested in examining what Chakrabarti labels Khurrana's more "outlier" films, as these, in turn, provide powerful glimpses into key political and cultural issues that have otherwise gone unaddressed in both mainstream and more *hatke* Hindi films. While these recent films featuring Khurrana provide comparatively progressive depictions of their respective themes and concerns, they also at times articulate certain tradeoffs and compromises, for instance, with broader Bollywood genre demands, which I would also like to examine here. In other words, this chapter explores how a relative newcomer like Khurrana has negotiated the fraught contemporary terrain of Bollywood and paradoxically made his name by starring in films that others may have been less willing to take up.

The Ayushmann Genre

In exploring Khurrana as a new type of "everyman" in contemporary Hindi cinema, Chakrabarti traces the "repeated narrative trajectory" that has emerged in several of the actor's films, one in which Khurrana appears as an "ordinary man with dysfunction" who, in turn, finds "provisional resolution to the apparent lack that lies beneath his dysfunction" (2020: 73). Along with a lack of education and erectile dysfunction, such issues have included writer's block (*Meri Pyaari Bindu* [2017]), failed love (*Bareilly ki Barfi* [2017]), and premature balding (*Bala* [2019]). Such themes, along with the "associated affects and identifications," have contributed, in turn, to "the core of Khurrana's star persona" (Chakrabarti 2020: 73). Part of this core, as Chakrabarti notes, is determined "by the very nature of the genre" in which Khurrana frequently performs, namely, sex comedy, in which the narrative crisis "always coalesces around a bodily element / affect, with the latter providing the moral catalyst that precipitates narrative action and resolution" (ibid.). Yet, even as an "Ayushmann genre" has emerged in the process, Chakrabarti questions whether there is "something more to Khurrana's career trajectory than simply the emergence of a (sub)genre" (ibid.). Chakrabarti also notes the "pedagogic intentions" of these films, which "make claims of dealing with 'social issues' in no uncertain terms" (ibid., 74). In many ways, these films appear to function as "petri dishes for *culturing* new social attitudes" (ibid., emphasis in original). Both of these points are salient to the discussion at hand and, in particular, to the expansion of the "Ayushmann genre" vis-à-vis consideration of what Chakrabarti may consider his more "outlier" films, that is to say, films that are not romantic comedies but which nonetheless also encapsulate the type of "pedagogic intention" that Chakrabarti describes in relation to Khurrana's romantic comedies. To again invoke the words of film theorist John Ellis, "There is always a temptation to think of a 'star image' as some kind of fixed repository of fixed meanings" (1982: 92). Khurrana's career trajectory, however, belies such a facile reading and problematizes the notion of an "Ayushmann genre," in which certain films/genres predominate and others function (merely) as "outliers." Indeed, one of the aims of this chapter is to explore how Khurrana simultaneously engages in both types of roles—those that accord with his eponymous genre as well as those seen as falling outside of it—and, furthermore, that such versatility and the accompanying willingness to explore alternatives both within and outside of such genres, are what increasingly inform his star text. Khurrana, in other words, has actively worked to expand the "core" element of his star persona and such roles, in turn, enhance earlier considerations of his career trajectory, in which there also seems to be "something more" (Chakrabarti 2020: 73). I thus begin my consideration of the range of Khurrana's recent roles with an analysis of one of the films Chakrabarti considers an "outlier" to Khurrana's filmography, *Article 15*.

Caste Politics and *Article 15*

Alternatively described as "an investigative drama where the audience too is an accused party" and a "punc[h] ... in the face" (NDTV 2019; Chatterjee 2019), Sinha's film is a gritty exploration of issues of caste and caste discrimination in the fictional small town of Laalgaon in India's most populous state, Uttar Pradesh (UP). The film, which is loosely based on the 2014 Badaun case, features Khurrana as the new Additional Superintendent of Police assigned to Laalgaon, apparently as punishment for being too flippant in his remarks to the chief minister of the state.[1] Upon first arriving in Laalgaon, Khurrana's character, Ayan Ranjan, a cosmopolitan, upper caste young man, is taken by the small town's rustic charm, texting his girlfriend Aditi back in Delhi that the countryside is "so beautiful" and reminds him of a "1980s Bollywood movie." Soon, however, upon discovering the corpses of two young Dalit girls hanging from a tree, Ayan changes his tune, telling Aditi, "It's like the wild West here."[2] The film viewer has arguably already come to this conclusion, as the film begins not with Ayan but with a powerful rendition of a folk song, voiced by a young woman who leads the others gathered around her singing and clapping in unison under a shanty in the pouring rain:

You'll get offended if I tell the truth
Rich people [*Bade bade log*] live in palaces
With a shining chandelier, separately [*alag se*]
We poor live in a hut, just a small hut
If a storm comes, it's enough to blow it away
Rich people enjoy delicious food
They even buy mineral water, separately [*alag se*]
We (poor) make do on chutney and roti
We drink unfiltered water
Rich people's kids go to big schools and college
They also take extra classes, separately [*alag se*]
While our kids toil hard, they say studies won't help them

The film literally begins with these words, voiced by the young woman[3] and repeated, in turn, by the men and women gathered around her, some of whom provide percussive rhythmic accompaniment to the singing. As the woman sings about the poor living in a hut, the camera cuts to external tracking shots of parts of the village, including images of pigs rummaging in the rain near debris-strewn pools of water. The camera continues cutting back and forth from the singers gathered under their hut to other images—to a hand-cranked pump, for instance, sitting idly in the rain as they sing of the rich drinking mineral water. About one minute in, the singing fades as the camera presents an extreme close-up of the rain falling on the pavement, tracking forward and up to a shot of a school bus passing by on a road, as ominous, *Sicario*-esque mood music replaces the earlier singing.[4] This is followed by a cut to a close-up of an anguished young girl's face being forcefully grabbed by a hand. The hand pulls the young girl's face toward the implied offscreen character, in the process revealing another young girl huddled at the back of the bus. As the girl in the foreground whimpers, she is pushed back and then slapped by the same hand. The camera (and the implied offscreen character) follows her as she crawls to the back of the bus, where she clutches the other young girl and they both breathe loudly and anxiously as the camera and character menacingly approach. A cut takes us back to the singers in the rain briefly and only then does the film title appear.

It is fair to say this opening packs many punches. Not only do the song's lyrics cut against the typical Bollywood ethos (typically aligned with the *Bade bade log* and their shining chandeliers) but its ensuing picturization shows us not glamorous images imbued with pastels but the subdued greys of a poor village, juxtaposed, in turn, to raucous singing skewering the privilege (and hypocrisy) of the rich. It is in this opening segment's segue to the interior of the bus—and, indeed, the bus itself—that a deeper punch is leveled, conjuring up as it does the spectre of the notorious Nirbhaya case.[5] This connotation would easily be grasped by a contemporary Indian audience, given the enormous amount of press coverage the Nirbhaya rape and assault case received, as well as the large number of ensuing demonstrations across the nation. Beginning a film with a song skewering the rich and then conjuring up the spectre of Nirbhaya as ominous mood music plays is not your typical Bollywood beginning. And while this opening scene alone packs a punch, the audience, as Sinha has noted, is also "an accused party" (NDTV 2019), precisely and paradoxically because, as a number of critics have observed, "There are no revelations here. We've read about such cases, we've sighed about these horrors" (Sen 2020a: 3).[6] It is precisely the (Indian) audience's familiarity with such images that paradoxically makes this opening sequence that much more discomforting, coming, as it does, on the heels of the opening song's refrain about the privilege and obliviousness of the rich. All of this is arguably not just "unusual in the context of Bollywood" (Vetticad 2019: 2) but, indeed, a direct assault on many of its most cherished conventions (and their underlying sentiments), particularly with regard to the use of song in this cinema.

Article 15 continues its unusual deployment of song in the sequence following the film's title, an aerial shot of a white police jeep moving along a highway accompanied by Bob Dylan singing his famous song, "Blowin' in the Wind," whose lyrics ("How many times can a man turn his back/ and pretend that he just doesn't see") take on an added resonance coming as they do after the film's opening song and the subsequent cut to the interior of the bus (and, in turn, its connotations of previous horrors). The audience, in keeping with the director's earlier claim, may very well feel implicated in and by everything they have thus far seen and heard, and are thus far more knowledgeable about the reality of this India than Khurrana's debonair character, to whom the camera cuts, sitting inside the white police jeep, texting his girlfriend about how beautiful the countryside is as he gazes out the window in dark sunglasses with a hint of a smile on his face. Ayan appears equally naïve to his police entourage when he asks them to stop at a roadside stand to buy a bottle of water. The policeman driving the jeep tells Ayan the stand is run by a lower caste from whom they cannot take water. Nevertheless, by the time he sees the two girls' bodies hanging from a tree, he, too, has become disabused of his earlier, naïve perspective. Khurrana's character functions as an integral element of what Chakrabarti describes as the "pedagogic intentions" of several of his films, including in an "outlier" to his oeuvre such as *Article 15* (2020: 74, 73). This is achieved by using Ayan as the film's narrative agent, the new Additional SP come to the hinterlands of UP from Delhi, still possessed by a slightly rose-tinted view of the countryside, and simultaneously by putting the audience one step ahead of him. Not only have viewers already seen the horrific reality of Laalgaon via the opening sequence but they are (thus) able to grasp the link between these images (unseen by Ayan) and the subsequent hanging bodies.

If the film, as film and media scholars Megha Anwer and Anupama Arora argue, "intends for its elite audience to receive, alongside Ayan, an anti-caste education" (2022: 632), then Ayan simultaneously functions as the police agent following clues and as a way for audiences to gauge their own advanced knowledge of (and hence, perhaps, complicity in) the atrocities at the heart of the film narrative: not only the repugnance of the caste system in operation (made even more repugnant by its quotidian nature, the way the police casually inform Ayan they cannot buy water from a certain roadside vendor) but the contingent horrors that lie behind it—the brutal rape and murder of the two young girls, and its particularly public nature, itself meant, as with lynchings in the American South, to send a (caste-ist) message, to teach a lesson. Thus, even as Ayan functions as the new sheriff in the "wild West" of rural Uttar Pradesh, with Khurrana, in turn, "underplay[ing] his part to great effect" (Chatterjee 2019), the film's ostensible detective narrative ultimately provides viewers with the opportunity to face what they may already know. As one critic noted, "*Article 15* is not a film in search of easy answers" (Sen 2020a). While Ayan is disabused of his romantic notion of Laalgaon resembling something from "1980s Bollywood," the viewer becomes aware of this from the get-go. The mystery, then, is not only what happened to the two girls but, in a deeper sense, how long it will take Ayan to realize what is happening all around him, that is, how he, as an upper caste Brahmin who enjoys the privilege of being unaware of his own and others' castes, is imbricated within the very caste system he is trying to "fix." And as film critic Raja Sen asks, "What do you do when the system is the bad guy?" (2020a). What Ayan soon learns about caste, in other words, at least some element of the audience (if not vast swaths of it) already know, not only because of the film's parallels to previous cases including that of Badaun but more broadly because of the caste system's arguable ubiquity in India.

Directly interrelated with the ubiquity of caste is the plague of official corruption that permeates *Article 15* and surrounds newcomer Ayan. At one point, attempting to better grasp the intricacies of the caste system, he questions his police officers regarding their and his caste status. As he grows increasingly frustrated with the apparent nebulousness of caste laws and subdivisions, he yells, "What the fuck is going on here?!"[7] As Ayan conducts his inquiry into the girls' deaths, he discovers how caste and corruption become insidiously intertwined, threatening to thwart his investigation and again silence the voices of the oppressed. When Gaura, the young woman singing the opening song, first approaches the police, requesting their assistance in locating three girls from their Dalit community who have gone missing, she is rebuffed by the upper caste Circle Officer Brahmadatt Singh (Manoj Pahwa) and both he and his lower caste subordinate officer Kisan Jatav (Kumud Mishra) repeatedly tell Ayan that the affairs of "inn logon" (these people) are, essentially, unimportant ("It's nothing," Brahmadatt tells him when Ayan initially asks about Gaura coming to him). Ayan, for his part—or, playing his part—subsequently lashes out at Jatav for constantly referring to lower castes as "these people"—"Where do they come from, Jupiter?" he demands. Jatav, in turn, assures Ayan that such things happen with "these people" all the time—"their girls run away, then come back." Ayan's investigation into the girls' deaths similarly hits a (caste-ist) roadblock when the lower caste female doctor performing the postmortem, Malti Ram, is, in turn, pressured by Brahmadatt not to disclose her report, which concludes that the girls were gang-raped repeatedly over two to three days and then hanged alive. Even as Ayan leads a search of the nearby pig swamp for traces of the third young Dalit girl, Gaura's younger sister Pooja, who remains missing, the broader stench of the cover-up begins to percolate. Gaura tells Ayan that after Pooja and the other girls had asked the upper caste construction supervisor, Anshu Naharia, for a three rupee raise, he had slapped Pooja, leading to all the other children refusing to work at his construction site. The local Dalit organization meanwhile tells Dalits to stop working in protest and trash begins mounting in the streets, creating a vivid metaphor as the police must literally walk through the accumulating waste surrounding their police station. The stench of corruption permeates the station itself, when Ayan interrogates Anshu about the missing girls. Anshu, whose father is a powerful local minister, remains unfazed during the interrogation, even as an unknown number repeatedly calls on Ayan's phone, sitting face up on the table between them, and Anshu informs Ayan that he has friends everywhere and that everyone has their place. Though Ayan does not pick up his phone, the message is clear.

Ayan's education is furthered when he meets with Nishad (Mohammed Zeeshan Ayyub), the local leader of the Bhim Shangharsh Sena (BSS), an activist group fighting for the rights of Scheduled Castes and seeking justice for the murders of the two Dalit girls. Nishad is a cynical critic of the state who claims that nothing has changed with regard to Dalits other than name changes. Nonetheless, he agrees to send men to clean up the clogged sewers after Gaura, whom he was to marry, tells him Ayan is searching for her missing sister, Pooja. Ayan subsequently discovers the school bus we first saw in the film's opening sequence and discovers it belongs to Anshu Naharia. The DNA samples tested by Dr. Malti Ram confirm that it was Anshu who raped the two girls and Ayan orders his arrest. Before he can be arrested, however, Anshu is shot dead in cold blood by Brahmadatt, who realizes that he, too, will be incriminated if Anshu is arrested, as it is eventually revealed that Brahmadatt and another police officer also took part in the gang-rape of the two Dalit girls. A further level of corruption is introduced when a CBI officer (Nassar) arrives in Laalgaon, accuses Ayan of "disturbing the peace," and suspends him from the case. Ayan nevertheless continues working on the case, even as Nishad, in turn, plans to flee for fear of being arrested for his group's opposition to an upcoming "pro-unity" rally organized by a Brahmin politician, Mahantji, in coordination with members of the local Dalit community.[8] Following an emotional scene with Gaura in which he laments his frequent feelings of hopelessness in the face of such overwhelming struggle, Nishad is apprehended by men in plainclothes who whisk him away in a jeep even as Gaura is left bereft.

The ensuing "pro-unity" rally, intercut with shots of Nishad being taken away, serves as the dramatic climax of the film, even as the ensuing crosscutting effectively belies the rally's proclaimed unity between upper and lower castes. Even as the hoardings for the rally literally cover over the "Missing" posters of Pooja that Ayan ordered placed on the town's walls, the saffron-clad followers of Mahantji cheer as he approaches the podium to speak. "This is the land of Shabri's Lord Ram, this is the land of Kevat's Lord Ram," Mahantji bellows, even as a cut takes us to Nishad being taken away in a jeep, where we are privy to his thoughts via a voiceover. "I wanted to be a writer, and a scientist, too," he says. "Then I thought I'd be a science writer but it came to nothing, because where I was born itself was a terrible accident." Following this is a cut back to Mahantji, who continues speaking, stating, "Whatever caste you belong to, it's time for Hindus to become one! It's also time to recognize the enemy." The camera continues to crosscut between these two characters who, via this crosscutting, could be seen as engaging in a dialogue of sorts, the words of one serving as both a sound bridge and rejoinder to the other.[9] "If anything happens to me, it will enrage you," Nishad says. "Make that anger your weapon but make sure you use no other weapon, friends [*doston*], because the day we take the path of violence, it'll be even easier for them to kill us." Cutting back to the "pro-unity" rally, another young leader clad in a saffron scarf says, "Friends [*Doston*], a few young anarchists in our community are spreading false rumors on WhatsApp and Facebook, in order to malign our unity. We must be aware of this!" The camera then cuts back to Nishad who says, "If anyone tries to raise their voice, they're accused of being a threat to national security and then killed." And this is precisely what happens, as the jeep comes to an abrupt halt on the side of the road and Nishad is gunned down, or "encountered," in broad daylight by the men, whom we can surmise are police officers following the orders of the organizers of the "pro-unity" rally. As the camera returns to this "pro-unity" rally, we see scarved infiltrators throwing Molotov cocktails at the stage and clashing with police, even as the rally organizers flee.

The film shifts back to Ayan for a follow-up meeting with the CBI inspector, who says the Dalits should not have engaged in violence, as it is they who will pay for it the most. "Who's doing the violence, sir?" Ayan asks, noting that sometimes, behind such outward violence, a quieter and more persistent violence is overlooked—the endemic violence of caste. "It becomes part of our culture," Ayan adds, noting that we don't call it violence then, we call it law and order. When the CBI inspector says, "You can't be neutral, can you?" Ayan replies that staying neutral when a fire is lit means standing with the ones who lit it, adding that the person repeatedly calling the CBI inspector for the past twelve hours is the one lighting it, as he hands him his phone records. The CBI chief looks at the dossier and smiles, asking Ayan if he has anything else to add—"otherwise," he says, "a clear case of honor killing."[10] Ayan then explains to the CBI inspector that the girls were only asking for a three rupee raise—"just a few sips of the mineral water you're drinking," he tells the inspector, who placidly sips his bottled water. They were raped for that mistake, Ayan says, adding that they were gang-raped to remind them of their place in society. They could have been thrown away but they were hung from a tree to remind all Dalits of their place, Ayan claims, then, rising, adds that he has the evidence, which he proceeds to show the CBI inspector. Building to his conclusion, Ayan tells the CBI inspector how "these people" (lower castes) constitute 70 percent of India's population and how the other thirty percent continues to subordinate them. "We all know this," Ayan adds, "We see it every day, we just don't remember it." Rising to leave, he hands his report to the CBI inspector, adding that he has already shared it with the other authorities, including the chief minister, the same one who allegedly punished him for his flippancy by sending him to Laalgaon. Following this speech, Ayan continues searching for Pooja, the upper-caste officer descending into the pig swamp with the others. Their search is ultimately successful and Ayan carries Pooja in his arms to the ambulance, following which we see Gaura performing an obeisant namaste to him as she is driven away with her reunited younger sister. Ayan then joins the other police officers for a shared meal, engaging in a group laugh as they casually violate caste-ist strictures.

To return to Chakrabarti's earlier question regarding Khurrana's career trajectory, we can indeed point to *Article 15* as effectively demonstrating that there is "something more" to this trajectory than sex comedies. Khurrana, a "lead actor with considerable star value," nevertheless manages to deliver a performance that is "underplayed" and, by being so, simultaneously marks his distance from the conventional Bollywood hero (Chatterjee 2019).[11] As film critic Raja Sen observes, in "eschew[ing] showiness," Khurrana stays "true to the part," even as he "build[s] on the everyman baggage of his earlier films" (2020a). Even as Khurrana does arguably "build on" and broaden his career trajectory as an "everyman" via this role, his character is not entirely immune from critique. While Anwer and Arora note the absence of all the "accoutrements of mainstream Bollywood's depiction" in this film, they nevertheless note that the "resolution to the caste question is framed within an overwhelmingly Brahmanical savior complex" (2022: 627–8). This is on display not only in overt images concluding the film, featuring Ayan carrying the rescued Pooja in his arms but also and more perniciously in the subsequent image of the Dalit Gaura performing an obeisant namaste to this Brahmin savior.[12] While such a gesture is problematic, I nevertheless believe, in response to Anwer and Arora's subsequent question—of whether the film is "governed by brahmanical hegemony" which, in turn, "ensures that upper-caste stories and characters invariably predominate, and [which] incapacitates the telling of Dalit stories" (ibid., 635)—that the crosscutting climax featuring Nishad's "rejoinders" via voiceover to the speech of Mahantji, does serve as a powerful critique of such "brahmanical hegemony," particularly as it is "voiced" by a Dalit (albeit mentally). As film critic Anna Vetticad observes, "There was a time when 'Mahantji' was a generic title, here though the allusion cannot be lost on any individual who has not been living under a rock in recent years" (2019). The allusion is of course to Yogi Adityanath, Chief Minister of Uttar Pradesh since 2017. As political scientist Christophe Jaffrelot has noted, Adityanath is "primarily the mahant (chief priest) of the Nath Hindu sect," and his coming to power created a situation in which "the head of the executive is also a religious leader and a militia chief" (2021: 222). We see all of this in *Article 15*'s Mahantji who, along with organizing a rally to unify Hindus (as a vote bank from which he will directly benefit), bears a striking physical resemblance to Adityanath, with his relatively short stature, saffron robes and shaved head—to paraphrase Vetticad, it would be impossible for an Indian audience not to recognize this reference.

It is paradoxically by allowing the Dalit Nishad to level the statements which, through the film's dynamic crosscutting, become effective rejoinders to Mahantji's superficial rhetoric that *Article 15* carves out at least some space for a lower caste protagonist to tell his story, complemented, in turn, by Khurrana "underplay[ing] his part" (Chatterjee 2019), both of which disallow the upper caste Ayan from completely predominating. This is also a shrewd choice by Sinha, given the overt parallel between Mahantji and Adityanath who, as Jaffrelot observes, has promoted "a form of state-sponsored vigilantism" in Uttar Pradesh where, if the police intervened, "it was more often to apprehend the victims rather than the instigators of violence," detaining them under the National Security Act (NSA), "intended for criminals posing a threat to state security" (2021: 227). This is precisely what we see happen to Nishad—he is apprehended for his opposition to the Mahant's "pro-unity" rally, which constitutes "a threat to state security" (or at least to the political fortunes of Mahantji). Jaffrelot cites a former police officer who notes that current political leaders in Uttar Pradesh "us[e] the police as their power arm to overawe the Dalits and minorities," notably including "encourag[ing] the police to open fire, in the name of law and order, on those suspected of a crime" (ibid., 227–8). Again, this is precisely what we see happen to Nishad, who is taken away and then killed in a so-called "encounter" by men who appear to be acting at the behest of the state.[13] By absenting the upper-caste Ayan from this moment, Sinha allows the Dalit Nishad to offer his own critique, simultaneously humanizing him and making his ensuing "responses" to the Mahant's rhetoric that much more powerful, culminating in his death, which serves as the ultimate indictment of the "police state" the religious head of state has currently created in Uttar Pradesh (ibid., 227). Simultaneously, Khurrana's "underplay[ed]," and "restrain[ed]" performance as Ayan demonstrates that there is more to the actor's career than sex comedies (Chatterjee 2019; Vetticad 2019). Yet, as we shall see in our discussion of his subsequent film, *Shubh Mangal Zyada Saavdhan* (2020), this does not mean Khurrana has forsaken his abilities in such a genre. Rather, in a testament to the elasticity of his star text and to Ellis' (1982) observation regarding the consolidation of a star's image, we see how Khurrana delivers nuanced performances in grittier dramas like *Article 15* even as he remains willing and eager to perform in, and recalibrate, the so-called "Ayushmann genre" of the sex comedy.

Queering the Patriarchy: *Shubh Mangal Zyada Saavdhan*

If caste serves as the key issue in *Article 15*, the primary focus of Hitesh Kewalya's *Shubh Mangal Zyada Saavdhan* (hereafter, *SMZS*) is "not homosexuality, but homophobia" (Jhunjhunwala 2020). This film follows its lead duo, Kartik Singh (Khurrana) and his boyfriend Aman Tripathi (Jitendra Kumar) as they take a train from New Delhi to Allahabad, to take part in wedding festivities for Aman's cousin, Rajni, aka "Goggles." The film commences with a lengthy disclaimer which begins by stating, "This film is intended for entertainment purposes only." Nevertheless, per Chakrabarti's earlier point about Khurrana's sex comedies, *SMZS* contains clear "pedagogic intentions," in this case, regarding homophobia (2020: 74). The film is also, unlike *Article 15*, much more influenced by a Bollywood idiom, which helps shape the discourse surrounding this topic. Indeed, if one of the ur-texts of *Article 15* is *Mississippi Burning*, a key ur-text for *SMZS* is Adiya Chopra's landmark Bollywood film, *Dilwale Dulhania Le Jayenge* (1995, hereafter *DDLJ*), to which the film pays multiple homages, even as it reworks several of the components of this earlier, quintessential, heterosexual Bollywood love story. The film's opening sequence itself is a tongue-in-cheek homage to *DDLJ*, as Kartik and Aman run, in matching Shaktiman outfits (donned for their jobs), to catch a train—Train 0377—heading from Allahabad to Gomti Nagar, where Aman's cousin's wedding is to take place.[14] After Aman jumps aboard the train, he extends his hand to Kartik, who runs to grasp it and board the train as well. In this sequence, and in this particular gesture, over which the film title appears, we see the first of many references to *DDLJ*, in which Bollywood superstar Shah Rukh Khan similarly extends his hand from a moving train to Kajol, who runs to grab it and climb aboard.

Following this reflexive opening sequence, the film moves back to the period just before Kartik and Aman leave for Allahabad. We see Kartik riding on the back of Aman's motorcycle in New Delhi one night, his arms clenched around him and his head resting on his back as a song plays on the soundtrack, one which the duo is presumably listening to on their shared earbuds. Kartik, who sports a nose ring and a triangle tattoo on his neck, convinces Aman that they both attend the upcoming wedding and from here we return to Train 0377, where the two lie sleeping on their seats. Awakened just in time, they get off and run to catch the connecting train to Gomti Nagar, still wearing their Shaktiman outfits and, as they board the train and greet Aman's extended family, another song commences—"Ooh la la"—to which the duo dances and Kartik lip synchs, along with all of Aman's relatives. At some point during this song, the duo moves to an isolated section of the train, where they engage in a passionate kiss. At precisely this moment Aman's father passes by and sees them kissing, then, startled, makes his way to the open train door, where he proceeds to vomit as the song ends and they arrive at Gomti Nagar. Here we see a vivid instance of what Chakrabarti describes as the "comic and obscene" element of such comedies, which he urges we take seriously (2020: 75). It is worth noting how this sequence utilizes a key element of the Bollywood idiom—the song and dance—and yet, how it soon morphs into something else, that is to say, is queered.[15] As Kartik and Aman discuss the possible fallout of Aman's father having seen them kissing on the train, Aman's father lies passed out inside the train, where other members of the extended family try to revive him, wondering what could have happened. Upon regaining consciousness and seeing the duo outside the train, Aman's father retches and again nearly vomits, reiterating this obscene gag reflex. Kartik urges Aman to explain their relationship to his father, claiming that Aman's dad is an educated man and will understand. Yet, when Aman approaches his father on the train platform, his father proceeds to douse him with a water hose, then tells him to stay away from "that boy" (Kartik), adding that what they are doing is "not right."

Later that evening, as the wedding celebrations ensue at the groom's residence, Kartik and Aman dance together but Aman soon stops as he notices his father surreptitiously watching their every move. Aman's father continues to follow and observe the duo throughout the festivities, even as they continue to dance and engage in revelry. The third song of the film, "Gabbru," comes during these festivities and again features Kartik, front and center, dancing and lip synching the Punjabi tune, soon accompanied by Aman and others. Aman's father then also joins the dancing, enacting a series of bodily gestures signifying "No," for example, crossing his arms repeatedly, which he aggressively directs at Kartik, who tries to respond with his own (counter-)gestures. The song culminates with Aman grabbing Kartik and kissing him flush on the mouth in front of everyone, at which point all of the singing and dancing stops. Here again we see how the conventional Bollywood wedding song and dance morphs into something else—as in the "Ooh la la" song aboard Train 0377, the dynamics of this sequence become queered and, in turn, such a moment, with its presumed heteronormativity, is defamiliarized. As the wedding guests stand and gawk in the ensuing silence at the still-kissing (gay) couple, Aman's uncle quickly tosses a jacket over the duo and starts chanting, claiming that this is how family members greet friends. Here we see another confluence of the "comic and obscene," in which the comic thrust entails "enjoy[ing] the resistance to the … alien object/situation" (Chakrabarti 2020: 75). Despite Aman's uncle's attempt at a cover story (and the equally dubious "covering up" of the kissing couple with a jacket), Aman's father drags Kartik away, telling his younger brother to take Kartik to the train station and see him off. The groom's family meanwhile refuses to proceed with the marriage due to Aman being gay.

It is at this moment that we witness a particularly compelling instance of the film's "pedagogic intentions" (Chakrabatri 2020: 74), as Aman gives a scientific jargon-laden speech to his parents, explaining how he felt an explosion of dopamine in his body when he first met Kartik, how he feels without him due to corticotrophin, how when he first kissed Kartik there was a burst of cortisol in his body. He tells his parents it is not him speaking now but rather the oxytocin, which is manufactured in the hypothalamus when one is in love. In this speech, we see not just an appeal to the pedagogical impulse on Aman's part but, in keeping with a Bollywood ethos, a hyperbolized rendition of such pedagogy, one which almost becomes a caricature of itself, what film scholar Sumita Chakravarty characterizes as "impersonation" (1993: 4).[16] The difference here—from earlier invocations in Bollywood films of such highfalutin language—is that Aman is seriously trying to explain his attraction to Kartik to his parents, who unfortunately respond to his scientific jargon-laden speech in a similar vein, with Kartik's mother stating that they will "get him treated." Aman rolls his eyes at this rejoinder, again taking recourse in scientific palaver, telling his mother, "Your oxytocin signals love and mine, a sickness [*bimari*]," before he leaves. Though his parents may remain confused, Aman's (and the filmmaker's) "pedagogic intentions" here are clear. Nevertheless, Aman's father insists on performing a "rebirth" ceremony for his son upon returning to Allahabad, making Aman pretend to be reborn as a (heterosexual) boy. Here we see how the accoutrements of Hindu ritual are deployed as a countermeasure by Aman's father, responding as it were to Aman's scientific explanation of his same-sex desire. Even more than Aman's speech, this "rebirth" ceremony is played for laughs and, furthermore, the comic thrust again is "to enjoy the resistance" Aman's father puts up in the face of the "alien object/situation" (Chakrabarti 2020: 75). Aman's father solemnly states that Aman's new name is "Chandravadhan," and that Aman is "dead for us."

It is precisely in the middle of this "rebirth" scene that Kartik returns to the Tripathi household, bare-chested and wearing a rainbow flag as a cape while clutching a bullhorn. Kartik proceeds to provide the film's most overt manifestation of its "pedagogic/ awareness-generating avocation" (Chakrabarti 2020: 73) as he stands bare-chested with pride flag hanging around his shoulders and bellows a lesson through his bullhorn from atop the family household's balcony, telling everyone assembled below that Shankar Tripathi (Aman's father) is suffering from an illness and that the illness he is suffering from is homophobia, a word he repeats through the bullhorn multiple times, adding that it is a disease that affects the mind (Figure 5.1).

While Aman smiles below as he watches his boyfriend's ostentatious performance, his father remains unamused and proceeds to fetch a stick with which he beats the bare-chested, rainbow flag-wearing Kartik, even as a remixed version of an older romantic Hindi song, "Kya karthe the saajna," plays

FIGURE 5.1 *Kartik gives a lesson about homophobia in* Shubh Mangal Zyada Saavdhan *(2020). Source: Screenshot from* Shubh Mangal Zyada Saavdhan, *directed by Hitesh Kewalya. 2020. AA Films. All rights reserved.*

on the soundtrack.[17] The idea conveyed by the use of the song here is one of sacrificial love, queering the original heterosexual notion of lovers lamenting their separation via Khurrana's willingness to take repeated blows from the Tripathi patriarch's *danda* (stick) for his homosexual love. In this vein, the song culminates with Kartik proclaiming, "My sexuality is my sexuality, not your sexuality," to Aman's father before collapsing. Despite Kartik's brief lesson about homophobia and his willingness to take repeated blows from Aman's father, Aman agrees to his parents' desire that he marry a local girl, Kusum (who herself loves another man). Kartik protests, asking Aman how long he intends to continue such a charade. In an additional reflexive comment, he refers to Aman's father as "woh Amrish Puri" (that Amrish Puri), the actor who plays the stern patriarch in *DDLJ* who refuses to let his daughter (Kajol) marry Shah Rukh Khan.

It is at this moment that Section 377 makes its appearance, on the back of a newspaper clipping upon which Aman writes, in red nail polish, that he will marry Kusum (so long as Kartik is not harmed). Reading about the pending Supreme Court decision on the legality of this section of India's Constitution (which is to be announced the following day), Aman's mother shows the clipping to her husband. Kartik meanwhile discovers a note left by Kusum, stating that she has taken her bridal jewelry and absconded. Laughing in disbelief, Kartik decides to take Kusum's place and comes out wearing the bride's red sari with his head covered and bowed submissively. He proceeds to sit beside Aman in front of the *havan*, or Hindu wedding fire, and prepares to circle it, per Hindu wedding ritual, with Aman. Aman's father, however, has doubts and, even as we get a reprise of the "Ooh la la" song, Aman's father repeatedly tries to unveil Kartik. Running away from Aman's dad, Kartik pulls off his head covering, revealing his identity as chaos ensues. Aman then confronts his father and, in a neat paraphrasing of Chakrabarti's (2020) contention, says everyone is laughing at *him*, not at them. In another interesting intertextual moment, however, Kartik approaches Aman even as the latter continues cursing at his father, saying, "What are you saying? This is your Papa."[18] Kartik then makes an(other) edifying statement, this time sans bullhorn, explaining that Aman's parents and others are only familiar with "Laila-Majnu, Shirin-Farhad, Romeo-Juliet stories," that is to say, heterosexual love stories. Aman then tells his father, "I love this boy, how does that change our (father-son) relationship?" He then takes Kartik's hand in his and leads him to the wedding fire, telling the Hindu pandit to proceed. The pandit refuses and so, in yet another intertextual moment, the duo proceeds to walk around the fire together as they sing, a cappella, another old Bollywood song, "Yeh Dosti Hum Nahi Todenge" (We Will Not Break this Friendship), from the Hindi blockbuster *Sholay* (1975).[19]

This reflexively repurposed queer Bollywood wedding is subsequently interrupted by the police, who arrive unannounced, with the mustachioed inspector clutching his stick as he announces that they have come to arrest "these two," invoking Section 377 and noting that being gay is a crime, which, he adds, is being openly committed here. Aman's uncle (a failed lawyer) then asks the police inspector if he has any proof that Aman and Kartik are gay, adding that if what they are doing is consensual, why is it anyone else's business? He notes that the law can change tomorrow (per the pending Supreme Court decision regarding Section 377) and the inspector, in turn, says he will wait for the decision to be announced the next day, adding that, until then, Aman and Kartik must remain in the Tripathi compound. Following this unexpected arrival of the law, another song ensues, this time signifying reconciliation as Kartik and Aman embrace, Kusum returns the bridal jewelry she had stolen, and Aman's father discovers worms nestled in the black cauliflowers he had genetically engineered to be worm-resistant.[20] The following morning the Supreme Court announces its unanimous verdict, decriminalizing consensual homosexual sex between adults.[21] Following this announcement there is much hugging and celebrating while Aman's father goes off by himself and burns all of his black cauliflower while silently weeping. He then catches up with Aman and Kartik on his motorcycle, offering them a lift to the train station, and they all ride together while the song of reconciliation continues to play. At the train station, Aman's father makes a brief speech to his son, saying, "I don't know if I'll understand all this but go and live your life," and then, in yet another reflexive homage to *DDLJ*, repeats to his child, "Jaa" (Go).[22] As Kartik watches Aman touch his father's feet and receive his blessing, he, too, is touched, watching Aman's father cry, and approaches the latter figure from behind to hug him. As Aman's father turns, Kartik also tearfully touches his feet and joins his hand in a humble namaste as the Tripathi patriarch holds Kartik's hands in his, then briefly nods before turning to go. Wiping away his tears, Kartik walks back to Aman and, in a final reprise of the famous sequence from *DDLJ*, extends his hand from the departing train to his lover. The film concludes on this freeze-framed image, while Kartik says, in voiceover, "We're running, for our own love. Just like Laila must've run for Juliet, Majnu for Romeo, Simran for Anjali, Veeru perhaps for Jai. Weddings happen at a fixed time," he concludes, "but there is nothing fixed about love."

In this resolution and, indeed, in *SMZS* overall, we witness a series of paradoxes: a certain degree of "radicalism" which, in turn, "has its limits" (Chatterjee 2020); a lack of subtlety and yet a "sensitive" treatment, particularly compared to previous depictions of homosexuals in Bollywood (Jhunjhunwala 2020; Sharma 2020);[23] a film that is "just so extra" in its depiction of two gay men in love, which simultaneously functions as the film's "drawback and delight" (Jhunjhunwala 2020). Like *Article 15*, *SMZS* draws upon contemporary events (the 2018 Supreme Court ruling decriminalizing consensual sex) even as it references earlier filmic texts. And while such references, including to *DDLJ*, are playful and playfully subversive in their queering of the earlier film's heterosexual love story, *SMZS*, like its straight Bollywood ur-text, pays obeisance to its patriarch, conjuring up an emotional register through song and acting that belies claims of such gestures merely being gestures or lip service. Though he stands up to Aman's father, Kartik also reproaches Aman for cursing him. And like Raj and Simran in *DDLJ*, both men truly seem to value the blessing of the patriarch. Thus, even as one could argue that *SMZS* may be seen as a step forward in progressively depicting homosexuality in Bollywood, and that Khurrana's "film choices, and his interpretation, continue to impress" (Jhunjhunwala 2020), one could simultaneously note, as some have, that, despite "pushing the boundaries," Khurrana is, "all said and done a mainstream Bollywood star" who can "go only this far and no further" (Chatterjee 2020). Yet, to return to Chakrabarti's analysis of Khurrana's earlier sex comedies, one can and should note that Khurrana's performance in *SMZS* (coming on the heels of his performance in the "outlier" *Article 15*) queers the sex comedy genre and, unlike earlier sex comedies in which "the narrative crisis always coalesces around a bodily element/affect" (2020: 73), effectively shifts the focus here to social mores—as he tells the Tripathi clan in his sermon from on high, homophobia is a disease of the mind. Through both *Article 15* and *SMZS*, we witness, in radically differing ways, what Chakrabarti calls "the traumatic occurrence of the modern" (2020: 82) as well as not only the radical differences in Khurrana's respective characters and performance styles but the radically different (yet, equally effective) ways in which his characters address these modern problems. In the final film I would like to discuss here, we will see how Khurrana continues to expand his star persona and the contemporary issues his characters address, in this case, the fraught cultural and political tensions of India's Northeast region.

Peace is a Subjective Hypothesis: *Anek*

The Northeast of India, as anthropologist Arkotong Longkumer notes, is "a region that has been largely ignored" (2021: 16). The struggles of this region vis-à-vis the Indian state have been ongoing since India gained independence in 1947 and, indeed, existed even prior to this date. The seven states comprising this region—Arunachal Pradesh, Assam, Nagaland, Manipur, Meghalaya, Mizoram, and Tripura—constitute an area rich in indigenous cultures and resistant to attempts by the Indian government to incorporate it into the collective national identity. As Longkumer observes, "Many in the Northeast question their 'Indian' identity, some even taking up arms to fight for independence from the Indian state" (ibid., 12). Such independence struggles, as historian Ramachandra Guha notes, have more or less continued over the past seventy years. New Delhi's so-called "Naga problem," despite being "much less known than its Kashmir problem," is just as old, if not older, than the latter and has proven to be just as intractable (Guha 2007: 267). Even as the Indian Constituent Assembly designated approximately 400 communities in this region as "scheduled tribes," their status in relation to the Indian mainland remains tenuous, both culturally and politically (ibid., 272). Compounding the region's alienation is its Christianity, with five of the seven states including a "sizeable Christian population" (Longkumer 2021: 27–8). Also contributing to its alienation is the fact that "few Indians" outside the region, and "virtually no foreigners," know much, if anything, about the region and its longstanding conflicts and concerns with the larger Indian state (Guha 2007: 282). The region has also generally remained unrepresented in popular Hindi cinema, apart from occasional (mis)representations of the region and its people, which have only contributed to preexisting stereotypes or, more broadly, to the region's erasure from the collective Indian consciousness.[24]

Anek sets out to change all of this. The film, directed by Anubhav Sinha, constitutes Khurrana's second collaboration with the director and also further reflects the actor's willingness to tackle so-called "outlier" roles in films falling outside of mainstream Bollywood (Chakrabarti 2020: 73). In this discussion, I want to examine not only the political and cultural issues the film raises with regard to the Northeast's troubled historical relationship with India but how it does so, that is, in comparison with what may broadly be called the "Bollywood idiom." Like Sinha and Khurrana's previous collaborative effort, *Article 15*,

Anek is not a Bollywood film. In tandem with a continued exploration of Khurrana's elasticity as an actor and his willingness to take on "outlier" roles, I want to examine how, by eschewing certain formulaic elements of the Bollywood idiom, *Anek* paradoxically provides a more vivid glimpse into the contemporary sociopolitical realities of this region and its people.

Unlike most of the previous films made about the Northeast, *Anek* was actually filmed in Assam and Meghalaya, and features numerous actors from the region, including its female protagonist, Aido (Andrea Kevichusa, in her debut role), who we first see at a nightclub with friends.[25] The police order the club closed when its owner refuses to pay off the police inspector who, in turn, tells the female officers to "arrest those Chinese lasses." One female officer repeatedly slaps Aido and calls her a prostitute, even as Aido glares back silently in a close-up. The female cop slaps her again and asks if she is Nepali. Aido again receives the slap in silence and continues to glare at the female officer, who remains offscreen, even as she orders Aido to lower her gaze, again slapping her and asking if she has come from Bangkok to give a massage.[26] In the beginning minutes of the film, we hear the pernicious stereotypes of women from the Northeast as "promiscuous by nature," due in part to stereotypes associated with their Christian faith as well as, more broadly, with Northeast women as "less moral" and "more available for male attention" (Dowerah and Nath 2018: 122; McDuie-Ra 2015: 312). A cut takes us to Aido boxing in the gym the following day while the Indian coach, in a side conversation with Aido's Northeast trainer, John, berates her for partying at a club the night before the selection day. The Indian coach, Avtar, makes a series of stereotypical jokes, asking John if his family drinks together while eating dog tikka. Even as John insists that Aido not only does not drink but went to the club for her cousin's birthday with his permission, furthermore noting that "no one in Asia can match Aido's technique," Avtar remains dismissive, saying he will not be selecting her for the Indian team this year, adding that Mary Kom remains dominant in her division and speculates, if Aido joined, whether the team would be Indian or Chinese.[27] Following this comment, he casually says, "Joke, joke." Yet, when John insists that Aido can knock out the star female Indian boxer, Gopa, who hails from Haryana, Avtar becomes incensed. When John relays Avtar's decision to Aido, she wordlessly packs her gym bag and prepares to leave but then pauses and announces to everyone that she will beat Gopa by knockout.

As with *Article 15*, it is only following this powerful opening sequence that the film title appears onscreen. Yet, already, within the opening minutes, the film telescopes many important themes regarding how Northeasterners, and Northeast women in particular, are perceived by those hailing "from" the Indian mainland (e.g., Avtar, the female cop). It is also only following the film title that we first hear Khurrana's voice, in a more conventional voiceover in which he explains that he has worked on secret missions for India for the past decade and that he was sent to the Northeast three years ago to ensure the signing of a peace accord between the Indian government and Tiger Sangha, who leads the most powerful rebellion movement which has been actively opposed to integration with mainland India for the past sixty years. Khurrana adds that the Indian government has been unable to defeat Tiger's army, which operates in three Northeastern states, and has been forced to negotiate with him as well as other separatist leaders. As this voiceover continues we see Khurrana walking up to an office, carrying a cardboard box. Arriving, he says to someone who remains offscreen, "Sorry, sir, I couldn't kill him," before the camera cuts to his boss, seated behind a desk. What we do not yet realize is that this moment is a flashforward to the film's conclusion, which will reappear roughly two hours later. The bulk of the film, in other words, recounts the period leading up to this moment, when Khurrana's character makes his announcement, even as it provides an explanation for his decision (not to kill).

In the meantime, the film cuts to Tiger Sangha's office, where a camera pans over numerous framed photos of Tiger meeting with various Indian government officials over the years. The photos are being filmed by an Indian television crew that has arrived for an exclusive interview with Sangha. Tiger (Loitongbam Dorendra Singh) proceeds to tell the female Indian journalist that, despite the arrival of the internet and WhatsApp, people still know nothing of his people's struggle. When the reporter claims that India is celebrated as the most diverse democracy in the world, Tiger replies, "You call us Chinkies, call Kashmiris Pakistanis, Khalistanis, Naxalite, etcetera, etcetera," then adds that Indians don't like people's local identity, telling the reporter that "in your definition, all Indians must be of the same color—that's not diverse democracy." When the reporter mentions violence, Tiger replies, "Violence? Did we send our troops to India?" then adds that, since Independence, India has sent 200,000 soldiers here, acting upon the Armed Forces Special Powers Act (AFSPA).[28] The reporter then says, "But this is India," and asks Sangha, "Aren't you Indian?" Tiger vehemently replies that he is not an Indian, adding that India does not want peace.[29] Again, just within this brief three-and-a-half minute interview, we learn quite a bit about the Northeast and its relationship with India. Following the interview, Khurrana proceeds to supplement this knowledge by continuing to explain in voiceover, as the camera cuts to aerial shots of the Northeast, that Tiger's was not the only group in the region, that there were thirty to forty active secessionist groups in the region, each with different methods, some friends, other enemies. Yet, Tiger's was the most powerful, Khurrana's character adds, controlling toll taxes, drugs and arms trafficking in the region. As he speaks, we see a group of young boys in shirts and ties riding their bicycles through the hilly landscape. Khurrana continues to explain that one group has become particularly active recently, a group named Johnson, whose mural we see painted on a wall as Khurrana emerges from his jeep.

Khurrana's look here is also worth noting. Sporting a beard, close-cropped hair and a slit through one eyebrow, his image deviates from both the mustached, suited and booted Ayan of *Article 15* as well as Khurrana's more metrosexual look in *SMZS*. Khurrana's character, whose name we now learn is

Joshua, has come to meet with Doko, a Northeasterner working for Johnson, who has stolen hashish from Tiger which he plans to sell in order to purchase arms for their struggle. Joshua agrees to help Doko with the deal and, as the police arrive, helps him make his escape. We again see the young boys approaching on their bicycles, apparently heading to school and, as they are caught in the ensuing crossfire between the police and Doko's men, we are presented with an image that vividly encapsulates the region's conflict, with innocent young boys literally stuck between two sides shooting at one another and with no place to take cover. The boys huddle on the ground, screaming and covering their heads as bullet fly above them. Yet, the camera then abruptly cuts to Khurrana's character, Joshua, laughing as he drinks a beer at a café. Such moments, or such juxtapositions, which emerge periodically throughout the film, have a jarring effect, abruptly shifting from one emotional register (panic and fear for the young boys) to another (Joshua's laughter over beers) which, by their being intercut in quick succession, creates a momentary sense of displacement through such contrapuntal editing. We then see Aido approaching, even as Joshua, in voiceover, says, "I wish Aido had never walked into my café," even as we hear her asking for Joshua.[30] As the two greet each other, with Joshus reaching out to hold Aido's hands, it becomes clear that they share some emotional bond. Aido tells Joshua she had an argument with her father, who again tells her India is not her country and not to compete in the challenge match. Joshua nods and listens and later tells a colleague that Aido will be useful to them. We are subsequently introduced to her father, Wangnao (Mipham Otsal), who appears to be a schoolteacher at a Johnson-supported local school and who tells the others gathered there that they must become self-sufficient and make use of their rich natural resources.

A cut takes us from the Northeast to New Delhi, where Tiger Sangha has arrived to meet with Mr. Abrar, Joshua's boss, and another man, a government minister, who pushes Tiger to accept the Indian government's conditions for autonomy, which include pledging allegiance to the Indian flag.[31] Following a cut we return to the Northeast where Aido, in voiceover, explains that her father says they are not Indian, that India lied and took over their state and has gone on to break its promises, leaving many people feeling cheated. As we hear her voice we see her running through the countryside, training. As she runs, she continues in her voiceover:

> India is fighting us but I want to talk to India. No one cares what I think, what I want for my state, my people. That's why I want to play for India's team. One day I will bring a gold medal for India, then everyone will listen to what I have to say. Then I'll talk to India, one on one.

Following this voiceover we get the first song of the film—a female rap in Hindi beginning with the lines, "Arre, ladna hai, ladna hai" (So, you want to fight, you want to fight) as we see Aido continue to train. The rap fades away after thirty seconds, however, providing just a taste, a teaser of sorts, of the full piece, which we will only hear at the very end of the film. As with the shot of Khurrana approaching his boss' desk and announcing his inability to kill a man, this brief musical interlude holds a latent promise of further development, further unfolding. It also clearly marks *Anek* as more of an "outlier" film in terms of its redeployment of one of Bollywood's most typical conventions—not only in the manner in which it appears (and quickly disappears) but in its form—a rap number performed by a woman, itself a rarity in Hindi cinema—and, in keeping with a *hatke* ethos, merely playing on the soundtrack rather than lip-synched by Aido, with whom the song is clearly associated. Thus, *Anek* provides a series of glimpses into multiple simultaneous moments—Tiger meeting with politicians in New Delhi, Aido training in the Northeast for her challenge match—all of which serve as pieces of a puzzle slowly being assembled, yet whose direct links are still unclear. In a similar vein, Joshua and Aido are friendly and flirt with one another while also maintaining a degree of distance, in part created by the alternating rhythms of this "web-of-life" plot,[32] never going beyond a certain point. This relationship, too, holds a latent promise, yet resists unfolding in a more conventional Bollywood pattern, for example, through a romantic duet.

In this vein (of the web-of-life plot) Joshua realizes his conflict even as he smiles when dropping Aido off at her home, then frowns as he sees her father, Wangnao, who gazes apprehensively at Joshua. The reason for this wary exchange of glances is not primarily due to the potential romantic relationship blossoming between Aido and Joshua, so much as it is informed by the respective backstories (and conflicting interests) of these two men, one an undercover agent for the Indian government and the other, a teacher at a school run by one of the region's secessionist groups. Joshua receives a phone call from his boss in New Delhi, Abrar (Manoj Pahwa), who informs him that Tiger is willing to negotiate. We also learn that Abrar and Joshua have created the Johnson group as a way to pressure Tiger to negotiate. In a subsequent voiceover Joshua explains that everyone in the local village worked for Johnson, including a local woman, Emma (Sheila Devi), who also serves as Joshua's comprador, primarily in exchange for Joshua looking out for her fourteen-year-old son, Niko (Thejasevor Belho). Even as Joshua explains this, we see young Niko taking packets of rice to soldiers affiliated with the Johnson movement, then singing a brief folk song praising the life of a farmer, which the soldiers clearly enjoy listening to, their leader exchanging his military cap with Niko's baseball cap as they leave on their patrol. Soon enough, even as the various strands of this plot begin to intertwine, Tiger's men attack Johnson's (in order to gain more leverage with Abrar). Joshua keeps the viewer informed of these convoluted plot developments, explaining in voiceover as the attacks occur, "If I couldn't control Johnson, Abrar would lose. Either way, Johnson's people would be defeated, by Tiger, the police, the army and me," even as we see Niko walking his bike past the ensuing violence.[33]

Seeing his Johnson cap, the leader of Tiger's troops arrests Niko and his mother, Emma, in turn, asks Joshua for help in securing her son's release. Arriving at the detention center, Joshua and the viewer are confronted by a

FIGURE 5.2 *Joshua walks through rows of imprisoned boys with bound hands in* Anek *(2022). Source: Screenshot from* Anek, *directed by Anubhav Sinha. 2022. AA Films. All rights reserved.*

second compelling image that effectively encapsulates the broader themes at play in *Anek*, as well as their repercussions. Through Joshua we see the brute reality of the young local boys' confinement by Tiger's troops (themselves sanctioned by the Indian government, seeking to negotiate a peace accord with Tiger). Endless pairs of bound hands emerge from two rows of bamboo cages on either side of a narrow path, even as we hear corresponding cries for help (Figure 5.2).

Following this, the camera pulls up for a high-angle wide shot, in which we see just how many bamboo cages there are here—over fifty at least—even as they appear to stretch beyond the camera frame, each holding what appears to be a dozen or so boys (based on the number of bound hands we see), in other words, over 600 youths being detained in these Guantanamo-like conditions.[34] The troops beat the boys with sticks, asking which is Niko. We see these troops not only repeatedly beating the boys but also dragging one away by his hair, even as Joshua, appearing momentarily stunned, takes all of this in.[35] Finally finding Niko, Joshua takes him back to his mother, who warns him what will happen to him, telling him to go to Delhi instead. Niko replies, "I won't go to India." Following a brief conversation with Joshua, who urges him to respect his mother, the third song of the film, "Oh Mama," begins to play as Niko subsequently walks up to his mother and embraces her while Joshua speculates in voiceover that all these kids might one day grow up to become Tiger—if they grew up. As with the earlier female rap, this song plays for less than a minute, a brief burst of a sentiment yet to be fully expressed, the song again foreshadowing future plot development associated with these characters.

As Tiger returns to the Northeast and the fighting escalates between his troops and Johnson's, we see preparations for the "Alliance" rally underway, in honor of the planned union between Tiger's movement and the Indian government. As with *Article 15*'s climax featuring the Dalit-Brahmin "pro-unity" rally, *Anek* crosscuts between clashes between the two sides and preparations for the unity rally, where women practice dance moves as the stage is literally set. Suddenly a bomb explodes at the site and, following the ensuing chaos, there is a cut to Abrar heading to the Northeast, commenting as he gazes out the window of his plane, on how beautiful it looks from up here. Abrar meets with Joshua, whose real name turns out to be Aman. Aman asks Abrar who was responsible for the bomb blast, adding that he doesn't believe Johnson was behind it. Abrar replies that whoever it was, it helped them but adds that he now requires calm in order to finalize his negotiations with Tiger. Following his meeting with Aman, Abrar meets with an old friend, Anjaiyaah (J. D. Chakravarthy), with whom he discusses the possibility that Aman is "soft" on Wangnao and the Johnson movement because of his affection for Aido. He orders Anjaiyaah to tap Aman's phone, even as the camera cuts to Wangnao hurriedly leaving his home, while Aido asks her father where he is going and why. To each of his daughter's questions Wangnao replies he cannot tell her. As he turns to go, Aido tells him he has to go to his fight but this, holding up her plane ticket to the challenge match in Delhi, is her fight and she must go for that. Abrar meanwhile tells Anjaiyaah to let Aido go to her challenge match, adding that she will serve as a "brand ambassador of happiness from the state," even as he, in turn, is trying to eliminate her father and the Johnson movement. As she packs for her trip, Aido catches Aman/Joshua taking photos of documents in her home and asks him who he is. She adds that he is doing the same thing to the people of her state as he is doing to her, adding, "I expected love and they expect peace," then concluding, "What a waste." As Aman/Joshua looks on wordlessly, she says, "I hope I never remember you," and leaves for her fight in Delhi.

In the ensuing scenes we alternately witness the coming of age of two young teenagers from this region—Aido and Niko—as the former flies alone to the nation's capital for her challenge match and the latter becomes increasingly indoctrinated in the fight against Tiger's troops. Even as Aido gazes out of a plane window, down below Niko watches as another soldier of Johnson's is killed and then, with a resolute look on his face, picks up the fallen soldier's rifle and begins firing at Tiger's soldiers. The ensuing dazed look on his young face marks his premature coming of age, as he and his allies drive past and gaze at the piles of dead bodies lying along the side of the road. Aman meanwhile goes to meet with Wangnao, revealing his true identity and telling him the Indian government will negotiate with him so long as his group does not take up arms, adding that if they do, more children will become orphans, including Aido. As Aman continues to plead with him, Wangnao walks toward a map of India hanging on the wall. "You Indians talk so much about the nation, sing songs, beating your chest, make [patriotic] films." Approaching the map, he says, "If I covered the names of Indian states on the map, how many Indians could put their finger on the correct state?" He goes on to note, in an echo of Tiger's comments in his earlier interview, how little Indians know about the Northeast, how tenuously it is linked to the mainland, by the so-called "Chicken's neck," in West Bengal, a twenty-two kilometer pass which he points out on the map even as the camera shows this in close-up. In all of this, *Anek* again provides, via Wangnao's speech to Aman, a primer to the audience about this overlooked region, literally showing us not only where it is on the map but just how isolated it is from the rest of India. Following this brief lesson, Wangnao concludes that it is easier to maintain war than peace, which, he adds, is why everyone makes war—Tiger Sangha and you, too, pointing his finger at Aman, who again looks taken aback. In many ways, then, it is not only Aido and Niko whose coming of age the film chronicles; Aman, too, is receiving an illusion-shattering education, its impact doubly powerful because of his own complicity in the events unfolding around him.

Aman's *tête-à-tête* with Wangnao is interrupted by the arrival of Indian troops whom Aman holds off while Wangnao escapes. Abrar's old friend Anjaiyaah also arrives with the troops and Aman takes him away at gunpoint in a car. In their ensuing car ride Anjaiyaah, who, in his introductory scene, explained to a confused soldier that "Peace is a subjective hypothesis," identifies himself as a member of the Indian Police Service (IPS) and asks Aman if Wangnao said anything about Johnson. Lowering his gun, Aman tells him what Wangnao said to him, then asks Anjaiyaah how one can define who is an Indian. The two then engage in a fascinating dialogue that again contributes both to Aman's and the viewer's ongoing enlightenment about the reality of the Northeast conflict:

Aman   What do we want to achieve—peace or a peace accord?

Anjaiyaah   Peace accord.

Aman   By silencing everyone's voices?

Anjaiyaah   Peace is a dirty business, officer. Mostly people confuse peace with control. When everything is in control, it looks like peace.

Aman   And when everything becomes peaceful then everything goes out of control?

Anjaiyaah   If you notice, peace is never achieved. Violence is achieved for peace—sorry, for control. I think humans don't like peace.

Aman nods his head at Anjaiyaah's last words and then, looking directly at the camera, adds, "We even murdered Gandhi." Then, after a pause, he adds that control is now in Abrar's hands and that he suspects there will be a lot of violence, followed by peace—sorry, he adds, smiling cynically, control. Following this Socratic dialogue, itself coming on the heels of Wangnao's lesson, we see Aman completing his learning process. Anjaiyaah also seems to recognize this evolution in Aman's final self-correction, substituting "control" for "peace," gazing at him and nodding in silence.

It is in the ensuing scene, following the deaths of Niko and the other Johnson soldiers by unseen snipers, that the film's most moving, and jarring, sequence takes place. Following a ten second long shot of their corpses, the song we previously heard in abbreviated form—"O Mama"—suddenly returns, a woman singing, "Writing's on the wall," even as the camera remains fixed on the pile of corpses. The sound of the woman's voice singing in English as well as the jazz-like arrangement of the song, accompanied by soft piano and a male voice in the background, serves as a jarring juxtaposition to the image of dead bodies. With the song's next line ("This wall has gotta fall") the camera cuts to a small bamboo-walled church in daylight which the camera slowly enters, where a Christian funeral service is taking place. As the breezy singing continues ("Say mama, see the other side/ See mama, it's shining bright/ See, mama, I'm bathing in the sun") we see photos of the fourteen people recently killed on display beside a priest. As the song continues ("O mama, the kids are having fun/ O, mama, the mighty pen is bleeding dry/ Mama, see the monster cry") we see Aman walking in the background and standing outside while, in the foreground, we see Emma, Niko's mother, mourning her dead son. Emma rises, even as the music fades, exiting the church and approaching Aman, whose gaze remains averted. Pulling his shirt she silently beckons him inside the church but Aman refuses. Emma then lets go of him and screams, "Niko died! He died!" and begins crying, telling Aman he promised he would look after Niko. "You said you people were working for peace," she adds. "Tell me," she says as she pushes him, "Is this peace?!" Aman remains silent as he gazes at her, as she cries, "This is all your people's doing!" and then screams multiple times before walking away, still crying, while Aman remains in the foreground, speechless but, again, clearly overwhelmed and barely suppressing his grief.

What makes this scene particularly powerful is the use of the "O Mama" song. Sinha, who wrote the lyrics, achieves a sense of defamiliarization at many levels, not only of unspeakable violence through its juxtaposition with song but, more particularly, of the typical use of song in Bollywood. "O Mama" being rendered in English, its invocation of Christian sentiment, along with its more Western musical arrangement, all contribute to its sense of incongruity with this moment. The film's brief juxtaposition of the song, following the ten second shot of Niko's and the others' corpses, is unsettling because both its overly sentimental (but non-Bollywoodized) rendering and its delayed yet accompanying response risk banalizing these very deaths. The "writing on the wall" is there for all of us to see and to wince at and the song puts an (over) emphasis on this. Thus, un/like Bollywood, the song risks being (seen as being) in "poor taste," that is, as too crude, too overt, in its sentiment as well as in its suddenness, in the abrupt transition not from the exalted to the commonplace but from the commonplace to the exalted, producing an almost ludicrous effect, that is to say, the definition of bathos. Yet, this very "mis-fit," the juxtaposition of silent death and smoothly rendered accompanying song paradoxically achieves a distancing effect, creating a jarring impact on the viewer expecting a more typical rendering of sentiment at this moment.

Even as Aman subsequently persuades Abrar to let him try to bring Wangnao in (without killing him), Abrar sends in Major Veer, an expert at "surgical strikes," to accompany Aman, along with Veer's covert team of soldiers. The surgical strike commences, with the chest-thumping Major Veer very much invoking Vicky Kaushal's character, Major Vihaan, from the 2019 Bollywood film *Uri: The Surgical Strike*, who repeatedly asks his troops, "How's the *josh* (zeal)?" The film's denouement is comprised of crosscutting between this surgical strike in the Northeast, where Aman is trying to save Wangnao's life, and Aido's boxing match in Delhi, which she eventually wins, even as Aman manages to successfully extricate Wangnao. It is at this point that the film comes back to the opening scene where Khurrana approaches Abrar with box in hand, saying he was unable to kill him. He now proceeds to pull out two files from the box, which he hands, in turn, to Abrar, explaining that the first file is Wangnao's and the second (larger) file is Tiger Sangha's, then adding that if either is to be arrested, both should be and, similarly, if either is to be negotiated with, then negotiations should take place with both. Before leaving a muted Abrar, Aman poses a question, which marks the culmination of his growing enlightenment: "Is it possible that no one wants peace?" Perhaps this is why, he adds, we haven't been able to solve this little problem for so long. He then repeats Aido's earlier line, "What a waste," as he submits his long-leave application and departs. Abrar then considers both files Aman has left him and places a call to someone, saying, "I'm sending you something—sources," then adds, "No quotes." A news anchor's voiceover subsequently informs us that the Northeast peace accord has again been put on hold, due to the government finding incriminating evidence against Tiger Sangha. We then see Abrar receiving a transfer from Police Services to Pay Advisory Commission and, one month later, Aman says in voiceover, the one winner in all of this was Aido, who we now see boxing for India in what appears to be the Olympics. As she fights, the earlier rap we briefly heard returns in full force, powerfully voiced by playback singer Sunidhi Chauhan:

> I have many names, many languages [*bhasha*]
> I can be weighed in gold, I have as many hopes [*asha*] as waves in the ocean
> I've deleted the word despair from my dictionary
> All my rivers flow into one
> Many [*anek*] are the characters but in this story there is one [*ek*]

I have many faces, I am one among many
Look at me, I am one among the many!

As the rap continues, the camera cuts to a bar where Aman and Abrar, along with many other Indians, watch Aido's match on TV and cheer. The rap concludes with the line, "Listen up, India! India! India!" as we see Aido has won her match. The camera cuts back to her in the ring, rising from her corner and walking to the center, where she slowly raises the Indian flag while looking down. As the image freeze-frames, the song continues. Yet, even as there is an ensuing transition to the film's end credits, a rectangular insert of Aman and Abrar at the bar appears on the left side of the screen as the credits continue rolling on the right and the song continues to play. As the song gradually fades, the diegetic sounds of the bar return and we hear Aman and Abrar engage in another dialogue in which Aman asks Abrar about all those who didn't win a medal—what, he asks, must they do for us to celebrate them? Pausing, he adds that it is their duty to celebrate us but whose duty is it to celebrate them? Abrar says nothing, silently sipping his drink. Aman continues his line of questioning, asking if we are all not Indian. Abrar continues to silently sip his drink as Aman adds, "Or are some Indians while others have to prove it?" then gestures toward the TV with his glass, saying, "Just like Aido." After a pensive pause, Abrar finally replies. "I agree with you. But-" And the rap song returns, cutting him off and continuing as the final image finally fades.

* * *

If an ur-text for *Article 15* is *Mississippi Burning*, a key ur-text to *Anek* is Mani Ratnam's 1998 film, *Dil Se*, which also addresses, albeit in a manner more closely approximating Bollywood, the conflicts and tensions of the Northeast. In comparing *Anek* to *Dil Se*, which I would briefly like to do as a way of concluding, one can see just how radical Sinha's film is, as well as how significantly Khurrana deviates in his performance from the typical Bollywood mould. While Ratnam's film (in)famously attempted to combine Bollywood elements such as song and dance with a more political narrative, *Anek* essentially eschews such typical Bollywood elements. In the process, Sinha avoids "the fine line" Ratnam had to walk between these two components ("a politically conscious film" and "Bollywood tropes and talent") which, in turn, allows *Anek* to avoid the "cinematic compromises" that constitute *Dil Se* (Mezey 2018: 30). Similarly, just as *Dil Se* "seizes upon the issue of center-state tensions in India," but is unable to fully explore these due to its "conformity to Bollywood conventions," the film's protagonist, Amar, played by superstar Shah Rukh Khan, comes across as "nothing so much as a Bollywood hero who finds that he is stuck in the wrong movie" (Mezey 2018: 36). As film scholar Jason Howard Mezey observes, one of the "foremost" examples of Ratnam's "adoption of a Bollywood idiom" is his casting of Khan as the male lead" (ibid., 45). We see the contrast with Sinha's casting of Khurrana, whose star text is less affiliated with and informed by a Bollywood sensibility and more aligned with a *hatke*, or offbeat, sensibility, made even more heterogeneous via Khurrana's eclectic role selections. While, in *Dil Se*, this impasse—between political thriller and Bollywood film—literally comes to a head at the film's climax, which ends with a bang, *Anek*, in its repudiation of typical Bollywood elements, including in its (brief) songs, remains more firmly ensconced within the terrain of a political thriller and, in turn, more clearly focused on the political issues at hand. Relatedly, while the role of the insurgent female protagonist in *Dil Se* has been criticized for the limitations of her agency (again due in part to Bollywood conventions) which, in turn, binds her to the male lead and disallows her from fully voicing (and effectively acting upon) her "specific political grievances" (ibid., 38), in Aido we see a young female protagonist who remains autonomous from Khurrana's character to a greater degree. Similarly, while the political commitments of Meghna, the female protagonist of *Dil Se*, are in some ways "reducible to her bodily identity," Aido, even as a boxer, never becomes reduced to her bodily identity in this way, retaining her personhood and expressing it forcefully in a variety of ways, not only physically but via voiceover and through the film's title song whose lyrics and energy become associated with her struggle and her aspirations. Aido is thus able to detach herself from Khurrana and succeed at both an individual and collective level as a female boxer from the Northeast representing India.

Nevertheless, despite such noteworthy elements, including its jettisoning of the conventional Bollywood form or, indeed, due to such cinematic choices, Sinha may have been right to note that *Anek* is "too political for any casual watch" (*Indian Express* 2022). While Sinha may have avoided the pitfalls Ratnam faced in trying to tell a political tale employing a Bollywood lexicon, sticking instead to what he set out to do without "add[ing] an unnecessary love angle" (Chopra 2022), *Anek* is arguably also a film that needs to be watched more than once in order to be fully grasped, not only due to its convoluted narrative but due to the convoluted history of the Northeast conflict and the average viewer's corresponding unfamiliarity with the region and its political struggles. That being said, *Anek* is, as one critic noted, "a welcome departure from the nationalistic jingoism that has ruled Hindi cinema and its box office in recent years" and, furthermore, a film that "spotlights Northeastern Indian stories" even as it "goes out of its way to refuse to condemn guerrilla fighters as terrorists" (Le 2022), a welcome departure from the handful of previous Bollywood films that have focused on the region, such as *Tango Charlie* (2005), which traffic in familiar tropes regarding this region and its peoples, framing the latter in a racist or derogatory manner even as the region's political concerns are essentially elided. Khurrana's growing evolution is on display not only via his character's political (re)education in *Anek* but, indeed, through the arc of his burgeoning career which has provided an impressive range of characters, from the naïve police officer of *Article 15*, to the queer pedagogue of *SMZS*, to *Anek*'s increasingly jaded undercover officer who continues questioning the foundations of Indian democracy even after the film has ended. The questions he poses are salient, particularly in light of the rising attacks and increasing incidents of "outright discrimination" against Christians during the Modi era

(Abdi 2023). In addressing such issues, which those in power may very well wish were left alone, Khurrana displays a willingness to engage with "traumatic occurrences of the modern" and an effectiveness in doing so (Chakrabarti 2020: 82). Suffice to say, there is clearly more to Khurrana's trajectory than mere sex comedies, as this versatile actor continues to provide compelling alternatives from the hinterlands of India and Bollywood to some of the more problematic contemporary trends on display in both.

Conclusion: The Modi Question

The two-part BBC documentary, *India: The Modi Question* (2023), which premiered on January 17 and 24, 2023, respectively, vividly shows, through compelling documentary footage, some of the key flashpoints informing Narendra Modi's tenure, both as chief minister of Gujarat (2001–14) and subsequently as prime minister of India (2014–present). These flashpoints include not only the controversial and wide scale attacks that took place against Muslims in Gujarat in 2002 but also more recent events including the abrogation of Article 370 in Kashmir, student protests against the government's Citizenship Amendment Act (CAA) and the ensuing heavy-handed attacks against demonstrators by the police, who raided universities and assaulted students. The documentary, which the Indian government called "a 'propaganda' film peddling a 'discredited narrative,'" was subsequently banned in India, demonstrating, among other things, Modi's sensitivity to images, particularly those casting him and his ruling Bharatiya Janata Party (BJP) in a negative light (Krishnan 2023).[1] The Modi question to Bollywood, meanwhile, is whether the latter can remain true to its defining spirit amidst the recent onslaught of Hindutva-ization that this study has chronicled, as well as whether it can engage in effective ways with the contemporary sociopolitical context. Perhaps the latter possibility remains a bridge too far (hence the advent of the *hatke* phenomenon) but even the first possibility—of remaining true to its defining (secular) spirit—seems equally challenging for Bollywood today. One day after the second part of *The Modi Question* premiered, Bollywood superstar Shah Rukh Khan (SRK)'s long-awaited return to the screen occurred with the release of *Pathaan* (2023), a big budget affair featuring several high profile Bollywood stars including SRK, Deepika Padukone and John Abraham. The film's release provides an interesting way to address these questions, which I would briefly like to do by way of concluding. It is worth noting, as many have, that SRK is in many ways the embodiment of Bollywood and thus *Pathaan* was seen not only as SRK's comeback (after a roughly four-year hiatus) but, indeed, as Bollywood's comeback, particularly in light of the recent success of films such as *The Kashmir Files* (2022).[2]

Before the film had even been released, controversy ensued following the pre-release of one of the film's songs, "Besharam Rang," which features SRK and Padukone dancing and lip synching, accompanied by numerous background dancers in a coastal Spanish setting. In keeping with a longstanding Bollywood tradition, SRK and Padukone both go through a number of costume changes during this brief (three minute) song sequence. Padukone's final outfit, an orange bikini dress, drew the ire of right-wing Hindus, who argued that the dress was saffron (a color associated with Hindutva) and, coupled with its skimpiness, was an affront to Hindu sensibilities. Even as the Indian Censor Board reviewed the film, SRK's effigy was burned by right-wing protestors who also, as is often the case, threatened to burn down any theatre that planned to screen the film (D. R. Chowdhury 2023: 75). SRK, as noted in the introduction, is unfortunately no stranger to such controversies which, in many ways, target him as the (secular, Muslim) embodiment of Bollywood. Resurrecting yet another contemporary trope, some Hindutva activists "even labeled the film as 'love jihad'" and "#BoycottPathaan" soon became a top trend on Twitter (K. Chowdhury 2023). As film critic Rahul Desai observed, the context surrounding the film could not be "divorced" from the film, in which

SRK plays the eponymous character, a government agent whose given name refers to a Muslim of Afghan origin (Sharma 2023). The film itself commences with the BJP-led government's abrogation of Article 370 in August 2019, which essentially stripped the state of Jammu and Kashmir, India's sole Muslim majority state, of the semi-autonomy it had since the 1950s.[3] When one of the film's villains, a rogue Pakistani general, hears of this decision, he decides to engage "the Devil," in this case, John Abraham's character, Jim, himself a former Indian solider who has subsequently grown disillusioned with the Indian state after it failed to pay a ransom to save his pregnant wife. In literally commencing with the abrogation of Article 370, we see how *Pathaan*, as a big budget Bollywood feature, is simultaneously concerned with one of the most controversial political decisions of Prime Minister Modi's second term. As in the first two features of Yash Raj Films' Spy Universe franchise, in which *Pathaan* is the most recent installment, SRK's character works with an operative of Pakistan's intelligence agency, in this case, Rubina Mohsin (Padukone) who, furthermore, as in the first two films of the franchise, becomes her Indian counterpart's love interest.[4]

For all of these reasons, as journalist Debasish Roy Chowdhury has observed, "by the time it was released, *Pathaan* had become less a film and more a civilizational test of India's multiculturalism" (2023: 75). Similarly, as film critic Desai notes, there is "no question" that *Pathaan* was written with SRK's "particular situation in mind"; as he goes on to point out, the "director and the writers all but admitted in interviews that *of course* it was made and designed around Shah Rukh Khan's comeback" (Sharma 2023, emphasis in original). This is also why, as Desai notes, if contemporary Hindutva forces wanted to "take down the idea of secularity," they had, in turn, to "take down the ultimate symbol of that as well," namely, SRK.[5] This is also why, particularly within a cinema as intertextual as Bollywood, there are several moments during the film in which "Pathaan, the hero, and Shah Rukh Khan, the actor, are almost indistinguishable" (K. Chowdhury 2023). *Pathaan* is not only about the eponymous character's resurrection and return to the fold, it is about SRK's similar return, following years of being attacked by the right-wing as a "Pakistani agent." Critics thus framed the ensuing popularity of the film as "pushback against the hate politics and the vitriolic hate agenda of the Hindu right-wing" BJP-led government (K. Chowdhury 2023) and, indeed, the film has gone on to become not only the most successful film at the Indian box office but indeed "the biggest film in the world, knocking down *Avatar: The Way of Water*, which had held the top spot for weeks" (Sharma 2023). Some critics also saw the film as "sort of subversive," in its casting of SRK (as "Pathaan") as the nation's hero, one who furthermore works with, rather than against, his Pakistani counterpart, played by Padukone (ibid.). All of this—SRK's conflation with Bollywood, his character as a secular Pathaan committed to protecting the nation, working (and, in turn, developing a romantic relationship) with his female Pakistani counterpart—would seem to be validated by the film's ensuing success and, in turn, may be seen as a repudiation of Hindutva discourses that have sought to frame both Bollywood and SRK as suspect. Yet, there are also tradeoffs, including SRK's adherence to a nationalist template, in which his character seems to outdo everyone as the uber patriot. If the success of *Pathaan* is seen as a "vindication," in other words, what precisely is being vindicated here?

This is where the particular form of *Pathaan* becomes relevant. Though featuring occasional Bollywood flourishes, for instance, in SRK's slow motion appearances, accompanied by triumphal music, in ensuing action sequences, such sequences, and the film overall, remain at heart committed to the action genre, part of a broader genrefication of the Bollywood form that dates back to the early twenty-first century, with one of John Abraham's first big hits, the motorcycle heist film, *Dhoom* (2004). SRK has also previously starred in such action-driven films, including the remake of *Don* (2006) and its sequel, *Don 2* (2011), through which one sees the ensuing diminution of the earlier Bollywood form and its simultaneous streamlining into the contours of the action genre.[6] The one song featured within the film itself, "Besharam Rang," which garnered so much advance controversy apparently due to the color and (lack of) coverage of Padukone's seventh costume in the sequence, is only approximately three minutes long. Yet beyond its number of costume changes, this shortened song sequence reveals even more salient issues that continue to inform the contemporary Bollywood playbook. Foremost among these are representations of (Hindu) women and, in turn, their interactions with (Muslim) men. India's Central Board of Film Certification (CBFC) issued a list of approximately a dozen requested modifications to be made to *Pathaan*, including several to "Besharam Rang," such as the removal of close-up shots of (Padukone's) "buttocks," "side pose (partial nudity)," and "sensuous dance movements" (Banerjee 2023). The CBFC requested that these, in turn, be replaced with "suitable shots" (ibid.). While there was speculation that the final moments featuring Padukone in her "saffron" attire would be excised altogether, shots of her in her orange outfit remained in the final version included in the film. Nevertheless, the sequence was modified and a handful of particular shots were removed from the final film version, including this one (Figure C.1).

FIGURE C.1 *Excised shot from "Besharam Rang" song, 2022. Source: Screenshot from "Besharam Rang Song," available online: https://www.youtube.com/watch?v=huxhqphtDrM (accessed May 6, 2023). Yash Raj Films.*

What the exclusion of this shot seems to suggest is that it is neither Padukone's costume nor its color so much as her bodily gestures—her moves—that are problematic for the patriarchal Hindutva mindset, particularly her physical coupling with SRK, the (Muslim) Pathaan. This is what makes the sequence "transgressive" to such (patriarchal, Hindutva) eyes: Padukone is sexually assertive and that, too, with a Muslim man. This is what triggers ensuing labels of "love jihad" by Hindutva activists, even as the image itself belies the logic informing such a trope, in which the Muslim man is purportedly the aggressor (cf. K. Chowdhury 2023). To be clear, then, women immolating themselves in order to escape the clutches of either Muslim or Christian men are not considered inflammatory but indeed noble (cf. Padukone in *Padmaavat* [2018], Ranaut in *Manikarnika* [2019], and Manushi Chhillar in *Samrat Prithviraj* [2022]). On the other hand, a Hindu woman dancing "sensuously," and with a Muslim, or Pathaan, in particular, while wearing a revealing orange dress, is considered "vulgar." In other words, a woman whose expression of desire culminates in her death is permissible, whereas expressions of female desire that do not result in death but only in artistic, sensuous poses (with a Muslim man), are impermissible. The invocation of "Indian culture" by Hindutva activists in objecting to such scenes becomes a club wielded against so-called unsuitable images, that is, of non-sacrificial female expressions of desire. Such images—of empowered and sexually expressive women—are disturbing to such viewers and framed, in turn, as "sexual perversions" (Ghosh and Kapur 2006: 94). What emerges as the enemy in such "controversies" are not only interfaith interminglings (particularly those of a "sensuous" nature) but women who refuse to appear passive and submissive. *Pathaan* has become a box office hit and, via its conflation with SRK, himself seen as "a symbol of secular Bollywood" (K. Chowdhury 2023: 4), is seen as the successful return of Bollywood, of its vindication over Hindutva forces bent on reshaping Bollywood in accordance with its own ideology, as we have seen throughout this study. Yet what is ultimately vindicated? And how much longer can SRK, now 58, continue to "save" Bollywood? As is revealed in the film's final reflexive exchange between SRK and fellow Muslim superstar Salman Khan, regarding who, if anyone, can take their place, there are no clear heirs apparent nor paths forward in the face of Hindutva forces and the ensuing Hindutva-ization of Bollywood. *Pathaan* has become a success but does its success portend the success of the erstwhile Bollywood form or its capitulation to a contemporary nationalist ethos in which each subsequent foray is an attempt to outdo the others in being the most patriotic?

SRK recently claimed that "what makes cinema" is "Amar, Akbar Anthony" (qtd in K. Chowdhury 2023). Yet that earlier, quintessential Bollywood film's climax commences with the film's title song which celebrates unity in diversity as the three estranged brothers—one Hindu, one Muslim, one Christian—fight together to uphold such erstwhile secular values of Bollywood and the nation. *Pathaan*, in turn, concludes with SRK saying "Jai Hind" (Hail Hindustan) as he watches Jim plummet to his death, then signing up for yet another mission, followed by a disconnected item song during the end credits. Who, or what, then, has won? Has the "King of Bollywood" also become coopted, as Bollywood arguably has, by the simultaneous upsurge of nationalism in film and this popular cinematic form's ensuing transformations? Is the King of Bollywood, in other words, still the King of "Bollywood"? Or has this latter form itself undergone such a change as to render it unrecognizable to erstwhile fans? These are questions that remain both salient and open. If, as one critic notes, box office numbers are, for better or worse, the "measuring stick for the conscience of the nation" (Sharma 2023), does the success of *Pathaan* signify the resurgence of (secular) Bollywood in the wake of (Hindu) nationalism, or its capitulation to the same? Is being "sort of subversive" sufficient? If both the content of *The Modi Question* and "India's censorial response" to it potentially function as a "wake-up call" (Steinfeld 2023: 1), what does *Pathaan*, replete with its own "modifications," function as? And is it sufficient if, as one film critic claims, "audiences may be consuming it without really realizing that it's not the kind of film they think it is" (Sharma 2023)?

NOTES

Introduction

1. Even Basu, by his own account, only provides "some sketches from Bollywood cinema" (2020: 201) which are quite cursory, only amounting to half a dozen pages (189–95) in the final chapter of his book.

2. Golwalkar also wanted a ban on the slaughter of cows, which he felt should be the "topmost priority" of the RSS campaign (Guha 2007: 624). This has increasingly become a rallying cry during the Modi era, which has seen a dramatic uptick of so-called cow vigilante groups who have increasingly targeted anyone suspected of killing cows.

3. The ur-text for Hindu–Muslim divisions in independent India is Partition (the partitioning of India, upon its independence, into the separate nations of India and Pakistan), during which up to 1 million people were "savagely murdered in riots that broke out all over north India" and up to 12 million people became refugees (Goldberg 2020: 134). As Goldberg notes, "the overwhelming social trauma of Partition remains a painful wound that continues to fester until today in the consciousness of the Indian nation" (ibid.). Godse feared Gandhi had given in to too many political demands of Muslims during Partition.

4. As Guha notes, "there is no evidence that the hero of the epic *Ramayan* was a historical person" (2007: 576).

5. As Gayatri Chakravorty Spivak has observed, *sati* means "good wife" (1988: 305). She also notes both "the nationalistic romanticization of the purity, strength, and love of these self-sacrificing women," and "the profound irony in locating the woman's free will in self-immolation" (ibid., 301, 303).

6. These two events also share a link, as Anand Patwardhan observes in his documentary, *Pitra, Putra, aur Dharmayuddha* (*Father, Son and Holy War*, 1995), as Ram's wife Sita is also forced to undergo a "trial by fire" by Ram to demonstrate her purity after rescuing her from the clutches of the demon king Ravana in the *Ramayan*. Sita's trial by fire is featured in the television serial.

7. Advani's Toyota was "fitted up to look like a rath (chariot)" for the journey and frequently stopped along the way to hold public meetings (Guha 2007: 626).

8. The Indian government conducted a study in the summer of 1992 and found that "flagrant violation of the law" was taking place in Ayodhya at this time (ibid., 628–9).

9   To return to a point political scientist Christophe Jaffrelot (2021) has made, Leidig also notes that "the Hindu Mahasabha [a Hindu nationalist political party founded in the early twentieth century] openly supported the Third Reich," and that "Savarkar, then president of the Hindu Mahasabha and close affiliate of the RSS, made continuous reference in writings and speeches to Germany's treatment of the Jewish population as a model for India's Muslim 'problem'" (2020: 222–3).

10 *Roja* was originally made in Tamil and later dubbed into Hindi.

11 The particular scene Bharucha has in mind comes near the end of the film, when the Hindu protagonist's Kashmiri / Muslim captors set the Indian flag on fire and the Hindu protagonist, Rishi Kumar, leaps onto the flag in an effort to douse the flames, his pants catching fire as he rolls on the ground in slow motion while Rahman's plangent soundtrack plays. Historian Nicholas Dirks claims that "the scene is framed, in a manner that seems clearly to set Islam against the principles of Indian nationalism, by shots of the main terrorist calmly praying to Allah" (2001: 161).

12 As film historian Sumita Chakravarty has observed, "The Bombay film has not so much addressed the Hindu–Muslim relationship as sublimated it by displacing it onto the canvas of history" (1993: 165).

13 Thackeray went on to call *Bombay* "a damned good film" (qtd in Vasudevan 2001: 198). An Indian film critic, writing at the time of the film's release, noted that "though the theme of communal conflict engulfs the film for nearly three fourths of its duration, there is no hint of the possibility of the entire episode in Bombay in 1993, having been an organized and planned pogrom against a minority" (qtd in Vasudevan 2001: 208n4). Also commenting on the film, screenwriter and lyricist Javed Akhtar stated, "If you make a film about Germans and Jews, and the Nazi party says it is a good film, then there must be something wrong" (1995: 30).

14 It was also during this period that explicit references to Pakistan began to be included in Bollywood films. According to film scholar Tejaswini Ganti, *Border* (1997) was one of the first Hindi films to include such a reference, explicitly naming Pakistan as the enemy (2013: 45).

15 As Chakravarty notes, "Concentrated within this metaphor [imperso-nation] are the notions of changeability and metamorphosis [...] Indian cinema [...] has made the drama of impersonation its distinctive signature" and one, furthermore that subsumes "the disavowal of fixed notions of identity" (1993: 4).

16 Kaul himself notes other films released during this period, including *Veer-Zaara* (2004) and *Main Hoon Na* (2004), which, despite ostensibly being "caught up in terrorism and warfare," nevertheless "try not to think of Pakistanis as villainous enemies" (2009: 193).

17 It is worth noting that the only "disclaimer" *Mughal-e-Azam* includes is the following statement: "History and Legend link the Story of our past. When both are fused in the

Crucible of art and Imagination, the spirit of this great Land is revealed in all its Splendour and Beauty."

18 "According to an official estimate, 13 million tickets are sold every day in the approximately 13,000 theatres nationwide, but the actual theatrical attendance may be around 26 million a day" (Pendakur 2003: 16).

19 According to a Central Board of Film Certification (CBFC) spokesman, CBFC members "suggest disclaimers only when a film has a historical/research-based/non-fiction premise [. . .] However it differs from case to case" (qtd in Lal 2019).

20 It is also worth noting that, as in the case of *Bajirao Mastani*, these increasingly lengthy disclaimers now not only appear onscreen but are simultaneously read aloud in Hindi voiceover. The disclaimer preceding *Jodhaa Akbar*, as Merivirta notes, did not prevent Rajput groups from demanding a ban on the film (2016: 462).

21 Pentecostals seek to be "filled with the Holy Spirit."

22 Though Srinivas claims that, "in general, the seeking out of a solitary movie experience is considered an anti-social and unnatural act," in India, she also notes that "men did admit to seeing movies by themselves," and that, in her own observances, she "routinely saw men at the theater who appeared to be alone" (2013: 381).

23 Discounting the five earliest statues erected before 1433 and considering only the seventy-one erected since Independence (1947), one sees a continual increase of monumental statues in India, nearly all of Hindu deities or leaders, over the ensuing decades, with the most, and the seventeen tallest, erected in the past twenty years (Jain 2021: Table FM.1). Furthermore, five of these seventeen statues have come since Modi took office, i.e., approximately 30 percent, thus belying Jain's claim to some extent.

24 "Investing leaders with divinity and magical powers," Pandian claims, "has a long tradition in Indian politics" (1992: 139).

25 As Vasudevan observes, "First [Modi's] speeches were shot, *then* the trucks went out; there is no reference to the streaming of the speech through satellite; but even if satellite streaming did take place, it would be streaming of *recorded, not live feed*" (2022: 381, emphasis in original).

26 While Rai includes descriptions of "poorly educated voters" who "stayed behind after rallies to check behind the dais to see if he [Modi] was really there" (2019: 323), Vasudevan includes a brief interview with Bollywood filmmaker Mani Shankar, who claims that audiences "are impressed by the hologram and they have a willing suspension of disbelief" (2022: 378).

27 It is not entirely clear how the authors' listed areas of specialization—management and finance—qualify them to make such an assessment.

28 After a fire broke out on a train carrying *kar servaks*, or Hindu volunteers, back from Ayodhya to Gujarat, in which fifty-eight people died, rumor spread that the fire was started by a Muslim mob and a "wave of retributory violence" ensued, in which over

2,000 Muslims were killed and at least 100,000 rendered homeless. As Guha notes, Hindu "vandals had lists of voters that allowed them to identify" Muslim homes and "ministers of the state government" directed these operations from police control rooms (2007: 647). Guha notes that this was only one of two actual pogroms committed in independent India and one "made possible by the wilful breakdown of the rule of law" (ibid., 648). Modi, who was Chief Minister of Gujarat at the time, subsequently compared the events to a puppy being run over by a car (Gottipati and Banerji 2013).

29 After a song and dance number from the film *Pathaan* (2023) was pre-released in December 2022, BJP leaders objected to its picturization, calling Padukone's performance while wearing a "saffron" dress and dancing with SRK, offensive to Hindu religious sentiments and threatening to block the film's release (*Times of India* 2022b). Subsequently, a Hindu seer from Ayodhya threatened to burn "Jihadi Shah Rukh Khan" alive, as well as any theatre that shows the film (ibid., 2022c).

30 While previously Guha felt India was a "*phipty-phipty* [50-50]" democracy, more recently he has stated, "I don't think India has any plausible claim to being the world's largest democracy anymore" (2007: 738; Agrawal 2022).

Chapter 1

1 Sumita Chakravarty has noted that, "Bombay film has not so much addressed the Hindu–Muslim relationship as sublimated it by displacing it onto the canvas of history" (1993: 165).

2 In *Goya's Ghosts*, Forman could be seen as invoking the Spanish Inquisition and its employment of torture to speak to the contemporary sanctioning of torture by the administration of George W. Bush during the so-called "War on Terror."

3 In some ways, this is similar to what Grant Farred, in his discussion of *Lagaan* (2001), calls a "double temporality" (2004: 99).

4 In describing cinematic spectatorship in an Indian context, Ravi Vasudevan claims that the spectator is provided with "certain conditions of knowledge" which "immerses the spectator in a play with the image of the social" (2010: 137).

5 Mediation, in this sense, entails "the relationship between the levels or instances"—in this case, between the two timeframes of *BM*—"and the possibility of adapting analyses and findings from one level to another" (Jameson 1981: 39).

6 The classic earlier instance of a film which directly addressed contemporary Hindu–Muslim strife, and consequently generated a huge amount of controversy, is Mani Ratnam's *Bombay* (1995), about the riots that ensued in 1992–3, following the destruction by Hindus of the Babri Masjid in Ayodhya.

7   As Mastani's father notes, she worships Allah and Krishna alike. In some ways, it is precisely such syncretism which is feared and repudiated by Hindus, including Bajirao's mother and the Hindu priest Krishna Bhatt, both of whom insist on essentializing Mastani as "Muslim" and (thus) essentially an "outsider."

8   This lady, Maya Kodnani, was the BJP MLA for Naroda who, according to eyewitnesses, got out of her car and told the Hindu mobs to "kill them," i.e., the Muslims. Kodnani and Bajrangi were both subsequently sentenced to life in prison for their actions (Marino 2014: 114).

9   Togadia, whose statements were tape-recorded, urged followers to "create an atmosphere of riot and spit on the [Muslim] family to get them to move out" (Manor 2015: 749).

10 As Manor notes, "Modi's usual response when Hindu extremists engage in provocative rhetoric and actions is silence" (ibid., 753).

11 Modi first addressed the killing of Ikhlaq approximately two weeks after the event had occurred (Barstow and Raj 2015).

12 Here again, we see the parallel to contemporary efforts by Hindu chauvinists under Modi's tenure to "polarise society along religious lines" (Manor 2015: 748). As Manor observes, one Hindu extremist, who was subsequently awarded a ministerial post under Modi, claimed during the 2014 election campaign that "the place for those who oppose Modi was Pakistan" (ibid.). Cf. also the attacks on SRK who, upon noting the growing intolerance in India under Modi, was labeled a "Pakistani agent" by BJP leaders (see Sahadevan 2015).

13 When Bajirao hears of Mastani's imprisonment by his own son, Nana Saheb, and declares his intention to go and release her, his lieutenant incredulously replies, "You will fight against your own family? You will turn against us for that Muslim?" Here again, we see the notion of fighting for the rights of (Indian) Muslims as betraying one's "own" country and people, a sentiment frequently enunciated by members of the BJP and the Hindu right.

14 Though he previously asserted that there was "growing intolerance" in India, in the wake of the backlash his comments faced from Hindu nationalists, Khan subsequently claimed that he never said India was intolerant (*Hindustan Times* 2015).

15 See Vasudevan (2001) and also Rangan (2012) for more regarding the controversies surrounding *Bombay*.

16 As Karen Gabriel has noted, "The control of the Thackeray family over the Bombay film industry is well known and accepted now as part of cinematic imperatives" (2010: 274).

17 It is precisely the fraught nature of these relations, however, that sets *BM* apart from *Jodhaa Akbar*, a film made after the defeat of the BJP in the 2004 general election, which "presents a post-Hindutva nation-building narrative advocating Hindu–Muslim harmony" (Merivirta 2016: 472).

18 Board members insisted on a disclaimer clearly stating that the film did not claim historical accuracy, nor subscribe to the practice of *sati*. The covering up of Padukone's midriff in the "Ghoomar" song, which Board chairman Prasoon Joshi called a "modification," was demanded in order "to make the depiction befitting the character being portrayed" (Reuters 2017). The request for the change to the title itself was allegedly to more accurately reflect the source material for the film, Jayasi's *Padmaavat*.

19 Film scholars David Bordwell and Kristin Thompson have also emphasized this point more generally, noting that, "very often people assume that 'form' as a concept is the opposite of something called 'content,'" an assumption they reject in their ensuing observation that "there is no inside or outside" and that "every component *functions as part of the overall pattern* that is perceived" (2003: 50, emphasis in original).

20 In an interview in late 2013, for instance, Bhansali stated, "Narendra Modi has something magical about him. I am enamoured by the nation being obsessed with him. [...] I need to be inspired. I need to follow you" (qtd in Gupta 2013).

21 In the contemporary Indian context, one might see here an instance of what Britta Ohm calls the "Modi-fication of democratic discourse," which engages in a form of "medialisation," i.e., the "increasing merging of mediated representations and social and political reality" (2011: 130).

22 Just as Riefenstahl utilized "16 cameramen, 135 technicians, and a rally stage-managed by Third Reich architect Albert Speer" in making *Triumph* (Tomasulo 2014: 84), Bhansali is equally renowned for the over-the-top nature of both his spectacles and his modes of promoting them, including assembling over 5,000 students from across India to create the biggest human formation of a mosaic image of Lord Ganesha, as part of his launch of the "Gajanana" song from *Bajirao Mastani* (YouTube 2015).

23 Sontag goes on to make a key point which is worth reiterating here and which this discussion of *Padmaavat* in many ways demonstrates, namely, that "such [fascist] art is hardly confined to works labeled as fascist or produced under fascist governments" (1980: 91). That being said, one may very well find, following Tomasulo's approach, a confluence between (fascist) text and (fascist) context, particularly given the context in which *Padma(a)vat(i)* was realized (and "modi-fied").

24 What one *doesn't* see in this sequence, as noted before, is Padukone's midriff, which was digitally covered up due to the CBFC's concerns of propriety, a point to which we shall return in the ensuing section. Ratan Singh's gaze, meanwhile, can be seen as a proxy for the omniscient gaze of Hindutva groups, e.g., those protesting Padukone's / Padmavati's exposed navel.

25 One would be remiss not to note the synchronic parallel the film invokes between Khilji's invading troops, marching under their black flags, and ISIS forces today, who similarly speak of reinstating a caliphate. Such Islamophobic imagery can also be seen in Khilji's "Khalibali" song, which at times resembles an ISIS promotional music video.

26 Cf. the particularly prevalent motif in Hindi films of "burning" in and for love, a sentiment more often than not enunciated by female figures.

27 As Schmid notes, "The average citizen had to be attracted by the beautiful spectacle and to be bound by ritual" (2005: 138). Or, in Qureshi's words, "Bhansali has given India's marketplace and current Hindu political classes precisely the kind of film they wanted" (2018: 49). The film's enormous box office success becomes particularly relevant here.

28 The only character who gets to dance irreverently is Khiji, in the previously noted "Khalibali" song. It is hard to avoid noticing the correlation (and ongoing Manichaean structuring) here, between dancing unabashedly and being immoral, on the one hand, and moving demurely (even if in a dance of death) and being morally superior, on the other.

29 It is one thing to romanticize Devdas' death but quite another to romanticize—indeed, ritualize—*jauhar*. Even the more palpable fascist aesthetic of *Bajirao Mastani* is tempered by its arguably subversive content, i.e., its metatextual critique of Hindutva.

Chapter 2

1 As film scholar Tutun Mukherjee has observed, Kumar "has taken special efforts to reflect an earthy quality and certain degree of 'ordinariness'" in his performances (2020: 209). These elements, as we will see, become key to Kumar's subsequent success as "the poster boy for Indian patriotism" (qtd in Mitra 2021: 289).

2 Though in the film Kumar's character is supposed to be 36, Kumar was actually 50 at the time while Pednekar was 28. Even as a 36-year-old, Keshav's older age causes at least some initial concern for Jaya's parents.

3 Following a disclaimer, the film begins with the following statement: "We are thankful to the team of Swachh Bharat Mission Gramin for their tireless efforts towards creating an India free from open defecation."

4 As Rao notes, "Open defecation causes huge costs to India's social and economic development," and has been "detrimental to the health and well-being of millions of people exposed to decomposing human waste in public spaces" (2019: 87).

5 As Rao observes, *Toilet* "met key criteria such as advocating patriotism and a social message that deemed it worthy of tax exemption" (2019: 81).

6 As Meskell goes on to note, 500 million people still defecate in the open in India, i.e., roughly half the entire population (2021: 153).

7 As Meskell observes, "Single or twin pit latrines ... once filled up, need to be cleaned out manually" (ibid.).

8 "Today for the world we're the tailender, tomorrow we can become opening batsman" (my translation).

9 As one film reviewer notes, Rupert is presented as "a caricaturish villain ... with an unholy accent," which illuminates the film's overall Manichaean structure, pitting good (read: native) Indians who engage in *jugaad* and are more authentic in their indirect speech, against bad (read: NRI) Indians who worship the West and, correspondingly, speak "unholy" Hindi (Sen 2020b).

10 "In less than it takes Hollywood to make a film, we reached Mars!" (my translation).

11 See Chapter 1 for a further discussion of *Padmaavat*.

12 As political scientist Christophe Jaffrelot observes, "For the Sangh Parivar, Hindus are—and have always been—victims of external assailants" (2008: 5). Such a discourse is not unique to Hindus in India today—one could also point to (white/ Christian) Trump supporters in the US today who increasingly claim to be "under siege" from "un-American" forces. The irony here is that those who feel they are increasingly "under siege" (from invaders who want to destroy their country) are the ones who invaded the Capitol on January 6, 2021, just as Hindus stormed the Babri Masjid on December 6, 1992.

13 Though Kumar invokes honor and duty and, in his typical deadpan voice, taunts the Pathan leader for bringing 10,000 men to fight 21, he also engages in subterfuge during the ensuing battle, placing concealed explosives on two captured Pathans, then returning them, gagged and bound, to the Pathan leader, so that when the hidden explosives detonate, they kill many of the other Pathans as well.

14 Cf. *Padmaavat*, *Panipat* (2019), and *Samrat Prithviraj* (2022), among others, as additional contemporary instances of such "normative nationalist texts."

15 That *Kesari* was released in the spring of 2019, coinciding with Holi, and *Mission Mangal* on Independence Day, August 15, does not override the broader shift I am tracing here, which is fed by, even as it feeds into, Kumar's elastic star text, capable of easily moving from one role to the next, one genre to the other, whether *desi* scientist or Sikh warrior, in collaboration with one or the other government initiative.

16 The previous films in this franchise are *Singham* (2011), *Singham Returns* (2014), and *Simmba* (2018), all of which, like *Sooryavanshi*, were blockbusters at the box office.

17 For more regarding these events, see the Introduction.

18 Ahmed says "Uun logon," i.e., "those people."

19 "First the 1993 serial bomb blast [in Bombay], then the 2002 Ghatkopar bus blast, in 2006, a train blast, and then Taj 26/11," the terrorist attacks on the Taj Hotel and other sites in Bombay in 2008.

20 Some of these elided attacks on Muslims include the 2002 pogrom in Gujarat, the Malegaon blasts of 2006, which killed Muslims after Friday prayers, and the 2008 Malegaon blasts, in which retired Indian army officers were implicated (Ayyub 2021).

21 According to Ayyub (ibid.), each time Kumar's character "sermonizes the Indian Muslim to fall in line, the audience in the theater where I saw the film [in India] whistled and applauded."

22 As Menon (2021) notes, "the only Muslims shown offering namaz are the terrorists."

23 The song's title translates to "Forget Yesterday's Issues."

24 Shetty's previous film in his Cop Universe series, *Simmba*, also ends with such a police "encounter," i.e., extrajudicial killing.

25 Though work on this project began under the Congress-led government in 2005–6, it was actually the BJP-led coalition government that, in 2004, "approved a 3,500 crore rupees budget to create a shipping channel" at the site of the Ram Setu (Jaffrelot 2008: 3). The film elides this detail by situating the story in 2007.

26 See the Introduction for a further discussion of the Hindutva gaze and the related concept of *darsan*.

27 It is worth noting here, as historian Ramachandra Guha has, that there is "no evidence that the hero of the epic Ramayan was a historical person" (2007: 576).

28 Another critic describes the arguments the film makes as "half-baked theories about India's past . . . that sound more like ill-informed pronouncements of a vote-seeking politician" (Chatterjee 2022).

29 In 2019, the Indian Supreme Court rendered a unanimous decision, giving the land where the Babri Masjid once stood to Hindu parties (Gangopadhyay 2023: 107).

30 As film critic Nandini Ramnath (2022) notes, of *Ram Setu*, "Aryan is deeply disturbed by the burning of the Jaffna Public Library in 1981, along with the blowing up of the Bamiyan Buddhas. About the destruction of another monument in India in 1992, Aryan, and the film, have nothing to say."

Chapter 3

1 These include *I Love NY* (2015), *Rangoon* (2017), *Simran* (2017), *Thalaivii* (2021), and *Dhaakad* (2022).

2 In a television interview in 2020, Ranaut said that India had won its true independence in 2014, when Modi was first elected Prime Minister, and not in 1947 (Konnikara 2022).

3 It is worth noting the contemporary Bollywood ecumene, in which such "film industry children" often have to undergo Hindi voice lessons and, in turn, mock Ranaut for her lack of "polished" English.

4 In her subsequent tweet, Ranaut stated, "This terrorist is porn singer @rihanna's friend ... he is accused of funding terroristic activities. There is a Khalistan in his head also. A porn star followed him and that's his biggest achievement" (DNA 2021).

5 Though Kumar frequently aligns himself with Modi and the BJP government on nationalist and social schemes, a more "nakedly political statement" of the kind Ranaut frequently deploys seems "off-brand" for him (Dore 2021). For more regarding Kumar's endorsements of Modi and the BJP, see Chapter 2.

6 Ranaut was permanently suspended from Twitter in May 2021, after the Trinamool Congress Party (TMC) defeated the BJP and swept elections in West Bengal. In a tweet following this election, Ranaut said the state's chief minister, Mamata Banerjee, was "like an unleashed monster," and called upon "Modi ji" to "please show your Virap roop from the early 2000s" to "tame her" (qtd in Konikkara 2022). As Konikkara (ibid.) notes, "Virat roop" is a reference to the majestic form the Hindu god Krishna took in the battle of Kurukshetra in the *Mahabharata*, while the allusion to "the early 2000s" is a thinly veiled reference to the anti-Muslim pogroms that took place in Gujarat when Modi was the state's chief minister.

7 The Doctrine of Lapse stipulated that any Indian territory would fall under British control if the ruler died without producing an heir. Khilnani describes this doctrine as "a typically British form of colonial legal brigandage—thievery sanctified by conversion into a doctrine" (2016: 168).

8 The precise age of both Manikarnika and Gangadhar Rao is hard to pinpoint. While most Indian historians list the former's date of birth as 1835, British records list her birth as occurring in 1827 (Singh 2014: 12). Khilnani, in turn, lists her year of birth as 1828 (2016: 165). We shall see how this issue is treated by subsequent film adaptations.

9 Though *Jhansi Ki Rani* is credited as being India's first Technicolor film (Singh 2014: 123), the only Technicolor version I have come across is the shortened English language version, titled *The Tiger and the Flame*.

10 While Singh describes this as a "montage of scenes," it could more accurately be described as a lap dissolve, that is, "a transition between two shots during which the first image gradually disappears while the second image gradually appears; for a moment the two images blend in superimposition" (Bordwell and Thompson 2003: 502).

11 The problematic nature of the ensuing age gap is arguably reinforced by the casting of actor Milind Gunaji in the role of Gangadhar Rao. A decade prior, Gunaji famously appeared as Kalibabu in Sanjay Leela Bhansali's *Devdas* (2002), in which his character is an upper class patron of the *kotha*, or harem, where (young) courtesans perform for the pleasure of men. This connotation of depravity arguably carries through here, at least for viewers familiar with Bhansali's blockbuster film, and inflects the child marriage with a sinister undertone. Gunaji also went on to play Gangadhar in a subsequent film version of the Rani's life, *The Warrior Queen of Jhansi*, released in 2019.

12 Adding to the irony, the name of this song is "Ishq hai javaan" (Love is Young).

13 Though both Jagarlamudi and Ranaut are attributed as directors of the film, I will continue to refer to Ranaut as the film's auteur, given that she replaced Jagarlamudi as director and apparently reshot several portions of the film in accordance with her own vision. After being removed as director Jagarlamudi subsequently tweeted, "I never thought I've to defend my ability of film making based on the manipulations and lies of one person" (qtd in Konikkara 2022).

14 The film's disclaimer notes that, "cinematic liberties have been sought and certain elements have been fictionalized for dramatization purposes." Simultaneously, the disclaimer notes that "references" for the film have been "vetted by our Historian consultants Prof. (Retd) S.P. Pathak head Of history department, Bundelkhand University & Prof. (Retd) Ramakant Verma." Nevertheless, the disclaimer's second paragraph begins by noting that "this film does not claim historical authenticity." We will return to the content of this disclaimer later in our discussion.

15 Jisshu Sengupta, the actor who plays Gangadhar in *Manikarnika*, was 41 at the time while Ranaut was 31, an age gap far exceeded by that between Baby Shikha, the child actor playing young Manu in *Jhansi Ki Rani*, and Mubarak, who played Gangadhar when he was 52, and by that between the child actress playing the young Manu in *Laxmibai* and Gunaji, who played Gangadhar when he was 51.

16 Making the owner of the baby calf a Dalit woman also functions as a form of Hindutva propaganda, paradoxically utilizing the revered animal as a way of patching over caste divisions, e.g., between the Brahmin Rani and the Dalit Jhalkari, who unsurprisingly goes on to become one of the Rani's most devoted supporters.

17 The saffron color is associated with Hindutva movements. Cf. both *Padmaavat* (2018), discussed in Chapter 1, and *Kesari* (2019), discussed in Chapter 2, for additional instances of such motifs, e.g., the fort under siege, and the "saffronization" of the ensuing battles.

18 Khilnani, "looking down from the battlements of Jhansi fort, at the place where a big metal sign marks the spot of the legendary jump," claims one "might feel a bit of vertigo" given the height (2016: 166). The film, however, does not show us the leap from the Rani's point of view, instead framing it in long shot from a low angle perspective.

19 "Mahadev" is a reference to the Hindu god Shiva, the remover of obstacles. Framing a war against British imperialism as a holy war is a particularly compelling instance of the simultaneous Hindutva-ization and "presentification" of Indian history. Whereas the earlier *Jhansi Ki Rani* features cries of "Har har mahadev" intermixed with "Allah o Akbar," thus conveying the "plurality and tolerance of the Hindu and the Muslim war cry" (Singh 2014: 127), in *Manikarnika* all we hear is the Hindu war cry.

20 See Chapter 1 for a discussion of *Padmaavat* and its culminating *jauhar*.

21 In responding to the Karni Sena's threats to protest against her film, Ranaut stated, "If they don't stop, they should know I am also a Rajput and I will destroy each one of them" (qtd in Konikkara 2022).

22 "There are," as Spivak goes on to observe, "female suicide bombers" (1999: 297). We see an instance of this in *Manikarnika* when the Rani's Dalit follower Jhalkari creates a ruse, letting the invading British troops believe she is actually the Rani and then exploding a bomb strapped to her when they surround her.

23 *Padmaavat*'s disclaimer states that the film "does not intend to encourage or support 'Sati' or such other practices."

24 *Samrat Prithviraj*'s disclaimer also claims that the film does not intend to "support, encourage or glorify 'Sati', 'Jauhar', or other such practices."

25 Comments on the YouTube page for "Yoddha," which has been viewed over 52 million times to date, include statements of praise for the actress and the female playback singer, including one that begins with "Goosebumps," followed by a heart emoji and the ensuing question, "What better could one ask for"? (available online: https://www.youtube.com/watch?v=uXS3sZdB2-I, accessed May 6, 2023).

26 If one critic wondered about "the impressionable viewer who ends up believing that Manikarnika rode a horse off the edge of a fortress and survived what appears to be a 30ft fall" (Bhatia 2019: 13), one can only wonder what impact Ranaut's concluding celebratory *jauhar* might have on viewers.

27 Ranaut claims that she was "fascinated by the power dynamics that came into play at the time," which "changed the way we view power," and which, in turn, was why she decided to make the film (qtd in *Hindustan Times* 2023).

28 Indira Gandhi did indeed take to All India Radio on the morning of June 26, 1975, announcing, "The President has declared Emergency. There is nothing to panic about" (qtd in Guha 2007: 491).

29 The producers of another film, *Ganapath*, directed by Vikas Bahl and starring Tiger Shroff and Amitabh Bachchan, have announced plans to release their film on October 20 (*Indian Express* 2023). Bahl previously directed Ranaut in *Queen*, one of her most successful films.

30 Cf. note 1 for a further listing of Ranaut's recent flops.

31 These include "the weakening, if not evisceration," of five crucial institutions: the political party ("Since 2014 ... Modi has established his total and complete authority over the BJP"); the Union Cabinet ("in India today there is no consultation within the Union Cabinet. What Modi says, goes"); the press (including "Prime-time TV," which "exuberantly praises the prime minister and relentlessly attacks the opposition," with "many independent-minded journalists ... jailed"); the bureaucracy ("whatever independence and autonomy that remained have been completely sundered" since 2014, with "95 percent of all politicians raided or arrested by the Central Bureau of Investigation since 2014" being from opposition parties); and the judiciary (according to the legal scholar Anuj Bhuwania, "During the Modi regime, not only has the [Supreme] court failed to perform its constitutional role ... it has acted as a cheerleader for the Modi government's agenda") (Guha 2022).

Chapter 4

1. Along with Chadha's film, Kher has appeared in ten additional English-language films, arguably making him one of the most prolific Indian actors to appear in non-Indian films and, in turn, earning him the moniker of "Hollywood's favourite desi" (Bamzai 2019). This split—between the Kher that "New York's liberals fete" and the one "Indian liberals abhor"—becomes a key component informing his diffuse star text (ibid.).

2. In February 2016, Kher, in a Twitter post, compared JNU student leaders Kanhaiya Kumar and Umar Khalid to "cockroaches and vermin that need purging from people's home[s]" and argued for a nationwide "pest control" program (Ghoshal 2017).

3. Bernert, who lives in India, previously played Sonia Gandhi on the Indian television series *7 RCR* (2014).

4. Swaraj, who had "campaigned vociferously against an Italian-origin prime minister," in turn, "dramatically threaten[ed] to shave her head" if Sonia became PM (Baru 2014: 4).

5. As Baru notes, Singh, who received a doctorate in economics from Oxford University and served as the finance minister in the early 1990s, "made history by becoming the first prime minister from a minority [Sikh] community" (2014: xiii).

6. While Singh does indeed have a soft-spoken voice, Kher's characterization of it is an exaggerated one, as are other elements, most notably his manner of walking.

7. Though very knowledgeable, C-3PO was also framed as an effeminate buffoon. Kher, in turn, is described by one critic as "minc[ing] through the film" (Gupta 2019) and one can draw parallels to some of Kher's earlier comic roles in which he similarly performs in an affected manner and, in turn, is framed as an object of ridicule (cf. *Ram Lakhan*).

8. As film scholar Donald Bogle observes, when Colbert's Miss Bea proposes Delilah have her own car and home, Delilah responds, "My own house? You gonna send me away, Miss Bea? I can't live with you? Oh, honey chile, please don't send me away" (2007: 57). When subsequently asked if she does not want her own home, Delilah replies, "No'm. How I gonna take care of you and Miss Jessie if I ain't here," adding, "I'se your cook. And I want to stay your cook" (ibid.). Here, we can see a parallel in *Accidental PM*'s presentation of Singh as beholden to Miss Sonia and Mr. Rahul, as well as how such submissiveness functions as justification for his ensuing exploitation, if not as a cook then as a PM. As Singh tells Baru both in the latter's book and near the end of the film, "I have come to terms with this. There cannot be two centres of power. That creates confusion. I have to accept that the party president is the centre of power" (2014: 270).

9. This framing—Sonia seated at Singh's hospital bedside and looking down at him—further conveys both the latter's weakened state and the former's position of power. And this look—looking down her nose, as it were, at Singh—becomes particularly associated with Sonia, arguably functioning as yet another instance of her vilification in/by the film.

10 Indira Gandhi's Emergency lasted from 1975–7, during which time "thousands were arrested under the Maintenance of Internal Security Act (MISA), known by its victims as the Maintenance of Indira and Sanjay Act," referring to an earlier mother–son duo who imperiously governed the Congress Party (Guha 2007: 492). For more regarding the Emergency, see Chapter 3.

11 This scene conflates two moments: a 2013 press conference regarding this UPA ordinance in which Rahul said it should be "torn up and thrown out," and an earlier (2012) rally in Lucknow, where he tore up a list of alleged promises made to other parties. Ironically enough, Gandhi was given a two-year jail sentence in March 2023 (for defaming Modi in a speech) and, due to this sentence and the absence of the earlier ordinance, expelled from Parliament, per the provisions of the 2012 Supreme Court ruling (cf. Baru 2014: 282–3).

12 See Chapter 3 for further discussion of Ranaut's forthcoming *Emergency*.

13 The Rashtriya Swayamsevak Sangh (RSS) is a right-wing Hindu nationalist organization and progenitor of other such groups including the BJP.

14 The film's critique of Professor Menon and of "ANU," clearly meant to stand in for "JNU" (Jawaharlal Nehru University), is in keeping with the BJP's broader attacks on this and other "left-leaning" universities. See Jaffrelot (2021: 176–83).

15 In light of the frequent invocations by characters of the term "genocide" to describe the plight of Hindu Pandits in *The Kashmir Files*, it is worth noting the title of Farooqi's writ petition, *Kashmir Holocaust* (1992) cited in Hussain (2021: 343).

16 It is worth noting that this National Front (NF) coalition government was supported by the BJP. See Chowdhury (2022).

17 Nevertheless, the totals listed by other sources not only generally cohere with the official figures cited by Kak but similarly reveal a sizable difference from "the figures conjured up by the right-wing" (Kak 2022). According to historian Ramachandra Guha, "several hundred Pandits" were killed during 1989–90 (2007: 642). Journalist Debasish Roy Chowdhury describes the number of Pandits killed as being "in the low hundreds," per related figures provided by both the government and Kashmiri Pandit organizations, rather than "the thousands" claimed by the film (2022). Similarly, with regard to the number of Pandits who left the Kashmir Valley, Guha approximates it as being "at least" 100,000 (2007: 642); which is much closer to the figure cited by Kak than it is to those invoked during "inflamed television debates," which even go up to a million.

18 As Kak (2022) notes, a massacre took place in Nadimarg in 2003, in which twenty-four men, women, and children were killed. Similarly, Guha cites reports documenting a woman being bisected by a mill saw during the violence of 1989–90 (2007: 642).

19 *The Kashmir Files* was the third highest grossing film in India in 2022. While its commercial success may be due in part to both Modi's plug, as well as related tax breaks for the film and paid holidays for government employees to attend screenings

(Raj 2022), we must also try to better understand how and why such a brutal film speaks to a contemporary Indian audience.

20 At a private White House screening, President Woodrow Wilson stated, "It is like writing history with lightning, and my only regret is that it is all so true" (qtd in Loewen 2007: 21). Cf. Modi's statement that *The Kashmir Files* "has shown the truth" (qtd in Kak 2022). As sociologist James Loewen notes, Griffith "would go on to use this quotation in successfully defending his film against NAACP [National Association for the Advancement of Colored People] charges that it was racially inflammatory" (2007: 21).

21 Shandilya is referring to the character of Alauddin Khilji in Sanjay Leela Bhansali's *Padmaavat* (2018). See Chapter 1 for a further discussion of this character and film.

22 Just as miscegenation is fetishized in *Birth*, the trope of "love jihad," the notion that Muslim men seduce Hindu women to convert them to Islam, is frequently invoked in *The Kashmir Files*, e.g., the older Muslim teacher's proposal to Sharda.

23 One sees the same vivid contrast, between the "pale beauty" of the white heroine and the "big black arms" of the menacing buck (Bogle 2007: 14) when the dark-skinned Farooq rips off Sharda's blouse from behind, revealing the pale white skin of her bare back. The sexual violence underlying this act is paradoxically enhanced by Farooq's previous denial of culpability to Krishna, when he claims that Sharda "was like a sister to me" and, in turn, by his earlier statement to Sharda, upon forcing her to eat the bloodstained rice in his outstretched hand, that, had Pushkar not been his teacher, he would have taken her for a bride.

24 Kak describes a man "wearing the saffron robes of a Hindu preacher" waving such a trident, a "traditional weapon of Hindu gods, inside a cinema following the screening of *The Kashmir Files* and telling the audience as he gestures to the screen with said trident, "You have all seen what happened to the Kashmiri Hindus … That is why Hindus must protect themselves against the treachery of Muslims and prepare to take up arms" (2022).

25 In describing viewers' reactions to such sequences, in which people are alternately presented with filmed images of allies and enemies of the state, Orwell notes "uncontrollable exclamations of rage" breaking out "from half the people in the room," when confronted with images of the latter, followed by people "leaping up and down in their places and shouting" (1950: 15). Cf. Bogle's descriptions of how *Birth* was calculated to "work audiences into a frenzy" and often ended up doing so (2007: 15).

26 Kashmiri Pandits observe January 19 as their "Holocaust Day," dating their exodus from the Kashmir Valley to this one day in 1990 (Kak 2022). Though Kher comes from a Kashmiri Pandit family, he himself was born in Shimla.

27 As early as 2015, Kher was publicly calling for the revocation of Article 370 and the resettlement of Kashmiri Pandits (Sharma 2015).

28 Describing her film, Riefenstahl said, "It is *history—pure history*" (qtd in Tomasulo 2014: 84). See Chapter 1 for a further discussion of *Triumph of the Will* in relation to Bollywood.

Chapter 5

1. The Badaun case involved two lower-caste teenage girls who disappeared in the eponymous town in Uttar Pradesh and whose bodies were subsequently found hanging from a tree the following morning. Though an investigation by the Central Bureau of Intelligence (CBI) concluded they had not been raped, the Protection of Children Against Sexual Offences (POCSO) court subsequently rejected the CBI report (Dubey 2018).

2. The term Dalit, which means "oppressed," is the preferred term of lower castes formally designated "untouchables" (Jaffrelot 2021: 2). In official parlance, they are referred to as "Scheduled Castes" (SC).

3. Sayani Gupta, who plays this young woman, Gaura, also provides the female playback for this rendition of the popular folk song, "Kahab toh lag jayee dhak se."

4. The score for the Hollywood thriller *Sicario* (2015) is by Icelandic composer Johann Johannson, who received an Academy Award for the score. *Article 15*'s background score is composed by Mangesh Dhakde, who has composed the scores for all four of Sinha's most recent films.

5. "Nirbhaya," meaning "fearless" in Hindi, was the name given by the Indian press to Jyoti Singh Pandey who, while returning home on a bus with a male friend on the night of December 12, 2012, was brutally beaten and gang-raped by five assailants on the bus as it drove around the outskirts of the nation's capital. Pandey subsequently died of her injuries. As film scholar Sangita Gopal has noted, news of the incident "spread like wildfire" and provoked "large-scale and nationwide protests and demonstrations" (2021: 43).

6. One instance of such knowingness is the frequent invocation of the Badaun case in reviews of *Article 15*.

7. This line as well as other broader elements summon what could be considered an ur-text for *Article 15*, Alan Parker's 1988 Hollywood thriller, *Mississippi Burning*, similarly based on the true story of killings—in this case of three civil rights workers in the eponymous state during the 1960s—and whose young, naïve protagonist, an FBI agent played by Willem Dafoe, similarly says, "What is wrong with these people?" after coming across yet another brutal scene of carnage at the (invisible) hands of the local white community. Sen (2020a) refers to *Article 15* as a "stirring tribute" to Parker's film. For more regarding parallels between caste-ism and racism in India and the United States, see Isabel Wilkerson's study, *Caste: The Origins of Our Discontents* (2020).

8. Nishad sees this promotion of inter-caste unity, engineered by the Brahmin politician Mahantji, as disingenuous. "Mahant" is a term for a religious superior or head of a Hindu temple or religious organization. We shall return to Mahantji shortly.

9. Nevertheless, even as the crosscutting in this scene creates the illusion of a dialogue between these two (Dalit Nishad and Brahmin Mahant), it is important to note the

asymmetrical nature of their respective "speech acts," with Mahantji's words expressed openly and publicly (and literally amplified) while Nishad's remain relegated to his thoughts, heard only by the viewer.

10   The CBI inspector is referring to the theory propagated by the police and the CBI inspector's team, that the two girls were murdered by their fathers upon being discovered in a lesbian relationship. We previously see the two Dalit fathers being coerced by the CBI inspector and his aides into recording such a confession, after which they are jailed.

11   One can imagine how, e.g., Akshay Kumar, a la *Sooryavanshi* (2021), would handle such a role. See Chapter 2 for a further discussion of this more conventional Bollywood hero and the equally more conventional Bollywood blockbuster, featuring police officers who engage both in "encounters" and accompanying celebratory song and dance numbers.

12   Anwer and Arora characterize this gesture by Gaura as a "grave error" on the part of the film, as it "undermines the film's self-espoused anti-caste politics" (2022: 639–40). This gesture stands in stark contrast to Gaura's bold singing of the folk song at the start of the film, in which she skewers the rich.

13   According to Jaffrelot, there were "reportedly 1,200 shootings of this kind—which are supposed to be preceded by a warning shot—between February 2017 and February 2018, a record" (2021: 28).

14   The train number itself references the section of the Indian Penal Code—377—which criminalized homosexuality.

15   It is worth noting that typically and until very recently, the (heterosexual) couple engaging in a song and dance in Bollywood would never actually kiss, no matter how close they may come to doing so. For more regarding kissing in Bollywood song sequences, see Prasad (1998).

16   Aman's scientific jargon-laden speech also calls to mind Amitabh Bachchan's spoken interludes in the song, "My Name is Anthony Gonsavles," from the classic Bollywood film *Amar Akbar Anthony* (1977), as, for instance, when Bachchan says, "The whole country of this system is juxtaposition by the hemoglobin in the atmosphere because you are a sophisticated rhetorician intoxicated by the exuberance of your own verbosity."

17   The song originally appeared in a Hindi film made for television, *Lal Dupatta Malmal Ka* (1989), and features a man and woman alternately singing stanzas of this romantic duet. Along with queering this heterosexual pairing, the remixed version, in a sign of the metrosexual times, features a bearded Khurrana sporting a manscaped torso (fully on display), while the man in the original version is clean-shaven but with ample chest hair.

18   In *DDLJ*, Shah Rukh Khan's character, Raj, similarly tells Simran (Kajol) that they must respect her father and receive his blessing, rather than just eloping, as Simran's mother suggests.

19 This song, which the film's male leads, Jai (Amitabh Bachchan) and Veeru (Dharmendra), famously sing to one another, has frequently been cited as a paean to the duo's homosocial bond and, in turn, has frequently been appropriated as a queer anthem celebrating a male bond (*dosti*) that signifies much more than friendship.

20 Kartik had also previously deployed this black cauliflower as a trope, using it to bless Aman's father and telling him, "This (cauliflower) is your science, and these worms, your nature. I want to see what kind of science can change your son's nature." Upon subsequently unearthing worms in his cauliflowers, Aman's father realizes the error of his ways.

21 The actual decision by the Indian Supreme Court, striking down the provision of Section 377 that made consensual homosexual sex a crime, was announced on September 6, 2018, in the case of Navtej Singh Johar vs. Union of India. While the BJP did not take an official position in this case, it has already signaled its opposition to the pending case before the Supreme Court petitioning for the legalization of same-sex marriage, which it told the court was "not compatible" with "the concept of an Indian family unit" (Pasricha 2023).

22 Amrish Puri, *DDLJ*'s patriarch, famously relents after refusing to let go of his daughter's wrist at the train station, releasing it suddenly and telling her, "*Jaa* (Go), and live your life."

23 For discussions of earlier depictions of homosexuality in Bollywood, see Gopinath (2005), Gehlawat (2010), and Dudrah (2012).

24 See, e.g., *Tango Charlie* (2005) and *Mary Kom* (2014).

25 Kevichusa received the 2023 Filmfare Award for Best Female Debut.

26 Kevichusa herself was born and raised in Nagaland.

27 Mangte Chungneijang Mary Kom, aka Mary Kom, is a Manipuri native who won the bronze medal in the flyweight category of women's boxing at the 2012 Olympic Games.

28 As Guha notes, the Indian Army operates under AFSPA in the northeast region which "allows its officers and soldiers immunity from prosecution by civil courts" and, in turn, has "encouraged aggressive behavior" (2007: 618).

29 Tiger Sangha's comments echo those of the long-time leader of the Naga independence movement, A. Z. Phizo, who famously stated:

> The Nagas have nothing to do with India. And the Indians have nothing to do with Nagaland. There is nothing in common between the Nagas and the Indians. The difference is too varied, the feeling is too deep, and the attitude is too wide and too malignant for the two nations ever to think to live together in peace much less to becomes 'Indian citizens.'
>
> Qtd in LONGKUMER 2021: 56

30 It would be reasonable to assume Khurrana's voiceover stems from the present, that is, after he has completed his mission, even as it is paired with his image during the time of the mission.

31 Here, too, the Indian politician's offer—local autonomy in exchange for allegiance to the Indian flag—essentially mirrors that of Indian political leaders stemming back to India's first prime minister, Jawaharlal Nehru, who had offered leaders of Northeast secessionist movements autonomy in return for allegiance to the Indian Union (Guha 2007).

32 Such a plot weaves together a large number of plotlines, often involving many characters. While the plotlines "may at first seem completely isolated from each another," they typically converge, revealing "unexpected causal connections" (Bordwell and Thompson 2003: 437). Such plot construction is also interesting for the corresponding audience expectation it creates, that is, to "reveal unforeseen relations" (ibid., 438).

33 This latter image, in turn, invokes the earlier image of the young boys on their bicycles, caught in the crossfire between the Indian troops and Johnson's men which, in turn, becomes a form of foreshadowing.

34 Unlike at the US detention center at Guantanamo Bay, Cuba, however, the Indian troops here are detaining their own citizens, and youths at that, as "enemy combatants."

35 Such scenes function as part of Joshua's backstory and learning process, leading to the present, in which he informs his boss that he was unable to kill.

Conclusion

1 As reporter Vidya Krishnan notes, the documentary, based on "thoroughly reported documents and interviews," holds Modi directly responsible for what occurred in Gujarat in 2002, even as it reveals, as Modi himself states in the included footage, that "his only regret" from that period was that he "did not control the media narrative" (2023).

2 See Chapter 4 for discussion of *The Kashmir Files*.

3 See Chapter 4 for further discussion of Article 370 and Kashmir.

4 Though Padukone plays a Pakistani agent (and is therefore presumably Muslim), the actress herself is Hindu, which may have stoked subsequent cries by Hindutva activists labeling the film as "love jihad," in which such activists see Muslim men as attempting to woo and convert Hindu women.

5   Just as SRK himself is the son of a Pathan, his Hindu wife and middle-class upbringing contribute to his star text as "a secular, sophisticated Indian Muslim" (Mitra 2020: 193). In the film, meanwhile, even though Padukone's character explicitly asks him if he is a Muslim, Pathaan demurs in his response, noting that he was an orphan and that "the country raised him." His filmic name is taken due to the kindness shown to him by members of an Afghan village he saves from destruction who, in turn, call him their adopted son.

6   One can also trace this growing shift in the YRF Spy Universe franchise, whose first entry, *Ek Tha Tiger* (2012) features three songs in addition to an end credits song and dance sequence. The subsequent films in the franchise—*Tiger Zinda Hai* (2017), *War* (2019), and *Pathaan* (2023)—all only feature a total of two songs apiece, reflecting, in turn, the growing dissolution of the erstwhile Bollywood form and its increasing fidelity to the dynamics of the action thriller.

FILMOGRAPHY

Aa Ab Laut Chalen. 1999. Dir. Rishi Kapoor. India: RK Films.
Aandhi. 1975. Dir. Gulzar. India: Mehboob Studio.
Accidental Prime Minister, The. 2019. Dir. Vijay Gutte. India: Bohra Bros Productions.
Amar Akbar Anthony. 1977. Dir. Manmohan Desai. India: Hirarwat Jain & Co.
Andhadun. 2018. Dir. Sriram Raghavan. India: Viacom 18 Motion Pictures.
Anek. 2022. Dir. Anubhav Sinha. India: AA Films.
Article 15. 2019. Dir. Anubhav Sinha. India: Zee Studios.
Asoka. 2001. Dir. Santosh Sivan. India: Dreamz Unlimited.
Bajirao Mastani. 2015. Dir. Sanjay Leela Bhansali. India: Eros International.
Bajrangi Bhaijaan. 2015. Dir. Kabir Khan. India: Eros International.
Bala. 2019. Dir. Amar Kaushik. India: AA Films.
Bareilly ki Barfi. 2017. Dir. Ashwiny Iyer Tiwari. India: AA Films.
Being There. 1979. Dir. Hal Ashby. USA: United Artists.
Bell Bottom. 2021. Dir. Ranjit Tewari. India: Pen Studios.
Bend It Like Beckham. 2002. Dir. Gurinder Chadha. UK: Fox Searchlight Pictures.
Birth of a Nation, The. 1915. Dir. D. W. Griffith. USA: Epoch Producing Co.
Bombay. 1995. Dir. Mani Ratnam. India: Aalayam Productions.
Border. 1997. Dir. J. P. Dutta. India: J.P. Films.
Devdas. 2002. Dir. Sanjay Leela Bhansali. India: Eros International.
Dhaakad. 2022. Dir. Razneesh Ghai. India: Zee Studios.
Dhoom. 2004. Dir. Sanjay Gadhvi. India: Yash Raj Films.
Dil Se. 1998. Dir. Mani Ratnam. India: Eros International.
Dilwale. 2015. Dir. Rohit Shetty. India: Red Chillies Entertainment.
Dilwale Dulhania Le Jayenge. 1995. Dir. Aditya Chopra. India: Eros International.
Don. 2006. Dir. Farhan Akhtar. India: UTV Motion Pictures.
Don 2. 2011. Dir. Farhan Akhtar. India: Reliance Entertainment.
Dum Laga Ke Haisha. 2015. Dir. Sharat Katariya. India: Yash Raj Films.
Ek Tha Tiger. 2012. Dir. Kabir Khan. India: Yash Raj Films.
Emergency. 2024. Dir. Kangana Ranaut. India: Manikarnika Films.
Fashion. 2008. Dir. Madhur Bhandarkar. India: UTV Motion Pictures.
Gangster: A Love Story. 2006. Dir. Anurag Basu. India: Vishesh Films.
Goliyon Ki Rasleela Ram-Leela. 2013. Dir. Sanjay Leela Bhansali. India: Eros International.
Goya's Ghosts. 2006. Dir. Milos Forman. USA: Warner Bros.
Haider. 2014. Dir. Vishal Bhardwaj. India: UTV Motion Pictures.
Happy New Year. 2014. Dir. Farah Khan. India: Yash Raj Films.
Hum Dil De Chuke Sanam. 1999. Dir. Sanjay Leela Bhansali. India: Eros International.
I Love NY. 2015. Dir. Radhika Rao and Vinay Sapru. India: T-Series.
Imitation of Life. 1934. Dir. John M. Stahl. USA: Universal Pictures.

India: The Modi Question. 2023. UK: BBC Two.
Indu Sarkar. 2017. Dir. Madhur Bhandarkar. India: Bhandarkar Entertainment.
Jhansi Ki Rani. 1953. Dir. Sohrab Modi. India: Minerva Movietone.
Jhansi Ki Rani Laxmibai. 2012. Dir. Rajesh Mittal. India: NH Studioz.
Jodhaa Akbar. 2008. Dir. Ashutosh Gowariker. India: UTV Motion Pictures.
Kabhi Khushi Kabhie Gham. 2001. Dir. Karan Johar. India: Yash Raj Films.
Kapoor & Sons. 2016. Dir. Shakun Batra. India: Fox Star Studios.
Kashmir Files, The. 2022. Dir. Vivek Agnihotri. India: Zee Studios.
Kesari. 2019. Dir. Anurag Singh. India: Zee Studios.
Lal Dupatta Malmal Ka. 1989. Dir. Ravinder Peepat. India: Zee Movies.
Laal Singh Chaddha. 2022. Dir. Advait Chandan. India: Viacom 18 Studios.
Lagaan. 2001. Dir. Ashutosh Gowariker. India: SET Pictures.
Lakshya. 2004. Dir. Farhan Akhtar. India: Excel Entertainment.
Main Hoon Ha. 2004. Dir. Farah Khan. India: Eros International.
Mangal Pandey: The Rising. 2005. Dir. Ketan Mehta. India: Yash Raj Films.
Manikarnika: The Queen of Jhansi. 2019. Dir. Kangana Ranaut and Krish Jagarlamudi. India: Zee Studios.
Mary Kom. 2014. Dir. Omung Kumar. India: Eros International.
Mephisto. 1981. Dir. Istvan Szabo. Hungary: Analysis Film.
Meri Pyaari Bindu. 2017. Dir. Akshay Roy. India: Yash Raj Films.
Mission Kashmir. 2000. Dir. Vishu Vinod Chopra. India: SET Pictures.
Mission Mangal. 2019. Dir. Jagan Shakti. India: Fox Star Studios.
Mississippi Burning. 1988. Dir. Alan Parker. USA: Orion Pictures.
Mughal-e-Azam. 1960. Dir. K. Asif. India: Sterling Investment Corporation.
Olympia. 1938. Dir. Leni Riefenstahl. Germany: Tobis.
Padmaavat. 2018. Dir. Sanjay Leela Bhansali. India: Viacom 18 Motion Pictures.
Panipat. 2019. Dir. Ashutosh Gowariker. India: Reliance Entertainment.
Pardes. 1997. Dir. Subhash Ghai. India: Mukta Arts.
Pathaan. 2023. Dir. Siddharth Anand. India: Yash Raj Films.
Pitra, Putra, aur Dharmayuddha. 1995. Dir. Anand Patwardhan. India: Anand Patwardhan Productions.
Queen. 2014. Dir. Vikas Bahl. India: Viacom 18 Motion Pictures.
Ram Lakhan. 1989. Dir. Subhash Ghai. India: Mukta Arts.
Ram Setu. 2022. Dir. Abhishek Sharma. India: Zee Studios.
Rangoon. 2017. Dir. Vishal Bhardwaj. India: Viacom 18 Motion Pictures.
Roja. 1992. Dir. Mani Ratnam. India: GV Films.
Samrat Prithviraj. 2022. Dir. Chandraprakash Dwivedi. India: Yash Raj Films.
Saugandh. 1991. Dir. Raj N. Sippy. India: Tridev Films.
Sholay. 1975. Dir. Ramesh Sippy. India: Sippy Films.
Shubh Mangal Saavdhan. 2017. Dir. R.S. Prasanna. India: Eros International.
Shubh Mangal Zyada Saavdhan. 2020. Dir. Hitesh Kewalya. India: AA Films.
Sicario. 2015. Dir. Denis Villeneuve. USA: Lionsgate.
Simmba. 2018. Dir. Rohit Shetty. India: Reliance Entertainment.
Simran. 2017. Dir. Hansal Mehta. India: AA Films.

Singham. 2011. Dir. Rohit Shetty. India: Reliance Entertainment.
Singham Returns. 2014. Dir. Rohit Shetty. India: Eros International.
Slumdog Millionaire. 2008. Dir. Danny Boyle. UK: Pathe.
Sooryavanshi. 2021. Dir. Rohit Shetty. India: Reliance Entertainment.
Star Wars. 1977. Dir. George Lucas. USA: 20th Century Fox.
Tango Charlie. 2005. Dir. Mani Shankar. India: Neha Arts.
Tanu Weds Manu. 2011. Dir. Aanand Rai. India: Viacom 18 Motion Pictures.
Tanu Weds Manu Returns. 2015. Dir. Aanand Rai. India: Eros International.
Thalaivii. 2021. Dir. A.L. Vijay. India: Zee Studios.
Tiger Zinda Hai. 2017. Dir. Ali Abbas Zafar. India: Yash Raj Films.
Toilet: Ek Prem Katha. 2017. Dir. Shree Narayan Singh. India: Viacom 18 Motion Pictures.
Triumph of the Will. 1935. Dir. Leni Riefenstahl. Germany: UFA.
Uri: The Surgical Strike. 2019. Dir. Aditya Dhar. India: RSVP Movies.
Veer-Zaara. 2004. Dir. Yash Chopra. India: Yash Raj Films.
Vicky Donor. 2012. Dir. Shoojit Sircar. India: Eros Entertainment.
War. 2019. Dir. Siddharth Anand. India: Yash Raj Films.
Warrior Queen of Jhansi, The. 2019. Dir. Swati Bhise. UK: PVR Pictures.

BIBLIOGRAPHY

Abdi, S. N. M. (2023), "Reading Modi's Face in Nagaland," *Deccan Herald*, March 13. Available online: https://www.deccanherald.com/opinion/in-perspective/reading-modi-s-face-innagaland-1199926.html (accessed May 10, 2023).

Abi-Habib, M. (2018), "Same Gun was Used to Kill Critics of Hindu Nationalists in India," *New York Times*, June 8. Available online: https://www.nytimes.com/2018/06/08/world/asia/india-lankesh-kalburgi-gun.html (accessed May 8, 2023).

Acland, C. (1998), "IMAX Technology and the Tourist Gaze," *Cultural Studies*, 12 (3): 429–45.

Agrawal, R. (2022), "Is India Losing Its Claim to Being a Democracy?" *Foreign Policy*, December 14. Available online: https://foreignpolicy.com/2022/12/14/india-democracy-decline-ramachandra-guha/ (accessed May 5, 2023).

Akhtar, J. (1995), "Lifting the Veil: A Daring Film Explores Hindu-Muslim Relations," *Asiaweek*, 21 (33): 30–1.

Anwer, M. and A. Arora (2022 [2020]), "Love, Interrupted: Caste and Couple-Formation in New Bollywood," *Quarterly Review of Film and Video*, 39 (3): 615–43.

Art Karat (2018), *Padmavati*, Old Bethpage, NY: Art Karat.

Ashraf, A. (2018), "Makers of *The Accidental Prime Minister* Complicit in BJP's Design to Disparage Manmohan Singh, Demonise Gandhis," *Firstpost*, December 28. Available online: https://www.firstpost.com/india/timing-of-the-accidental-prime-minister-no-accident-its-makers-complicit-in-bjps-design-to-disparage-singh-demonise-gandhis-5807331.html (accessed May 5, 2023).

Ayyub, R. (2021), "Why an Indian Film's Success at the Box Office Should Worry Us All," *Washington Post*, November 16. Available online: https://www.washingtonpost.com/opinions/2021/11/15/why-an-indian-films-success-boxoffice-should-worry-us-all/ (accessed May 5, 2023).

Baishya, A. (2021), "Passions of the Political (Review of Anustup Basu's Hindutva as Political Monotheism)," *boundary 2*, November 5. Available online: https://www.boundary2.org/2021/11/amit-r-baishya-passions-of-the-political-review-ofanustup-basus-hindutva-as-political-monotheism/ (accessed May 5, 2023).

Baksi, S. and A. Nagarajan. (2017), "Mob Lynchings in India," *Newslaundry*, July 3. Available online: https://www.newslaundry.com/2017/07/04/mob-lynchings-in-india-a-look-atdata-and-the-story-behind-the-numbers (accessed May 11, 2023).

Bamzai, K. (2019), "The Double Life of Anupam Kher," *The Print*, January 1. Available online: https://theprint.in/opinion/the-double-life-of-anupam-kher-fanboy-to-bjp-and-desi-uncleto-hollywood/171381/ (accessed May 5, 2023).

Banaji, S. (2018), "*Vigilante Publics*: Orientalism, Modernity and Hindutva Fascism in India," *Javnost: The Public*, 25 (4): 333–50.

Banerjee, D. (2023), "Censor Board Asks for 12 Cuts in 'Pathaan' Including 'Close-Up Shot' of Deepika's 'Buttocks,'" *Storypick*, January 5. Available online: https://www.storypick.com/pathaan-censor-board-cuts/ (accessed May 10, 2023).

Barstow D. and S. Raj (2015), "Indian Writers Return Awards to Protest Government Silence on Violence," *New York Times*, October 17. Available online: https://www.nytimes.com/2015/10/18/world/asia/india-writers-return-awards-to-protestgovernment-silence-on-violence.html (accessed May 8, 2023).

Barthwal, S. and V. Sharma (2023 [2022]), "New-Age Media and the Genesis of Hindutva," *Quarterly Review of Film and Video*, 40 (6): 702–24.

Baru, S. (2014), *The Accidental Prime Minister*, New Delhi: Penguin Books.

Basu, A. (2020), *Hindutva as Political Monotheism*, Durham, NC: Duke University Press.

Benjamin, W. (2019 [1936]), "The Work of Art in the Age of Mechanical Reproduction," in H. Arendt (ed.), *Illuminations*, 166–95, Boston, MA: Mariner Books.

Bharucha, R. (1994), "On the Border of Fascism: Manufacture of Consent in *Roja*," *Economic and Political Weekly*, 29 (23): 1389–95.

Bhaskar, I. and R. Allen (2009), *Islamicate Cultures of Bombay Cinema*, New Delhi: Tulika.

Bhatia, U. (2019), "How Bollywood is Rewriting History," *Mint*, December 1. Available online: https://lifestyle.livemint.com/news/talking-point/how-bollywood-is-rewritinghistory-111641421170823.html (accessed May 10, 2023).

Bogle, D. (2007), *Toms, Coons, Mulattoes, Mammies, and Bucks: An Interpretive History of Blacks in American Films*, New York: Continuum.

Bollywood Hungama (2008), "Jodhaa Akbar Not Being Screened in Rajasthan," February 16. Available online: https://web.archive.org/web/20080302234437/http://www.bollywoodhungama.com/news/2008/02/16/10908/index.html (accessed May 11, 2023).

Bordwell, D. and K. Thompson (2003), *Film Art: An Introduction*, New York: McGraw-Hill.

Bose, N. (2009), "Between the Godfather and the Mafia: Situating Right-Wing Interventions in the Bombay Film Industry (1992–2002)," *Studies in South Asian Film and Media*, 1 (1): 23–43.

Brosius, C. (2002), "Hindutva intervisuality: Videos and the Politics of Representation," *Contributions to Indian Sociology*, 36 (1&2): 265–95.

Carroll, N. (1990), *The Philosophy of Horror, or Paradoxes of the Heart*, New York: Routledge.

Cesaire, A. (2000 [1955]), *Discourse on Colonialism*, New York: Monthly Review Press.

Chakrabarti, B. (2020), "'This Sperm Hits the Bllseye': Bollywood, Youth and Male (Im) potency as a Neoliberal Game," *Studies in South Asian Film and Media*, 11 (1): 71–85.

Chakravarty, S. (1993), *National Identity in Indian Popular Cinema, 1947–1987*, Austin, TX: University of Texas Press.

Chakravarty, S. (2000), "Fragmenting the Nation: Images of Terrorism in Indian Popular Cinema," in M. Hjort and S. Mackenzie (eds.), *Cinema and Nation*, 209–24, New York: Routledge.

Chatterjee, S. (2019), "*Article* 15 Movie Review," *NDTV*, June 28. Available online: https://www.ndtv.com/entertainment/article-15-movie-review-ayushmann-khurranaleads-an-effective-cast-in-this-radical-film-4-stars-out-2060019 (accessed May 5, 2023).

Chatterjee, S. (2020), "*Shubh Mangal Zyada Saavdhan* Movie Review," *NDTV*, February 21. Available online: https://www.ndtv.com/entertainment/shubh-mangal-zyadasaavdhanmovie-review-ayushmann-khurrana-jitendra-kumar-carry-the-film-2-5-stars-2183647 (accessed May 5, 2023).

Chatterjee, S. (2022), "*Ram Setu* Review," *NDTV*, October 25. Available online: https://www.ndtv.com/entertainment/ram-setu-review-akshay-kumars-film-is-about-afloating-stone-but-has-no-clue-how-to-stay-afloat-1-star-3460792 (accessed May 5, 2023).

Chaudhuri, S. (2019), "Feminist Historical Desire and the Politics of Biopic Adaptations: Review of *Manikarnika: The Queen of Jhansi*," *Neo-Victorian Studies*, 12 (1): 181–9.

Chopra, S. (2022), "Review: Ayushmann Khurrana's 'Anek' Has Its Heart in the Right Place," *The Quint*, May 27. Available online: https://www.thequint.com/amp/story/entertainment/movie-reviews/anek-reviewayushmann-khurrana-anubhav-sinha-andrea-kevichusa (accessed May 6, 2023).

Choudhury, G. (2014), "Launch of Modi's Make in India Campaign," *Hindustan Times*, September 25. Available online: https://web.archive.org/web/20140925055526/http://www.hindustantimes.com/businessnews/live-coverage-launch-of-modi-s-make-in-india-campaign/article1-1268119.aspx (accessed May 6, 2023).

Chowdhury, D. R. (2022), "*The Kashmir Files*: How a New Bollywood Film Marks India's Further Descent into Bigotry," *Time*, March 30. Available online: https://time.com/6162035/kashmir-files-india-hindu-muslim/ (accessed May 6, 2023).

Chowdhury, D. R. (2023), "Bollywood's Code Orange," *Index on Censorship*, 52 (1): 74–7.

Chowdhury, D. R. and J. Keane (2021), *To Kill a Democracy: India's Passage to Despotism*, New York: Oxford University Press.

Chowdhury, K. (2023), "Bollywood Film 'Pathaan' Pushes Back against Modi Regime's Hate Agenda," *The Diplomat*, February 14. Available online: https://thediplomat.com/2023/02/bollywood-film-pathaan-pushes-back-against-modiregimes-hate-agenda/ (accessed May 9, 2023).

Creekmur, C. (2005), "Bombay Boys: Dissolving the Male Child in Popular Hindi Cinema," in M. Pomerance and F. Gateward (eds.), *Where the Boys Are: Cinemas of Masculinity and Youth*, 350–76, Detroit, MI: Wayne State University Press.

Creekmur, C. (2007), "Remembering, Repeating, and Working through *Devdas*," in H. R. M. Pauwels (ed.), *Indian Literature and Popular Cinema*, 173–90, London: Routledge.

Daily Star (2023), "'I Didn't Want to Give Them the Pleasure of My Pain'—Kangana Ranaut," January 21. Available online: https://www.thedailystar.net/entertainment/tv-film/news/ididnt-want-give-them-the-pleasure-my-pain-kangana-ranaut-3226686 (accessed May 6, 2023).

Das Gupta, U. (2022), "A New Kangana Ranaut Movie Revisits the Anger and Anguish of the Emergency," *Business Standard*, July 25. Available online: https://www.businessstandard.com/article/beyond-business/a-new-kangana-ranaut-movie-revisits-the-angerand-anguish-of-the-emergency-122072500996_1.html (accessed May 9, 2023).

Dasgupta, P. (2020), "Kangana Ranaut Speaks Like any Right-Wing Politician, But Why is It Extra Disappointing?" *Huffpost*, September 18. Available online: https://www.huffpost.com/archive/in/entry/kangana-speaks-like-any-right-wing politician-but-why-is-it-extra-disappointing_in_5f63934bc5b618455868224d (accessed May 6, 2023).

Dasgupta, R. (2014), *Capital: The Eruption of Delhi*, New York: Penguin Press.

Deccan Chronicle (2019), "It's a Big Slap on Movie Mafia's Face: Kangana on Manikarnika's Global Selection," June 14. Available online: https://www.deccanchronicle.com/entertainment/bollywood/140619/its-a-big-slap-onmovie-mafias-face-kangana-on-manikarnikas-glob.html (accessed May 6, 2023).

Dirks, N. (2001), "The Home and the Nation: Consuming Culture and Politics in *Roja*," in C. Pinney and R. Dwyer (eds.), *Pleasure and the Nation: The History, Politics and Consumption of Public Culture in India*, 161–85, New Delhi: Oxford University Press.

DNA (2021), "Netizens Massively Troll Kangana Ranaut for Sharing Bikini Photos of Rihanna," February 4. Available online: https://www.dnaindia.com/bollywood/report-netizens-massively-troll-kangana-ranautfor-sharing-bikini-photos-of-rihanna-calling-her-porn-star-2873117 (accessed May 6, 2023).

Dore, B. (2021), "The Player: Akshay Kumar's Role as Hindutva's Poster Boy," *The Caravan*, January 31. Available online: https://caravanmagazine.in/reportage/akshay-kumar-rolehindutva-poster-boy (accessed May 6, 2023).

Dowerah, S. and D. Nath (2018), "Cinematic Regimes of Otherness: India and Its Northeast," *Media Asia*, 44 (2): 121–33.

Dubey, P. (2018), "Badaun Gang Rape and Mmurder," *Scroll.in*, December 21. Available online: https://scroll.in/article/906291/badaun-gang-rape-and-murder-this-book-investigateshowthe-cbi-tried-to-bury-the-case (accessed May 6, 2023).

Dudrah, R. (2012), *Bollywood Travels*, London: Routledge.

Dutt, B. (2018), "'Padmaavat' is Pure Misogyny Dressed Up in Diamonds and Drama," *Washington Post*, February 6. Available online: https://www.washingtonpost.com/news/global-opinions/wp/2018/02/06/padmaavatispure-misogyny-dressed-up-in-diamonds-and-drama/ (accessed May 6, 2023).

Dwyer, R. (2006a), *Filming the Gods: Religion and Indian Cinema*, New York: Routledge.

Dwyer, R. (2006b), "The Saffron Screen? Hindu Nationalism and the Hindi Film," in B. Meyer and A. Moors (eds.), *Religion, Media, and the Public Sphere*, 273–87, Bloomington, IN: Indiana University Press.

Dyer, R. (1998 [1979]), *Stars*, London: British Film Institute.

Ellis, J. (1982), *Visible Fictions: Cinema, Television, Video*, London: Routledge.

Farred, G. (2001), "The Double Temporality of *Lagaan*," *Journal of Sport & Social Issues*, 28 (2): 93–114.

Gabriel, K. (2010), *Melodrama and the Nation*, New Delhi: Women Unlimited.

Gangopadhyay, R. (2023), "'The Surgical Strike that Shook the Mughal Empire': Evacuation and Distortion of Histories in Contemporary Hindi Screen Cultures," in S. Gopinath and R. Deshmukh (eds.), *Historicizing Myth in Contemporary India*, 102–22, New York: Routledge.

Ganti, T. (2013), *Bollywood: A Guidebook to Popular Hindi Cinema*, New York: Routledge.

Gehlawat, A. (2010), *Reframing Bollywood: Theories of Popular Hindi Cinema*, New Delhi: Sage Publications.

Gettleman, J. (2018), "A Young Girl's Rape in India becomes a Crisis for Modi," *New York Times*, April 14. Available online: https://www.nytimes.com/2018/04/14/world/asia/india-girl-rape.html (accessed May 8, 2023).

Ghosh, S. and R. Kapur (2006), "The Violence of Censoring," in B. Bose (ed.), *Gender and Censorship*, 94–7, New Delhi: Women Unlimited.

Ghoshal, S. (2017), "Why Anupam Kher's Appointment As FTII Chairman Is Problematic," *Huffpost*, October 12. Available online: https://www.huffpost.com/archive/in/entry/whyanupam-khers-appointment-as-ftiichairman-is-problematic_in_5c10c763e4b09dcd67fc30ed (accessed May 6, 2023).

Girish, D. (2021), "'Sooryavanshi' Review: Cops on a Crusade," *New York Times*, November 8. Available online: https://www.nytimes.com/2021/11/08/movies/sooryavanshi-review.html (accessed May 6, 2023).

Goldberg, E. (2020), "Cultural Horror in *Dev*: Man is the Cruelest Animal," in E. Goldberg, A. Sen, and B. Collins (eds.), *Bollywood Horrors: Religion, Violence and Cinematic Fears in India*, 115–39, New York: Bloomsbury.

Gopal, S. (2021), "Lethal Acts: Bollywood's New Woman and the Nirbhaya Effect," in M. Anwer and A. Arora (eds.), *Bollywood's New Woman*, 40–53, New Brunswick: Rutgers University Press.

Gopinath, G. (2005), *Impossible Desires*, Durham, NC: Duke University Press.

Gopinath, S. and R. Deshmukh (2023), "Introduction," in S. Gopinath and R. Deshmukh (eds.), *Historicizing Myths in Contemporary India: Cinematic Representations and Nationalist Agendas in Hindi Cinema*, 1–20, New York: Routledge.

Gottipati, S. and A. Banerji (2013), "Modi's 'Puppy' Remark Triggers New Controversy over 2002 Riots," Reuters, July 12. Available online: https://www.reuters.com/article/narendramodipuppy-reuters-interview/modis-puppy-remark-triggers-new-controversy-over-2002-riotsidINDEE96B08S20130712 (accessed May 6, 2023).

Guha, R. (2007), *India After Gandhi: The History of the World's Largest Democracy*, New York: Harper Perennial.

Guha, R. (2022), "The Cult of Modi," *Foreign Policy*, November 4. Available online: https://foreignpolicy.com/2022/11/04/modi-india-personality-cult-democracy/ (accessed May 6, 2023).

Gupta, P. (2013), "When I am Not Being Watched, I too am a Loud Gujarati: Sanjay Leela Bhansali," *Times of India*, 12 November. Available online: https://timesofindia.indiatimes.com/entertainment/hindi/bollywood/news/sanjay-leelabhansali-hum-dil-de-chuke-sanam-saraswatichandra/articleshow/25591828.cms (accessed May 8, 2023).

Gupta, S. (2008), "Jodhaa Akbar Banned in MP," *Times of India*, February 23. Available online: https://timesofindia.indiatimes.com/india/jodhaa-akbar-banned-inmp/articleshow/2806303.cms (accessed May 11, 2023).

Gupta, S. (2019), "The Accidental Prime Minister Movie Review: A Shoddy Propaganda Film," *Indian Express*, January 12. Available online: https://indianexpress.com/article/entertainment/movie-review/the-accidental-primeminister-review-rating-anupam-kher-5533067/ (accessed May 6, 2023).

Gupta, S. (2022), "Ram Setu Review: Akshay Kumar Film is Very Amar Chitra Katha-cum-Indiana Jones, Minus the Story-telling Skills," *Indian Express*, 28 October. Available online: https://indianexpress.com/article/entertainment/movie-review/ram-setu-moviereview-akshay-kumar-8228574/ (accessed May 6, 2023).

Harlan, L. (1992), *Religion and Rajput Women*, Berkeley, CA: University of California Press.

Hasan, K. (ed.) (1992), *Kashmir Holocaust: The Case against India, Text of a Writ Petition Filed by Bahauddin Farooqi, Former Chief Justice of the Jammu and Kashmir High Court*, Lahore: Dotcare.

Hebbar, P. (2017), "Sanjay Leela Bhansali's 'Padmavati' Set Attacked Once Again," *Huffpost*, March 15. Available online: https://www.huffpost.com/archive/in/entry/sanjayleelabhansalis-padmavati-set-attacked-once-again-thi_in_5c0f6cece4b0d42cf23510a2 (accessed May 8, 2023).

Hindu, The (2018), "'Padmaavat' Glorifies Rajputs, Says Shri Rajput Karni Sena," February 3. Available online: https://www.thehindu.com/news/national/other-states/padmaavatglorifies-rajputs-says-karni-sena-withdraws-protest/article61484585.ece (accessed May 8, 2023).

Hindustan Times (2015), "Shah Rukh Khan Makes a U-turn, Claims He Never Said India is Intolerant," November 25. Available online: https://www.hindustantimes.com/bollywood/never-said-india-is-intolerant-shah-rukhkhan/story-TcX7o5ZYefPqSf4JSXGkxL.html (accessed May 8, 2023).

Hindustan Times (2017), "Beheading, Burning," November 20. Available online: https://www.hindustantimes.com/india-news/beheading-burning-the-many-threatsagainst-bhansali-padukone-for-padmavati-movie/storyMm01APDFzjLOvEECKatsfI.html (accessed May 8, 2023).

Hindustan Times (2023), "Kangana Ranaut Calls Emergency Musical Drama," January 7. Available online: https://www.hindustantimes.com/entertainment/bollywood/kanganaranaut-calls-emergency-musical-drama-i-might-just-have-the-longest-song-ever101673083303402.html (accessed May 6, 2023).

Hogan, P. (2008), *Understanding Indian Movies*. Austin, TX: University of Texas Press.

Hussain, S. (2021), *Kashmir in the Aftermath of Partition*, New York: Cambridge University Press.

Huxley, A. (2000 [1958]), *Brave New World Revisited*, New York: Harper Perennial.

Indian Express (2018a), "Despite CBFC Clearance, Rajasthan, Gujarat and Now Haryana Won't Screen Padmaavat," January 16. Available online: https://indianexpress.com/article/entertainment/bollywood/padmaavat-release-date-banrajasthan-gujarat-madhya-pradesh-sanjay-leela-bhansali-5025520/ (accessed May 8, 2023).

Indian Express (2018b), "Padmaavat Box Office Collection," February 19. Available online: https://indianexpress.com/article/entertainment/bollywood/box-officecollection/padmaavat-box-office-collection-5069970/ (accessed May 8, 2023).

Indian Express (2022), "Anubhav Sinha on Polarizing Response to Ayushmann Khurrana's Anek, Box Office Failure 'It's too Political for Casual Watch,'" June 30. Available online: https://indianexpress.com/article/entertainment/bollywood/anubhav-sinha-onayushmann-khurrana-anek-polarising-response-box-office-failure-7998196/ (accessed May 6, 2023).

Indian Express (2023), "Kangana Ranaut Seethes as Queen Director Vikas Bahl's Ganapath Blocks Emergency Release Date," February 23. Available online: https://indianexpress.com/article/entertainment/bollywood/kangana-ranaut-changesemergency-release-date-amitabh-bachchan-ganapath-clash-8461699/ (accessed May 6, 2023).

Jacob, P. (2009), *Celluloid Deities: The Visual Culture of Cinema and Politics in South Asia*, Lanham, MD: Lexington Books.
Jaffrelot, C. (2008), "Hindu Nationalism and the (Not So Easy) Art of Being Outraged: The Ram Setu Controversy," *South Asia Multidisciplinary Academic Journal*, 2: 1–17.
Jaffrelot, C. (2021 [2019]), *Modi's India: Hindu Nationalism and the Rise of Ethnic Democracy*, Princeton, NJ: Princeton University Press.
Jain, K. (2021), *Gods in the Time of Democracy*, Durham, NC: Duke University Press.
Jain, K., I. Sharma, and A. Behl (2021), "Voice of the Stars—Exploring the Outcomes of Online Celebrity Activism," *Journal of Strategic Marketing*: 1–22.
Jameson, F. (1981), *The Political Unconscious*, Ithaca, NY: Cornell University Press.
Jameson, F. (1986), "Third World Literature in an Era of Multinational Capitalism," *Social Text*, 15: 65–88.
Jhunjhunwala, U. (2020), "Film Review: Shubh Mangal Zyada Saavdhan Tackles Issues on the Rainbow Spectrum with Confidence, Humor," *Mint*, February 21. Available online: https://www.livemint.com/industry/media/film-review-shubh-mangal-zyada-saavdhantackles-issues-on-the-rainbow-spectrum-with-confidence-humour-11582291460286.html (accessed May 6, 2023).
Joshi, N. (2015), "Bajirao Mastani: A Historical Leap," *The Hindu*, December 18. Available online: https://www.thehindu.com/features/cinema/bajirao-mastani-a-historicalleap/article8004323.ece (accessed May 8, 2023).
Kak, S. (2022), "The Dangerous 'Truth' of The Kashmir Files," *Al Jazeera*, April 13. Available online: https://www.aljazeera.com/opinions/2022/4/13/the-dangerous-truth-of-thekashmiri-files (accessed May 6, 2023).
Kasbekar, A. (2006), *Pop Culture India! Media, Arts, and Lifestyle*, Santa Barbara, CA: ABC-CLIO.
Kaul, S. (2009), "Book Review: *Filming the Line of Control: The Indo-Pak Relationship through the Cinematic Lens*," *Studies in South Asian Film and Media*, 1 (1): 192–4.
Khilnani, S. (2016), *Incarnations: India in Fifty Lives*, New York: Farrar, Straus, Giroux.
Koepnick, L. (2008), "0-1: Riefenstahl and the Beauty of Soccer," in N. C. Pages, M. Rhiel, and I. Majer-O-Sickey (eds.), *Riefenstahl Screened*, 52–70, New York: Continuum.
Komireddi, K. S. (2019), *Malevolent Republic: A Short History of the New India*, London: Hurst & Company.
Konikkara, A. (2022), "The Warrior Queen," *The Caravan*, May 31. Available online: https://caravanmagazine.in/film/kangana-ranaut-role-in-bjp-battle-for-bollywood (accessed May 6, 2023).
Krishnan, V. (2023), "What the BBC's 'Modi Question' Reveals about India," *The Caravan*, January 27. Available online: https://caravanmagazine.in/commentary/bbc-documentarygujarat-riots-narendra-modi (accessed May 6, 2023).
Kumar, A. (2022), "'Ram Setu' movie review," *The Hindu*, October 26. Available online: https://www.thehindu.com/entertainment/movies/ram-setu-movie-review-a-bridge-too-far-tocross-for-akshay-kumar/article66056431.ece (accessed May 6, 2023).
Lal, N. (2019), "Wary Movies Play Safe with Ever-expanding Disclaimers," *Times of India*, August 18. Available online: https://timesofindia.indiatimes.com/entertainment/hindi/bollywood/news/wary-moviesplay-safe-with-ever-expanding-disclaimers/articleshow/70713908.cms (accessed May 6, 2023).

Le, P. (2022), "Anek Review," *The Guardian*, May 25. Available online: https://www.theguardian.com/film/2022/may/25/anek-review-gunfights-boxing-andwhat-it-means-to-be-indian (accessed May 6, 2023).

Leidig, E. (2020), "Hindutva as a Variant of Right-wing Extremism," *Patterns of Prejudice*, 54 (3): 215–37.

Loewen, J. W. (2007), *Lies My Teacher Told Me: Everything Your American History Textbook Got Wrong*, New York: Touchstone.

Longkumer, A. (2021), *The Greater India Experiment: Hindutva and the Northeast*, Stanford, CA: Stanford University Press.

Mahajan, K. (2021), "India's Streaming Auteurs," *New York Review of Books*, July 1. Available online: https://www.nybooks.com/articles/2021/07/01/indias-streamingauteurs/ (accessed May 6, 2023).

Majumdar, N. (2022), "Staging the Screen, Screening the Stage: Mediation and the Problem of Cinematic Self-Reflexivity," in N. Majumdar and R. Mazumdar (eds.), *A Companion to Indian Cinema*, 495–513, Hoboken, NJ: Wiley Blackwell.

Mankekar, P. (2013), "'We are Like this Only': Aspiration, *jugaad,* and Love in Enterprise Culture," in N. Gooptu (ed.), *Enterprise Culture in Neoliberal India*, 27–41, New York: Routledge.

Manor, J. (2015), "A Precarious Enterprise?" *South Asia*, 38 (4): 736–54.

Marino, A. (2014), *Narendra Modi: A Political Biography*, Noida: HarperCollins.

Masand, R. (2019), "Mission Mangal Movie Review," *News18*, August 16. Available online: https://www.news18.com/news/movies/mission-mangal-movie-review-akshay-kumarvidya-balan-deliver-an-entertaining-account-of-a-complicated-mission-2272027.html (accessed May 6, 2023).

Maurya, P. and N. Kumar. (2020), "*Manikarnika*: The Queen of Jhansi and Its Topicality," *South Asian Popular Culture* 18 (3): 247–60.

Mazumdar, R. (2007), *Bombay Cinema*, Minneapolis, MN: University of Minnesota Press.

McDuie-Ra, D. (2015), "'Is India Racist?': Murder, Migration and Mary Kom," *South Asia*, 38 (2): 304–19.

Menon, A. (2021), "Akshay Kumar's 'Sooryavanshi' and the Criminalisation of 'Normal Indian Muslims,'" *The Quint*, November 8. Available online: https://www.thequint.com/entertainment/bollywood/sooryavanshi-indian-muslimsakshay-kumar-rohit-shetty-islamophobia-terrorism (accessed May 6, 2023).

Menon, N. (2020), "Hindu Rashtra and Bollywood," *South Asia Multidisciplinary Academic Journal*, 24/25. Available online: https://journals.openedition.org/samaj/6846 (accessed May 10, 2023).

Merivirta, R. (2016), "Historical Film and Hindu–Muslim Relations in Post-Hindutva India: The Case of *Jodhaa Akbar*," *Quarterly Review of Film and Video*, 33 (5): 456–77.

Meskell, L. (2021), "Toilets First, Temples Second: Adopting Heritage in Neoliberal India," *International Journal of Heritage Studies*, 27 (2): 151–69.

Mezey, J. (2018), "The Pyrotechnics of Gender and Terrorism in Mani Ratnam's *Dil Se*," *South Asian Popular Culture*, 16 (1): 29–49.

Mishra, U. (2019), "Accidental Prime Minister Review," *Rediff.com*, January 11. Available online: https://www.rediff.com/movies/report/accidental-prime-minister-review-didmanmohan-fight-with-sonia/20190111.htm (accessed May 6, 2023).

Mishra, V. (2002), *Bollywood Cinema*, New York: Routledge.

Mitra, S. (2020), "The Question of Minority Citizenship: Shah Rukh Khan as the 'Global Indian'," in A. Ray and I. Banerjee-Dube (eds.), *Nation, Nationalism and the Public Sphere*, 191–213, New Delhi: Sage Publications.

Mitra, S. (2021), "#ModiWithAkshay: 'Brand Modi', Social Media and Bollywood," *Celebrity Studies*, 12 (2): 282–98.

Mohan, R. (2018), "A Template for Hate," *Harper's Magazine*, September: 34–40.

Mourenza, D. (2020), *Walter Benjamin and the Aesthetics of Film*, Amsterdam: Amsterdam University Press.

Mukherjee, T. (2020), "Akshay Kumar: The *Khiladi* of the Box Office," in A. Viswamohan and C. Wilkinson (eds.), *Stardom in Contemporary Hindi Cinema*, 195–213, Singapore: Springer.

Nandy, P. (2020), "The Campaign to Silence Bollywood," *New York Times*, October 7. Available online: https://www.nytimes.com/2020/10/07/opinion/bollywood-attackmodi.html (accessed May 6, 2023).

NDTV (2019), "Details about Ayushmann Khurrana's Next Film *Article 15* By *Mulk* Director," March 6. Available online: https://www.ndtv.com/entertainment/detailsaboutayushmann-khurranas-next-film-article-15-by-mulk-director-2003588 (accessed May 6, 2023).

O'Donoghue, D. (2023), "The Tiger's Roar: The Crossover Success of S.S. Rajamouli's *RRR*," *Cineaste*, 48 (2): 4–9.

Ohm, B. (2011), "Forgetting to Remember: The Privatization of the Public, the Economization of Hindutva and Medialization of Genocide," in S. Banaji (ed.), *South Asian Media Cultures*, 123–43, London: Anthem.

Oldenburg, V. T. (1994), "The Continuing Invention of the Sati Tradition," in J. Hawley (ed.), *Sati, the Blessing and the Curse*, 159–73, New York: Oxford University Press.

Orwell, G. (1950 [1949]), *1984*. New York: Signet.

Palat, L. (2019), "Manikarnika Movie Review," *India Today*, 15 March. Available online: https://www.indiatoday.in/movies/reviews/story/manikarnika-movie-review-kanganaranaut-excellent-as-queen-of-jhansi-film-not-so-much-1439057-2019-01-25 (accessed May 7, 2023).

Pandian, M. S. S. (1992), *The Image Trap: M.G. Ramachandran in Film and Politics*, New Delhi: Sage Publications.

Panikkar, K. M. (1961), "Introduction," *Baji Rao I: The Great Peshwa*, by C. K. Srinivasan, ix–xv, Bombay: Asia Publishing House.

Panjwani, V. (2017), "Sanjay Leela Bhansali: In the Realm of Innovative Cinematic Experiences," in A. Viswamohan and V. John (eds.), *Behind the Scenes: Contemporary Bollywood Directors and their Cinema*, 110–28, New Delhi: Sage Publications.

Paranjape, M. (2022), "The Kashmir Files Creates a New Language and Aesthetics of Protest," *Firstpost*, March 17. Available online: https://www.firstpost.com/entertainment/offcentre-the-kashmir-files-creates-a-new-language-and-aesthetics-of-protest10466481.html (accessed May 7, 2023).

Pasricha, A. (2023), "Indian Government Opposes Legalizing Same Sex Marriage, but LGBTQ Community Optimistic," *VOA News*, March 14. Available online: https://www.voanews.com/a/indian-government-opposes-legalizing-same-sex-marriagebut-lgbtq-community-optimistic/7003694.html (accessed May 7, 2023).

Pendakur, M. (2003), *Indian Popular Cinema*, Cresskill, NJ: Hampton Press.

Pillai, S. (2018), "Kangana Ranaut on Manikarnika, Turning Director, and Why She's Done Playing the Conventional Heroine," *Firstpost*, December 19. Available online: https://www.firstpost.com/entertainment/kangana-ranaut-on-manikarnika-turningdirector-and-why-shes-done-playing-the-conventional-heroine-5758291.html (accessed May 7, 2023).

Prasad, M. M. (1998), *Ideology of the Hindi Film: A Historical Construction*, New Delhi: Oxford University Press.

Qureshi, B. (2018), "The War for Nostalgia: Sanjay Leela Bhansali's *Padmaavat*," *Film Quarterly*, 71 (4): 46–51.

Rai, S. (2019), "'May the Force Be with You': Narendra Modi and the Celebritization of Indian Politics," *Communication, Culture & Critique*, 12: 323–39.

Raina, A. (2016), "What's Wrong with Anupam Kher Becoming the Dominant Voice for the Kashmiri Pandit Story," *Scroll.in*, February 7. Available online: https://scroll.in/article/803109/whats-wrong-with-anupam-kher-becoming-the-dominantvoice-for-the-kashmiri-pandits (accessed May 7, 2023).

Raj, S. (2022), "Film on Expulsion of Kashmir's Hindus is Polarizing and Popular in India," *New York Times*, May 26. Available online: https://www.nytimes.com/2022/05/26/world/asia/india-film-kashmir-files.html (accessed May 7, 2023).

Rajagopal, A. (2001), *Politics After Television: Religious Nationalism and the Reshaping of the Indian Public*, Cambridge: Cambridge University Press.

Ramnath, N. (2019), "'Kesari' Movie Review," *Scroll.in*, March 21. Available online: https://scroll.in/reel/917358/kesari-movie-review-Akshay-kumar-flexes-his-vocal-cordsin-underwhelming-ode-to-bravery (accessed May 7, 2023).

Ramnath, N. (2022), "'Ram Setu' Review," *Scroll.in*, October 25. Available online: https://scroll.in/reel/1035804/ram-setu-review-a-feature-length-whatsapp-forward-withvfx-thrown-in (accessed May 7, 2023).

Rangan, B. (2012), *Conversations with Mani Ratnam*, New Delhi: Penguin Books.

Rao, M. (2020), "Waif to Warrior—Kangana Ranaut," in A. Viswamohan and C. Wilkinson (eds.), *Stardom in Contemporary Hindi Cinema*, 215–28, Singapore: Springer.

Rao, P. (2019 [2017]), "*Soch aur Shauch*: Reading Brahminism and patriarchy in *Toilet: Ek Prem Katha*," *Studies in South Asian Film and Media*, 9 (2): 79–96.

Ravetto, K. (2001), *The Unmaking of Fascist Aesthetics*, Minneapolis, MN: University of Minnesota Press.

Rediff News (2005), "UP Govt to Consider Ban on 'Mangal Pandey'," *Rediff.com*, August 14. Available online: https://www.rediff.com/news/2005/aug/14mangal.htm (accessed May 11, 2023).

Reuters (2017), "'Padmavati', Now 'Padmavat', Gets Censor Board Nod," *Huffpost*, December 31. Available online: https://www.huffpost.com/archive/in/entry/padmavati-nowpadmavat-gets-censor-board-nod_in_5c10ad4be4b06e80c3f8dbce (accessed May 8, 2023).

Safi, M. (2017), "Controversial Hindu Priest Chosen as Uttar Pradesh Chief Minister," *The Guardian*, March 19. Available online: https://www.theguardian.com/world/2017/mar/19/uttar-pradesh-yogi-adityanath-hindupriestchiefminister#:~:text=Controversial%20Hindu%20priest%20chosen%20as%20Uttr%20Pradesh%20chief%20minister,This%20article%20is&text=A%20firebrand%20Hidu%20priest%20who,run%20India's%20most%20populous%20state (accessed May 8, 2023).

Sahadevan, S. (2015), "Shah Rukh Khan on Dilwale Boycott," *Indian Express*, 15 December. Available online: https://indianexpress.com/article/entertainment/bollywood/shah-rukhkhan-on-dilwale-boycott-inshallah-sab-kuch-acha-hoga-hamari-film-ke-saath/ (accessed May 8, 2023).

Saltz, R. (2015), "'Bajirao Mastani', a Bollywood Forbidden Romance," *New York Times*, 17 December. Available online: https://www.nytimes.com/2015/12/18/movies/reviewbajirao-mastani-a-bollywood-forbidden-romance.html (accessed May 8, 2023).

Saltz, R. (2018), "'Padmaavat' and All that Useless Beauty," *New York Times*, January 26. Available online: https://www.nytimes.com/2018/01/26/movies/padmaavat-review.html (accessed May 7, 2023).

Sarkar, S. (1993), "The Fascism of the Sangh Parivar," *Economic and Political Weekly*, 28 (5): 163–7.

Schmall, E. and H. Kumar (2022), "Israeli Filmmaker's Critique of Popular Bollywood Film Draws Fierce Backlash," *New York Times*, November 29. Available online: https://www.nytimes.com/2022/11/29/world/asia/india-film-kashmir-files.htm (accessed May 7, 2023).

Schmid, U. (2005), "Style versus Ideology: Towards a Conceptualisation of Fascist Aesthetics," *Totalitarian Movements and Political Religions*, 6 (1): 127–40.

Sen, R. (2020a), "Article 15 Movie Review," *Hindustan Times*, May 25. Available online: https://www.hindustantimes.com/bollywood/article-15-movie-review-ayushmannkhurrana-stands-tall-in-this-essential-film-about-cops-and-caste-4-5-stars/storyfivzSl1g0IV7kGnY2IXISO.html (accessed May 9, 2023).

Sen, R. (2020b), "Mission Mangal Movie Review," *Hindustan Times*, June 15. Available online: https://www.hindustantimes.com/bollywood/mission-mangal-movie-review-vidya-balanand-akshay-kumar-carry-off-an-oversimplified-film/sttnNIFcymIgTecUfm3KkPiM.html (accessed May 7, 2023).

Shandilya, K. (2019), "The Gaze of the Raping Muslim Man: Love Jihad and Hindu Right-wing Rhetoric in Sanjay Leela Bhansali's *Padmaavat*," *Studies in South Asian Film and Media*, 9 (2): 9–112.

Sharma, A. (2015), "Remove Article 370 to Solve Kashmir problem, Says Anupam Kher," *Indian Express*, December 27. Available online: https://indianexpress.com/article/india/indianews-india/remove-article-370-to-solve-kashmir-problem-says-anupam-kher/ (accessed May 7, 2023).

Sharma, D. (2020), "Shubh Mangal Zyaada Saavdhan Movie Review," *Filmfare*, 9 May. Available online: https://www.filmfare.com/reviews/bollywood-movies/shubh-mangalzyada-saavdhanshubh-mangal-zyada-saavdhan-movie-review-39164.html (accessed May 7, 2023).

Sharma, K. (2019), "Supporting Role," *The Caravan*, April 1. Available online: https://caravanmagazine.in/perspective/how-bollywood-acted-under-modi-government (accessed May 11, 2023).

Sharma, S. (2023), "Breaking down Pathaan, the Most Popular Movie in the World," *Vox*, February 10. Available online: https://www.vox.com/culture/23592808/pathaan-shahrukhkhan-bollywood (accessed May 7, 2023).

Singh, H. (2014), *The Rani of Jhansi*, Delhi: Cambridge University Press.

Singh, H. K. (2017), "Sanjay Leela Bhansali Assaulted on *Padmavati* Sets, Bollywood Demands Action," *NDTV*, January 28. Available online: https://www.ndtv.com/india-news/sanjayleela-bhansali-slapped-his-hair-pulled-by-protesters-on-padmavati-sets-in-jaipur-1653520 (accessed May 8, 2023).

Singh, S. (2013), *Lonely Planet India*, Singapore: Lonely Planet Publications.

Sontag, S. (1980), *Under the Sign of Saturn*, New York: Farrar, Straus, Giroux.

Spivak, G. C. (1988), "Can the Subaltern Speak?" in C. Nelson and L. Grossberg (eds.), *Marxism and the Interpretation of Culture*, 271–313, Urbana, IL: University of Illinois Press.

Spivak, G. C. (1999), *A Critique of Postcolonial Reason*, Cambridge, MA: Harvard University Press.

Srinivas, L. (2013), "Active Audiences and the Experience of Cinema," in K. M. Gokulsing and W. Dissanayake (eds.), *Routledge Handbook of Indian Cinemas*, 377–90, New York: Routledge.

Srinivas, L. (2016), *House Full: Indian Cinema and the Active Audience*, Chicago, IL: University of Chicago Press.

Srinivasan, C. K. (1961), *Baji Rao I: The Great Peshwa*, Bombay: Asia Publishing House.

Stam, R. (1992), *Reflexivity in Film and Literature*, New York: Columbia University Press.

Steinfeld, J. (2023), "Can India Survive More Modi?" *Index on Censorship*, 52 (1): 1.

Subramanian, S. (2022), "Screen Test: When the Hindu Right Came for Bollywood," *New Yorker*, October 10. Available online: https://www.newyorker.com/magazine/2022/10/17/when-the-hindu-right-came-forbollywood (accessed May 7, 2023).

Tieri, S. (2021), "Sikh Martiality, Islamophobia, Raj Nostalgia, a Pinch of Saffron: *Kesari*'s Nationalist Cocktail and the Power of Trailers," *Sikh Formations*, 17 (3): 358–86.

Times of India (2006), "Thackeray Suggests Indian Alternative to V-Day," February 13. Available online: https://timesofindia.indiatimes.com/india/thackeray-suggests-indianalternative-to-v-day/articleshow/1413417.cms (accessed May 8, 2023).

Times of India (2015), "Bajirao Mastani: Three Shows Cancelled in Pune amidst BJP Protest," December 18. Available online: https://timesofindia.indiatimes.com/bajirao-mastanithree-shows-cancelled-in-pune-amidst-bjp-protest/etphotostory/50228203.cms?from=mdr (accessed May 8, 2023).

Times of India (2022a), "Kangana Ranaut's 'Emergency' Lands in Controversy as Congress Objects," July 20. Available online: https://timesofindia.indiatimes.com/entertainment/hindi/bollywood/news/kanganaranauts-emergency-lands-in-controversy-as-congress-objectsreport/articleshow/92997560.cms (accessed May 7, 2023).

Times of India (2022b), "Pathaan Song Besharam Rang Row," December 17. Available online: https://timesofindia.indiatimes.com/entertainment/hindi/bollywood/news/pathaan-songbesharam-rang-row-sc-lawyer-files-complaint-with-ib-ministry-says-deepika-

padukoneand-shah-rukh-khan-have-hurt-the-religious-sentiments-of-hindus-by-performing-anobscene-dance/articleshow/96294955.cms (accessed May 12, 2023).
Times of India (2022c), "'Pathaan' Row," December 22. Available online: https://timesofindia.indiatimes.com/city/lucknow/pathaan-row-ayodhya-seer-threatens-toburn-srkalive/articleshow/96412297.cms#:~:text=Calling%20for%20boycott%20 of%20the,I%2will%20burn%20him%20alive (accessed May 12, 2023).
Tomasulo, F. P. (2014), "The Mass Pychology of Fascist Cinema," in B. K. Grant and J. Sloniowski (eds.), *Documenting the Documentary*, 81–102, Detroit, MI: Wayne State University Press.
Tuteja, J. (2021), "Sooryavanshi Review." *Rediff.com*, November 5. Available online: https://www.rediff.com/movies/review/sooryavanshi-review/20211105.htm (accessed May 7, 2023).
Vanina, E. (1999), "Bajirao and Mastani: A Family Tragedy in Eighteenth-Century Maharashtra," in I. Glushkova and R. Vora (eds.), *Home, Family and Kinship in Maharashtra*, 101–12, New Delhi: Oxford University Press.
Varughese, A. M. (2003), "Globalization versus Cultural Authenticity? Valentine's Day and Hindu Values," in R. Sandbrook (ed.), *Civilizing Globalization*, 53–8, Albany, NY: State University of New York Press.
Vasudevan, R. (2001), "*Bombay* and Its Public," in C. Pinney and R. Dwyer (eds.), *Pleasure and the Nation*, 186–211, New Delhi: Oxford University Press.
Vasudevan, R. (2010), *The Melodramatic Public*, New Delhi: Permanent Black.
Vasudevan, R. (2022), "Infrastructures of Political Address," in N. Majumdar and R. Mazumdar (eds.), *A Companion to Indian Cinema*, 360–85, Hoboken, NJ: Wiley Blackwell.
Vetticad, A. (2019), "Article 15 Movie Review," *Firstpost*, June 28. Available online:https://www.firstpost.com/entertainment/article-15-movie-review-ayushmann-khurranasrestraint-fits-this-gutsy-overwhelming-take-on-dalit-abuse-6888671.html (accessed May 7, 2023).
Vetticad, A. (2022), "Ram Setu Movie Rreview," *Firstpost*, October 25. Available online: https://www.firstpost.com/entertainment/ram-setu-movie-review-a-hindutva-projectpretending-to-be-scientific-with-aspirations-to-being-a-baahubali-11509891.html (accessed May 7, 2023).
Viswanath, G. (2002), "Saffronizing the Silver Screen: The Right-Winged Nineties Film," in J. Jain and S. Rai (eds.), *Essays in Indian Cinema*, 39–51, Jaipur: Rawat Publications.
Vohra, R. (2008), "'Jodha Akbar' and Street Censorship," *The Hindu*, March 16. Available online: https://communalism.blogspot.com/2008/03/jodha-akbar-and-streetcensorship.html (accessed May 7, 2023).
Wilkerson, C. (2020), *Caste: The Origins of our Discontents*, News York: Random House.
Wright, N. S. (2015), *Bollywood and Postmodernism*, Edinburgh: Edinburgh University Press.
YouTube (2015), "Bajirao Mastani Gajanana Full Song Out." Available online: https://www.youtube.com/watch?v=YLhx-KXUQJY (accessed May 8, 2023).
Zain, A. (2023), "Celebrity Capital and Social Movements," *Southern Communication Journal*, 88 (3): 240–56.

INDEX

Aandhi 135
Abraham, John 210–12
Accidental Prime Minister, The 142–50
Adityanath, Yogi 62, 179–80
Advani, L.K. 10
Agnihotri, Vivek 152, 158, 164–6
Akhtar, Javed 218 n.13
Amar Akbar Anthony 215, 233 n.16
Ambedkar, B.R. 139
Anek 189–206
Article 15 (Indian Constitution) 43
Article 15 167–8, 170–81, 204
Article 370 (Indian Constitution) 42–3, 142, 151–2, 209, *see also* Kashmir
   in *The Kashmir Files* 155
   and Anupam Kher 164–5
   in *Pathaan* 211
audience, film
   of *Anek* 199
   of *Article 15* 170, 172–3, 180
   of *The Birth of a Nation* 162–3
   foreknowledge 80, 87
   in India 24, 29–30, 35, 37, 74
   of *The Kashmir Files* 161, 163–4
   of *Manikarnika* 124–5
   of *Padmaavat* 71
   of *Pathaan* 215
   and spectatorial competence 49–50, 126
aura 31–2
   and Modi hologram 34
   and IMAX Hindutva 108–9
Ayodhya 8–15
   and Akshay Kumar video 111
   and *Sooryavanshi* 100–1, 103
Ayyub, Rana 103, 106

Babri Masjid, *see* Ayodhya
Bachchan, Amitabh 16, 233 n.16
Badaun case 170, 232 n.1
Bajirao Mastani (*BM*) 45–6, 50–60, 75, 223 n.29
   disclaimer 25–6, 46–7, 219 n.20
   metatext 49–50
Bajrangi Bhaijaan (*BB*) 59–60
Baru, Sanjaya 42, 142, see also *The Accidental Prime Minister*
Benjamin, Walter 30–2, 34
"Besharam Rang" 210, 212–14
Bhansali, Sanjay Leela
   attacks by Hindutva groups 5, 62–4
   and *Bajirao Mastani* 45–8, 56–9
   endorsement of Modi 222 n.20
   and *Padmaavat* 61–4, 69–72
   filmmaking style 64–5, 74–7
Bharatiya Janata Party (BJP) 2, 46
   antecedents 8
   ascent 9–11
   female leaders 143
   and Bombay film industry 17, 19–21, 37, 92
   new media policy in Kashmir 151
   and same-sex marriage 234 n.21
Bharucha, Rustom 14–16
Birth of a Nation, The 43, 68, 95, 162–4
Bollywood
   aesthetics 71, 73–5, 212
   and BJP 19–21, 92
   and Hindutva 28, 33, 37, 44, 215
   and historical accuracy 21
   idiom 181–2, 184
   in 1990s–2000s 15–21
   masala format 3, 18–19, 205
   outsized role in India 3
Bombay (city) 11–12, 41, 100–1
Bombay 16, 18, 59, 218 n.13, 220 n.6
boycotts 2, 17, 39, 163

of Aamir Khan 4–5
of Shah Rukh Khan 4, 47, 58, 210

Carroll, Noel 161–3
caste 37, 43, 54, 142
   in *Article 15* 170, 173–80
   in *Manikarnika* 227 n.16
   in *Toilet* 82, 84
catharsis 76, 163–4
censorship (in India) 4, 18, 36, 59, 74, 215, *see also* CBFC
Central Board of Film Certification (CBFC) 5, 64, 148, 210, 213, 219 n.19
Cesaire, Aime 14
Chakravarty, Sumita 18–21, 73, 184
Chauhan, Sunidhi 203
Chowdhury, Debasish Roy 211
Christians (in India) 1, 190–1, 206
Citizenship Amendment Act (CAA) 6, 209
Clean India mission, *see* Swachh Bharat Abhiyan
cow vigilante groups, *see gauraksha*

Dalits 1, 82, 85, 126, *see also* caste
darsan 27, 29, 31–3
Dil Se 18, 204–5
Dilwale Dulhania Le Jayenge (DDLJ) 181–2, 186, 188–9
disclaimers (in Bollywood) 5, 21–7, 36–7, 219 n.19
   in *The Accidental Prime Minister* 143
   in *Bajirao Mastani* 46–7
   in *The Kashmir Files* 152–3
   in *Kesari* 92
   in *Manikarnika* 131, 227 n.14
   in *Padmaavat* 64, 66, 70, 222 n.18, 228 n.23
   in *Ram Setu* 107
   in *Sooryavanshi* 100
Dwyer, Rachel 27–30
Dyer, Richard 80, 87, 89, 115, 124, 137–8

Ek Tha Tiger 236 n.6
Emergency (1975–7) 42, 134–5, 139, 148, 230 n.10
Emergency 42, 134–8, 140
encounters, police (in India) 160
   in *Article 15* 177, 180
   in *Sooryavanshi* 105–6

fascism 12–13, 15–16, 32, 34, 36–7
fascist aesthetics 40, 61–2, 65–71, 75–6, 129–30
"fort under siege" 95, 97, 126

"Gajanana" 40, 54–9
Gandhi, Indira 42, 134–5, 139, 148–9, 228 n.28
Gandhi, Mahatma 8
Gandhi, Rahul 42, 143, 147, 230 n.11
Gandhi, Sonia 42, 143
gauraksha 124–6, 217 n.2, *see also* Mohammed Ikhlaq
genocide 13, 152, 154, 156, 159–60, 230 n.15
"Ghoomar" 64, 67, 72, 222 n.18
Golwalkar, M.S. 7–8
Griffith, D.W. 43, 162, 231 n.20
Guha, Ramachandra 8–11
   and "cult of Modi" 34, 139
   and Hindi films 44
   and "Naga problem" 190
Gujarat
   2002 pogrom 36, 46, 56, 209, 219 n.28, 226 n.6

Haider 72
Happy New Year 73
hatke cinema 210
   and *Anek* 195
   and Ayushmann Khurrana 167–8, 205
   and Kangana Ranaut 113, 117
Hindi cinema (popular), *see* Bollywood
Hindutva 1, 37
   and Bollywood 19–20, 38–9, 215
   distinction from European fascism 13

gestation period 7–9
and Hindutva film 28, 39
and Hindutva-ized history 21, 25, 100, 111
and IMAX 108–10
meta-discourse 95, 97–8
and patriarchy 122–3, 133
and "soft Hindutva" 92
historical film 22–6, 35, 60, 126
and transhistorical critique 48
holograms, *see under* Modi
homophobia 43
in *Shubh Mangal Zyada Saavdhan* 181, 185–6, 189
homosexuality (in India) 44, 234 n.21
horror cinema 161–3
Huxley, Aldous 34–5

Ikhlaq, Mohammed 57, 62
IMAX, *see under* Hindutva
India
and cinema (*see* Bollywood)
rise of sectarian violence in 1–2 (*see also* Ayodhya, Gujarat, vigilantism)
India: The Modi Question 209–10, 215
Indu Sarkar 135–6
Instagram, *see* social media
intertextuality 49

Jaffrelot, Christophe 3, 110–11, 151–2, 179–80, 224 n.12
Jagarlamudi, Krish 114, 123, 227 n.13
Jain, Kajri 30–1
Jameson, Frederic 48
Jammu and Kashmir, *see* Kashmir
jauhar 37, *see also sati*
in *Kesari* 97
in *Manikarnika* 127–31
in *Padmaavat* 61, 66–70
in *Samrat Prithviraj* 132–3
Jawaharlal Nehru University (JNU) 6, 142, 230 n.14
Jhansi ki Rani 119–22, 129, 226 n.9
Jhansi ki Rani Laxmibai 121–3

Jodhaa Akbar 23–5, 60
Johar, Karan 5, 38
jugaad 88–90

Kabhi Khushi Kabhie Gham (*K3G*) 19–20
Kanwar, Roop 9
Kapoor, Shahid 67, 71–3
Karni Sena 62–4, 130
Kashmir 142, 150–2, 158–61, 163–4, 211
Kashmir Files, The 142, 152–8, 160–6, 210
Kesari 92–8
Kevichusa, Andrea 191, 234 n25
Khan, Aamir 4–5, 18, 23, 80
Khan, Aryan 6
Khan, Salman 18, 59, 80, 215
Khan, Shah Rukh (SRK) 4, 37, 47, 58, 210–12, 214–15
Kher, Anupam 42–3, 150, 165–6
Kashmiri Pandit advocacy 142, 164–5
previous roles 141
as Manmohan Singh 144–5
social media activity 141–2, 165, 229 n.2
Khilji, Alauddin 5, 37, 61–2
Khilnani, Sunil 118–19
Khurrana, Ayushmann 43–4, 167–8
in *Anek* 190–1, 193, 204–7
in *Article 15* 173–4, 178–80
and "Ayushmann genre" 168–70
in *Shubh Mangal Zyada Saavdhan* 189
Kumar, Akshay 40–1, 79–80, 111–12
in *Kesari* 93
in *Mission Mangal* 86–7, 89
interview with Modi 90–2
in *Ram Setu* 106–7
Ram Temple video 111
in *Sooryavanshi* 101
star text 80–1
in Swachh Bharat PSA 85–6
in *Toilet* 83–4

Laal Singh Chaddha 5
Longkumer, Arkotong 2, 189–90
love jihad 53, 102, 210, 214, 231 n.22

Make in India initiative 87–8, 89, 111
Malhotra, Jagmohan 158–9
Mangal Pandey: The Rising 22–3
Manikarnika: The Queen of Jhansi 114, 118, 123–31, 134
Mephisto 165
MGR 36
military (Indian) 11, 158–60
Mission Mangal 86–90, 99
   Modi's appearance in 89–90
Mississippi Burning 232 n.7
Modi, Narendra
   campaign statements 82, 149
   as divisive figure 46, 51
   endorsement of films 83, 158, 162, 165
   as Gujarat chief minister 46, 56
   use of holograms 33–4
   as intensifying pathologies 36
   selfie with Bollywood stars 38
   silence of 37, 46, 50, 57, 112
   speaking style 89–90
Modi, Sohrab 119
Mughal-e-Azam 24, 26
Muslims, *see also* love jihad
   in India 1, 12–13, 46, 56, 62
   in Kashmir 152, 158–60
   in *The Kashmir Files* 153, 157–8, 162–3
   in *Kesari* 93–5, 97
   in *Padmaavat* 61, 68
   in *Sooryavanshi* 101, 104, 106

Nirbhaya 172, 232 n.5
Northeast region (India) 189–90

Oldenburg, Veena Talwar 130
"O Mama" 201–2
Orwell, George 164

Padmaavat 40, 61, 66–71, 75–7, 94–5, 129
   making of 62–3
   protests against 63
   requested changes to 64
Padukone, Deepika 5–6, 37, 63, 73–4, 210, 213–14

Pakistan 5, 19, 101, 218 n.14
Pandian, M.S.S. 33, 36
Panipat 3
Partition 12, 76, 217 n.3
Pathaan 44, 210–15
Pednekar, Bhumi 81, 85
Phizo, A.Z. 234 n.29
propaganda 37, 77, 140
   and *India: The Modi Question* 209
   and *The Kashmir Files* 165
   and *Kesari* 95
   and *Manikarnika* 227 n.16
   and *Mission Mangal* 89
   and *Ram Setu* 110
   and *Sooryavanshi* 104, 106
   and Swachh Bharat PSA 86
   and *Toilet* 85
   and *Triumph of the Will* 32

Qureshi, Bilal 74–5

Rajput, Sushant Singh 5–6
Ramayan (TV series) 9
Ram Janmabhoomi movement 8, 11
Ram Setu 106–111
Ranaut, Kangana 41–2, 117, 123, 133, 135, 139–40
   early career 113, 115
   in *Emergency* 137
   in *Manikarnika* 124
   as Rajput 130
   social media activity 113–14, 116, 138
   star text 114–15, 118, 124, 137–8
Rani of Jhansi 118–19, 129, 130
Rashtriya Swayamsevak Sangh (RSS) 7–9, 18
Ratnam, Mani 16, 205–6
Riefenstahl, Leni 32, 65, 77, 165
Rihanna 116
Roja 16
Roshan, Hrithik 18, 23, 80

Samrat Prithviraj 132–3, 214
Sangh Parivar 13, 15, 21, 111, 224 n.12

Sarkar, Sumit 7–8, 12–15
sati 9, 37, 66, 71, 121, 217 n.5, *see also* jauhar
Savarkar, V.D. 7
scheduled castes, *see* Dalits
Section 377 (Indian Penal Code) 234 n.21, *see also* Shubh Mangal Zyada Saavdhan
Shah, Amit 151, 164
Shiv Sena 16–17, 19, 46, 58, 62
Shubh Mangal Zyada Saavdhan (SMZS) 181–9
    Section 377 in 186–7
Singh, Harleen 119–21
Singh, Manmohan 90, 142–3, *see also* The Accidental Prime Minister
Singh, Ranveer 51, 68, 75, 104
social media 2, 10, 38–9, 151, 163, 210, *see also* Anupam Kher, Kangana Ranaut
Sontag, Susan 65–7
Sooryavanshi 100–6
Spivak, Gayatri Chakravorty 130–1
Stam, Robert 49–50
Swachh Bharat Abhiyan 79–81, 83–4, 85

tax exemption (for films) 37, 42, 83–4, 89, 162
Thackeray, Bal 16, 60, 144
Toilet: Ek Prem Katha 81–5, 89, 111
Tomasulo, Frank 65–6, 76
Triumph of the Will 32, 65–7, 165
Trump, Donald 34, 62, 114
2014 elections (India) 221 n.12
2019 elections (India) 91, 150
Twitter, *see* social media

Uri: The Surgical Strike 3, 202
Uttar Pradesh 10, 180

"Vande Mataram" 20
Vasudevan, Ravi 33–4, 58–9
vigilantism (in India) 1, 36, 126, 180, *see also* Ayodhya, *gauraksha*, Karni Sena
Vishwa Hindu Parishad (VHP) 8–9, 11

Wilson, Woodrow 165, 231 n.20

"Yoddha" 133, 228 n.25